Participatory Practices
in Adult Education

Participatory Practices
in Adult Education

Edited by

Pat Campbell
Centre for Research on Literacy
University of Alberta

Barbara Burnaby
Faculty of Education
Memorial University of Newfoundland

2001

LAWRENCE ERLBAUM ASSOCIATES, PUBLISHERS
Mahwah, New Jersey   London

Lawrence Erlbaum Associates, Inc., Publishers
10 Industrial Avenue
Mahwah, New Jersey 07430

Cover design by Kathryn Houghtaling Lacey

Library of Congress Cataloging-in-Publication Data

Participatory practices in adult education / edited by Pat Campbell, Barbara Burnaby.
     p. cm.
   Includes bibliographical references.
   ISBN 0-8058-3704-3 (alk. paper) – ISBN 0-8058-3705-1 (pbk. : alk. paper)
     1.   Adult education—Social aspects—Canada—Case studies. 2. Adult education—Social
Aspects—United States—Case studies. 3. Popular education—Canada—Case studies. 4.
Popular education—United States—Case studies. 5. Functional literacy—Social
aspects—Canada—Case studies. 6. Functional literacy—Social aspects—United
States—Case studies. I. Campbell, Pat, 1958- II. Burnaby, Barbara.

LC5225.S64 P37 2000
374—dc21

                                                                                    00-064046

Printed in the United States of America
10   9   8   7   6   5   4   3   2

Contents

Preface

AIMS

This book is a celebration and sharing of experience, new knowledge, lessons learned, and reflections from the practice of participatory adult education. We, the editors, see a major gap of communication between, on the one hand, the large body of general literature within the field of adult education about work with people who are marginalized in various ways and, on the other hand, the everyday practice of workers, learners, and citizens engaged in participatory adult education activities. People at the front lines of adult education want to learn from the practical experiences of their counterparts who have attempted to implement the compelling calls to action reflected in the literature. To address this need, we have joined with practitioner colleagues in Canada and the United States to document successes and network about ideas from active projects, past and present, that have had a participatory component. The aim is to provide concrete models and suggestions to practitioners and participants in a wide variety of adult education settings who want to increase the participatory nature of their activities. It is also expected that people just starting out in situations like those described here might get some guidance from these experiences. Some chapters provide detailed descriptions of the triumphs and challenges in individual projects, whereas other chapters are more a reflection on years of experience and theoretical analysis. All, however, are rooted in and give examples from specific action.

SCOPE

Participation

In focusing on participation, we have sought out projects and practices in which taken-for-granted relationships among individuals involved are purposefully changed. In the projects described, possibilities, options, and power to create and use knowledge, to act, and to make decisions are deliberately distributed more equally among a wider range of stakeholders than would normally be the case. Under some circumstances, such shifts in relationships are attempted in only specific aspects of broader activities, whereas in others, efforts are made to make sweeping changes in various facets of an undertaking. New projects are outlined here that were intended to be highly participatory from the beginning, as well as established projects that are moving slowly from less to more participation. Opportunities and responsibilities are shared or shifted in some instances from teachers, administrators, and other traditional decision makers to students, learners, and citizens who, in the past, have had less influence over how actions were taken. Other examples are given in which initiatives are taken up afresh by learners and citizens to take action where there had been none before.

Sectors of Adult Education

Adult education is a vast field. Our scope for this collection covers activities involving learning, acting, growing, and creating in community and explicit teaching and learning settings. Children as well as adults are implicated in many of the community-based projects; however, learning and action by adults are the main emphasis in this book. Moves to increase participation by stakeholders are being made in many kinds of settings in our society. For example, there is a strong trend in business and government organizations: (a) to remove the middle levels of management so there are fewer levels of decision making, and (b) to create self-managing teams rather than the traditional supervisor and worker structures. This kind of development is not addressed here because the ultimate goal for such changes is the enhancement of the effectiveness of the organization. Instead, the projects covered in this book were initiated with the intention that greater participation, especially by those previously excluded from positions of control, would be of benefit to the individuals and groups empowered, not the organization itself (even thought that might happen as well). Therefore, although a number of the cases outlined in this book relate to activities in the workplace, they are mainly about relatively formal projects for workers' learning that benefit the workers at least as much as the organization.

In recent years, two books in North America, Fingeret and Jurmo's (1989) *Participatory Literacy Education* and Auerbach's (1992) *Making Meaning, Making Change: Participatory Curriculum Development for Adult ESL Literacy* have been widely used and cited in support of participatory practices in adult education. These two volumes focus on the general adult literacy and English as a Second Language (ESL) adult literacy fields with an emphasis on programs in formal education settings or community-based literacy projects. Most of the projects cited in our book, as well, are about literacy, ESL, and adult basic education, but we have broadened the range of material to include an extensive variety of settings of programs (such as workplace, prisons, schools, and community development), kinds of activities (such as photo-stories, conferences, teacher training, and community research), and discussions of the depth to which contextual factors contribute to unique solutions (such as the involvement of management in workplace programs, grassroots self-help and activism within the restrictions of prison life, and the linking of workers in different countries). In addition, chapters have been included on participatory community development that do not involve basic education, and participatory formal education for adults, even in a university graduate school.

ORGANIZATION OF THE BOOK

Each of the chapters in this book involves authors' comments on crucial concepts about participation as seen in light of specific instances of practice. To support readers in finding the parts that might interest them the most, we have organized the contributions to this book into six parts. The first and last parts were chosen for their emphasis on principles as a kind of lead into and tying together of the discussion in the other chapters. The remaining chapters are divided on the basis of the kinds of locations of the practice described.

In the first part, Reflections on Foundations, Sauvé distills essential principles of participation from her rich experience in ESL, adult basic education, and development in formal programs, community, and workplaces. Particular moments and projects (such as ESL, literacy, community, and workplace) in her work illustrate the grounding of these principles in action.

The second part, Adult Basic Education, ESL, and Literacy, includes four chapters in which participatory practices have been introduced into projects that ostensibly aim at ESL, literacy, and numeracy learning. Barndt shows the potential of photography and other image making in various forms of popular education, including ESL, and ESL literacy. Campbell and Horseman describe two different projects in which learners in community literacy organizations have been involved in the direction and administration of these organizations. Norton talks about literacy learners moving from the learner to the teacher role.

Community is the title of the third part and it is the location of the action described in its two chapters. Scott and Schmitt-Boshnick focus on an Alberta women's community development project in which group planning directs basic skills learning and local action. Zacharakis-Jutz covers community political action, but on a fairly small scale, and he directs our attention to the ways decision making can be facilitated.

The fourth part, Workplace, includes three examples of formal education programs in the workplace. Belfiore and Folinsbee, and Nash recount projects in which management and workers (and unions in some cases) are drawn into dialogues about the establishment of skills training in such a way that the interests of the parties are addressed. Pharness extends this theme, showing how the active involvement of all parties, especially management, in learning over time led to escalating phases of the project.

The fifth part, Institutions, was included because of the unique location of the projects and the special aspects of adult education that were revealed. A university doctoral program in adult education studies is the location of the chapter by de Avila et al., in which students and faculty struggle to enact adult education principles by overcoming traditional hierarchies of power entrenched in university structures. Davidson provides a detailed history of learning projects undertaken in prisons and with prisoners over several centuries.

The sixth part, Reflections on Practice, includes two chapters that tie together many of the issues and themes raised in the preceding chapters.

Auerbach quotes questions and observations from students in a graduate course on second-language teaching to reflect on her own learning about participatory practice throughout her dynamic career in various kinds of adult education and community action. Burnaby, in the final chapter, offers her observations on some themes that emerged throughout the book.

ACKNOWLEDGMENTS

The experience of contacting colleagues to contribute to the book has been a warm and enriching one for us. Although we hear bits and pieces of information about the challenges and successes of our fellow workers in the enterprise of participatory adult education, the work of putting this book together has given us a welcome opportunity to learn in detail about their projects. We wish to thank all the contributors to this book most sincerely for the wealth of experience they have shared, for the considerable trouble they have gone to in creating these chapters, and for their patience in dealing with us as editors.

REFERENCES

Auerbach, E. (1992). *Making meaning, making change: Participatory curriculum development for adult ESL literacy.* Washington, DC: Center for Applied Linguistics.
Fingeret, A., & Jurmo, P. (Eds.). (1989). *Participatory literacy education.* San Francisco, Jossey-Bass.

Pat Campbell
Barbara Burnaby

Introduction

Pat Campbell
Centre for Research on Literacy
University of Alberta

This book describes participatory practices in many environments, including educational and penal institutions, community-based programs, workplace settings, literacy, and English as a Second Language (ESL) programs. In these environments, the term *participatory practices* refers to education and management, or both. Participatory education is a collective effort in which the participants are committed to building a just society through individual and socioeconomic transformation and ending domination through changing power relations. As educators and students work toward building a just society, participants share, create, analyze, and act on their knowledge and experiences. Participatory management involves the representation of marginalized individuals in an organization's democratic decision-making process. Educators and students, and employers and employees, who work toward creating a democratic organization challenge the hierarchical social relations and power structures that create boundaries among individuals.

The origins of participatory education can be traced to popular education, a model and approach to learning developed in Latin America and pioneered by a Brazilian educator named Paulo Freire. Popular education has been used throughout Latin America to promote literacy and to help people educate and organize themselves around issues such as health care, agriculture, elections, and working conditions. Participatory education and popular education are both based on socialist principles of equality and justice, with the goal of building a new, more humane, democratic, and just society. As well, both models involve a dialectical, collective process of sharing, analysis, and action. Popular education tends to be highly creative, relying on cultural forms (drama, drawing, music, stories, photos) as educational tools.

The major difference between popular education and participatory education is that they have evolved from different contexts: Popular education is from Latin America whereas participatory education is from North America. Freire's work in literacy was rooted in developing countries; the literacy campaigns he organized occurred in the context of revolutionary social change. The specific historical, political, cultural, social, and economic factors that fueled these literacy campaigns are different from those in the relevant contexts in North America. Nonetheless, North American programs have incorporated and modified aspects of his pedagogy, with the understanding that this approach is likely small-scale social change, rather than revolutionary social change.

Freire denounced liberal and conservative approaches to literacy education by arguing that these ideologies subjugate literacy to the political and pedagogical imperatives of social conformity and domination. These ideologies, he maintained, resulted in literacy programs that "reduced[d] the process of reading, writing and thinking to alienating, mechanical techniques and reified social practices" (Giroux, 1983, p. 226). Specifically, Freire argued that the conservative discourse linked literacy development to meeting the economic interests of the state, whereas the liberal discourse viewed literacy development as an opportunity to "help" marginalized people fit into mainstream society. Freire offered, instead, an emancipatory theory of literacy along with a transformative pedagogy.

Although Freire published some of the initial literature that critiqued traditional forms of education, the principles of participatory education have been applied in North American contexts since the early 20th century. In 1902, under the sponsorship of Frontier College, educators worked in the labor camps alongside the laborers, trying to establish educator–student relationships where both parties learned from each other (Cook, 1987; Krotz, Martin, & Fernandez, 1999). The Antigonish Movement in the later 1920s and early 1930s in Nova Scotia advocated nonformal approaches to education for economic development (Cameron, 1996; Laidlaw, 1961). In 1932, Horton (Horton & Freire, 1990; Horton, Kohl, & Kohl, 1990) founded the Highlander Centre, an adult educational center dedicated to helping people address and solve socioeconomic and political problems by mining their own experience and awareness. The Highlander Centre has been integral to major social movements such as labor organizing in the 1930s and 1940s, the civil rights movement in the 1950s and 1960s, and environmental activism in the 1970s and 1980s.

Since Freire, many educators, both in developing countries and in North America, have developed, critiqued, and added to his theory. Freire's concept of empowerment and dialogue is problematic among feminists because he viewed class as the principal source of oppression. He maintained that dialogue would be possible only when educators and students were treated as equally knowing subjects with common interests and goals. This rationalistic stance does not make room for differences of privilege or oppression, meaning it does not "address the power dimension within which people are imbedded" (Horsman, 1988, p. 87). Feminists, on the other hand, assert that although dialogue and empowerment are fundamental elements of critical pedagogies, they are difficult to sustain or obtain when groups have a heterogeneous composition (Ellsworth, 1989; Lewis, 1990; Lewis & Simon, 1986; Narayan, 1988; Weiler, 1991). This is because race, class, and gender and the power, privilege, and oppression embedded within these subject positions affect the way individuals hear, speak, and understand the other members of a group.

Feminists promote a critical pedagogy that addresses trust, safety, and risk. To build a safe atmosphere where people can trust one another across divisive social differences, we must begin to name the inequalities in the classroom and devise ground rules for communication (Narayan, 1988). Weiler (1991) contended, "This is a validation of both difference and conflict, but also an attempt to build coalitions around common goals rather than a denial of differences" (p. 470). Participatory and critical pedagogy are similar, for both believe that naming the power dynamics within educational settings will act as a catalyst to begin addressing the power dynamic outside of the educational environment.

PARTICIPATORY PRACTICES IN ADULT EDUCATION

Within the field of adult education, the term *participatory* has been linked with education, communication, research, evaluation, planning, development, and decision making. With each passing year, the term participatory is connected to different fields such as health and agriculture, as well as to the private and public sectors evidenced in participatory models in the workplace or of government. It could well become the buzz word of the millennium, which means the danger exists that the essence of participatory practices may be distorted.

The terms *participatory practices* and *participatory education* made their debut in the literature during the 1980s (Jurmo, 1987; Sauvé, 1987). The notion of participatory practices has evolved, particularly within the field of adult basic education. Between 1987 and 1992, four significant pieces of literature on participatory practices were published (Auerbach, 1992; Finge-ret & Jurmo, 1989; Jurmo, 1987; Sauvé, 1987), creating a foundation for edu-cators and learners to build on.

Sauvé (1987), a community educator and ESL instructor, defined partici-patory education as:

> a learning/teaching process wherein all participants are involved in and com-mitted to defining their own learning needs and wants, working out an ap-proach to addressing them, and evaluating that process as they live out of and into it, all within a context of making life better for themselves and those around them. (p. 19)

In her publication, entitled *From One Educator to Another: A Window on Par-ticipatory Education*, Sauvé vividly described the struggles, tensions, and joys of working *with* the participants to create a learning community based on the participants' strengths, interests, and knowledge. In her work as a participatory educator, Sauvé emphasized the role of praxis, a dialectical process between thought (theory) and action (practice).

Auerbach (1992) believed that although the bottom line in a participa-tory approach is action, the term needs to be defined broadly. In her early work as a participatory educator, Auerbach postulated action needed to be "some form of concrete, visible social change outside the classroom—that addressing an issue didn't 'count' if it wasn't followed by an immediate at-tempt to transform conditions in students lives" (p. 101). As she gained more experience, Auerbach realized that action is a nonlinear, nonsequen-tial process that develops unevenly over time. Action can encompass changes at the personal, classroom, and community levels, including gain-ing self-confidence, determining curriculum content, and writing letters to the editor.

Jurmo's (1987) doctoral dissertation, *Learner Participation Practices in Adult Literacy in the United States*, identified efficiency, personal develop-ment, and social change as the major arguments supporting participatory practices in the program components of instruction and management. The participatory model provided opportunities for learners to engage in demo-cratic decision making, which led to a more efficient program responsive to learners' needs. With respect to personal development, Jurmo found that participatory practices enhanced critical thinking, self-esteem, and the abil-ity to work collaboratively with others. The participatory approach created a mileu in which learners and educators could work together to analyze and challenge the status quo.

The concept of changing power relationships between students and edu-cators was introduced in the early literature on participatory practices (Fingeret & Jurmo, 1989; Sauvé, 1987). Traditional adult basic education programs, for example, do not usually *give* students a voice in the conduct of the program because students are viewed as passive recipients of services. Often, marginalized people such as those with low literacy skills are simply excluded from the opportunity to participate because the "literate society uses literacy as an indicator of the ability to reason and, therefore, to actively participate in the human social world" (Fingeret, 1983, p. 141). The early literature slid over the slippery question of how to change power relationships; the underlying assumption seemed to be that participatory literacy practices formed a locus in which power relationships between literacy workers and students were altered, and this created new roles for both parties.

Campbell's (1994) study of five literacy programs indicated that identity politics played a pivotal role in the transformation or reproduction of power relationships between literacy workers and students. In other words, the question, "Who are we in relation to the students and their issues?" needs to be posed so that literacy workers can recognize and explore their privileged position in relation to that of the students (Campbell, 1996). This question enables one to move beyond descriptors such as "student" and "educator" and to look at how class, gender, and race constitute social identity. Before there can be any possibility of moving from inequitable to equitable relationships, educators and students need to engage in dialogue about identity politics.

Interesting, the early literature on power relationships presumed singular, essential, authentic, and stable notions of identity among students. In contrast, rather than seeing power as a relationship only between students and educators, contemporary literature has expanded the sphere of power to include power relationships among students (Campbell, 1994, 1996). Campbell's findings indicate that when differences among multiple social locations are not examined by students and literacy workers, or both, tensions and misunderstandings often arise. A discussion of differences creates a stronger sense of community among students. She advocated opportunities for literacy workers and students to collectively explore the questions of social identity and privilege.

Earlier frameworks of participatory education that promoted students' "right to speak" and voice their views did not problematize the multiple identities and positions of students that, in turn, determine who speaks and who listens. Contemporary frameworks of participatory education, shaped by postmodernism and critical pedagogy, have explored how the intersection of class, race, and gender plays a significant role in students' participation and their willingness to speak their minds (Ellsworth, 1989; Giroux, 1993; hooks, 1988; Narayan, 1988; Weiler, 1991). Campbell's (1996) findings indicate that, as educators, we need to shift our gaze away from the individual to look at how systemic factors play a significant role in silencing people. We need to examine the roots of silence, rather than attributing it to a lack of confidence or "shyness."

As the participatory model has gained momentum, educators have been documenting their successes, dilemmas, challenges, and questions (Auerbach, 1992, 1996; Demetrion; 1993; Norton & Campbell, 1998; Toroshenko, 1998). Sometimes, the vision of participatory practices collides with the reality of the classroom, as educators and students are constrained by lack of administrative support and limited time, funding, and space.

THEMES

Despite the disparate backgrounds of the contributing authors and rich diversity of this book, the participatory educators who penned these chapters share a strong vocation; they are committed to the vision of building a just society through individual and socioeconomic transformation and ending domination through changing power relations. In their work with groups and communities toward this vision, they strive for democratic participation and construct settings that fosters respect, honesty, compassion, trust, and risk taking.

The themes of community, social relations, and pedagogy woven throughout this collection of chapters reflect their common philosophy. Although these three themes are presented as separate entities, they are intertwined and interrelated, creating a gestalt.

COMMUNITY

Participatory educators who work in community-based literacy and ESL programs stressed the building of community (e.g., Barndt; Campbell; Sauvé; Scott & Schmitt-Boshnick; Zacharakis-Jutz). The term *community*, according to the *Oxford English Dictionary*, stems from the Latin word *communis*, meaning the abstract quality of fellowship and the sharing of common relations or feelings. Although this definition speaks to unity and harmony, we know that unity oppresses and excludes individuals and represses differences. The contributing authors, while addressing the participants' need for community in participatory education, acknowledge differences of race, class, gender, language, and intellectual and physical ability among community members. They raise questions of how to form bridges across and give a voice to differences among participants to ensure that individuals will not be reduced to silence or be excluded. In their practice, the authors embrace the need for common ground and goals within a community of learning, while acknowledging the diversity among individuals.

Zacharakis-Jutz and Belfiore and Folinsbee raise the issue of representation in the democratic decision-making process within a community or workplace. The term *representation* is widely used to call attention to the ways in which the "other" is positioned and represented by dominant sectors of society. Often, the "other" is presented as part of a dualistic framework in which they (the other) are the problem. Therefore, they (the other) are not invited into the conversation or dialogue and are represented by dominant groups who believe they have the solution to the alleged problem. Zacharakis-Jutz considers carefully the gender, ethnicity, length of residency, language, income, age, physical abilities, education, marital status, and sexual orientation of individuals who are representing a community because he is cognizant that *who* speaks is even more important than *what* is said.

Sauvé, and Scott and Schmitt-Boshnick describe the isolation and loneliness among women who are poor and they advocate the practice of community. Barndt believes educators must see every learning event as a moment for nurturing connections and countering the fragmentation that permeates Western society, particularly for those on the fringes. Campbell discusses the different perspectives of students versus educators as these relate to building community: Students stressed a balance of "being and doing" when building community, whereas educators stressed the need "to do." These different perspectives are not surprising, because literacy workers are positioned within a product-oriented discourse that rewards action-oriented behavior.

These chapters raise questions: Why do individuals who are marginalized seek community? Is building community a means of reducing the isolation in their lives? Do individuals living on a fixed income or in poverty seek community more than those who lead comfortable lives? Why do these individuals feel so alone in the world? In what ways does their poverty prevent them from connecting with others? To what extent is their sense of isolation heightened by popular culture? For instance, how does a marginalized person respond to images on TV, in magazines, and on billboards that do not reflect his or her daily realities? Zacharakis-Jutz links the decline of the community to the society's focus on individualism, consumerism, and popular culture. Perhaps, through community and participatory practices, individuals can overcome their loneliness by sharing their stories, knowledge, and skills; analyzing their realities; and taking action to create a more just society.

SOCIAL RELATIONS

Among participatory educators, there is a belief in democratic participation and social relations within workplace, educational, and community settings. Yet, how can democratic participation exist when the multiple identities of group members are considered? Throughout this book, you see how social identity plays a pivotal role in the transformation or reproduction of power relationships between and among educators and students, employers and employees, faculty and staff, facilitators and participants. The participants' social identities—based on race, gender, class, intellectual and physical ability, location, and language—influence their social relations. Moreover, the participants' social identities and the power, privilege, and oppression embedded within these identities affect how they process information, what they can accomplish, and how comfortable they are in expressing themselves.

No easy answers present themselves concerning the problem of how to address the multiple identities of educators and students. Barndt uses photo-story production processes as a way of generating discussions about differences among learners. Through these photo-story productions, she recognizes that the facilitators' sensitivity and skills are tools as important as the camera. In her work, Horsman is dissatisfied with the "us-and-them" framework that divides educators and students, because this division draws attention away from the students' multiple identities. There are bound to be tensions, divisions, and hierarchies within a heterogeneous community of students who differ in class, race, gender, and ability. If the students do not examine how their differences are affecting their interactions, there may be, as Horsman suggests, criticism from others or self-blame when their efforts to work together are unsuccessful. Horsman brings up the pragmatic need to design a wide range of activities to build connections among learners. These activities include an exploration of their commonalities and differences, and an examination of what creates divisions and competition among learners.

Sauvé and Norton point to the cultural and class differences between educators and students. For educators to position themselves on common ground with learners, Sauvé believes we need to seek out and break the bonds that have kept us from moving in a broader world of experience. For both Sauvé and de Avila et al., this process requires educators and students to abandon their familiar comfort zones and experience discomfort as they move out of self into the larger world, as they hear and come to understand the multiple and contradictory voices.

Several authors discuss power imbalances among participants (de Avila et al.; Norton; Scott & Schmitt-Boshnick; Zacharakis-Jutz). Scott and Schmitt-Boshnick and de Avila et al. employ a similar technique in their quest for democratic participation: Negotiation and dialogue are used as a means of working across differences among community members and between faculty and staff. Zacharakis-Jutz describes a "round robin" technique that ensures that no one can dominate a dialogue. He stresses the importance of creating a safe environment so that people of different classes and cultures feel comfortable enough to participate in the decision-making process. These authors understand that differences in an individual's experience of privilege and oppression in relation to the other members of a group influence his or her decision to enter into dialogue.

Nash and Belfiore and Folinsbee discuss differences among individuals in terms of the range of experience, language, and knowledge that people bring to the table. Nash describes how language is a process that mediates relationships and can be used to privilege some groups and diminish others. Pharness uses samples of employees' writing to illustrate how their language development has enabled them to be more effective and confident in talking with others in group settings. Certainly, access to and participation in forums of power depends on knowing the dominant language of these forums.

Social identity is an important aspect of participatory education because it influences communication, relationships, interactions, and decision making among participants in educational, institutional, community, and workplace settings. As participatory educators, the authors are cognizant of tensions that arise within educational, community, and workplace environments because of differences among participants in social identities and power. The authors raise esoteric and pragmatic questions as they discuss social identity, power, and voice: Who makes decisions and how are decisions made? How do we silence and control others without being aware of it? How do we begin to explore privilege and oppression? How do we unravel and address the tensions that arise from the students' and educators' different subject positions? Does participation on boards and committees increase learners' sense of powerlessness because they do not speak the language of educators? Although the authors may not have answers, they will engage you, the reader, in the process of seeking to integrate a new way of thinking and being into the fabric of your pedagogy.

PEDAGOGY

If you are new to participatory education, you will find there are no pat solutions to the question about "how to do it"; there is no method to follow or prescription to rely on. Your practice, instead, needs to be grounded in a vision that rests on egalitarian social relations, community and democratic participation, and a vision for a just society in which it is not "us" against "them." To work toward this vision, many of the contributing authors base their practice on a cyclical model of sharing, analysis, and action in which personal experience becomes a springboard for political action.

In each of the chapters that follow, the contributing authors discuss their own variation of this model and the challenges and struggles in trying to implement it. Participatory education is a cyclical process that begins with sharing the participants' experiences and knowledge, analyzing and building on the experiences to find commonalities and differences, planning for action, and reflecting on the action. Auerbach summarizes this approach as a process where students look at what is, ask why it is that way, and ask what can be done about it. Zacharakis-Jutz refers to the cyclical process of reflection, study, and action. As you read each author's account, you will see that all share the challenge of reaching the phase that requires "action." In their work with a community-based program, Scott and Schmitt-Boshnick have come to see that the movement toward action is a gradual process:

> Since the mid-1970s, Barndt has used the powerful combination of storytelling and photos as a means for participants to name and make sense of their realities. More recently, Barndt has put herself in the naming process, so that she too must reveal her stories. By doing this, Barndt challenges the traditional boundaries and borders that separate students and participants from educators and facilitators. It takes a lot of courage to break away from the ethos of professionalism that stops us from sharing our personal experiences.

Campbell provides an in-depth discussion linking educators' fear of focusing on the personal to their discomfort in moving out of the safe terrain of "being a teacher." Auerbach and Campbell also confirm that among educators, there is an assumption that listening to personal narratives is a form of therapy outside the realm of "education." Auerbach relates how some educators believe listening to personal problems is tedious, and she frames their resistance within the North American discourse of optimism, in which individuals prefer to avoid conflict. In her study on participatory practices, Campbell also identifies that educators want answers to the pragmatic question: How do educators facilitate a process that moves from the personal to the political? Sauvé discusses how, as a facilitator, it is challenging to move participants beyond their stories.

Although it is tricky to incorporate the cyclical process into the workplace, Nash recalls how she connected employees' personal experiences with barriers and walls to a workplace issue about a pending merger between two hospitals, which, in effect, symbolizes a wall coming down. Out of this discussion came an action in the form of a document entitled *Our Merger Survival Handbook*. Pharness narrates how the sharing and critical analysis of personal experiences was used with youth at risk and in diversity workshops to engage employees in the issue of racism. The challenge of moving beyond critical analysis to action becomes apparent in many workplace settings as participants are constrained by limited class time and the functionalist approach to education aimed at satisfying the employers' needs.

According to Davidson, the notion of being a participatory educator within a prison setting is implausible because the correctional ethos does not allow for the democratization of the curriculum, social relations, and decision making. In the history of prison education, Davidson documents only two examples in which educators attempted to move storytelling to critical analysis and action. He advocates prisoner-organized education because of the improbability of introducing in any other way a participatory model within prison schools.

As you read this book, you will discover that participatory practices within educational and workplace settings face a spectrum of barriers, ranging from material to ideological constraints. Packaged as a whole, these barriers could overwhelm and deter you from engaging in participatory practices. Yet, if you view participatory practices as a vision rather than as a set of goals, and place importance on the process rather than the product, you will be more accepting of the challenges ahead. By connecting with other participatory educators, you will create a community in which to share your visions, struggles, and successes.

REFERENCES

Auerbach, E. (1992). *Making meaning making change: Participatory curriculum development for adult ESL literacy*. McHenry, IL: Center for Applied Linguistics and Delta Systems.

Auerbach, E. (1996). *Adult ESL/literacy from the community to the community: A guidebook for participatory literacy training*. Mahwah, NJ: Erlbaum.

Cameron, J. D. (1996). *For the people: A history of St. Francis Xavier University*. Montreal & Kingston, Canada: McGill-Queen's University Press.

Campbell, P. (1994). *Participatory literacy practices: Having a voice, having a vote*. Unpublished doctoral dissertation, University of Toronto, Toronto, Canada.

Campbell, P. (1996). Participatory literacy practices: Exploring social identity and relations. *Adult Basic Education, 6*(3), 127–142.

Cook, G. L. (1987). Educational justice for campmen: Alfred Fitzpatrick and the foundation of Frontier College, 1899–1922. In M. R. Welton (Ed.), *Knowledge for the people: The struggle for adult learning in English-speaking Canada, 1828–73* (pp. 35–51). Toronto, Canada: OISE Press.

Demetrion, G. (1993). Participatory literacy education: A complex phenomenon. *Adult Basic Education, 3*(1), 27–50.

Ellsworth, E. (1989). Why doesn't this feel empowering? Working through the repressive myths of critical pedagogy. *Harvard Educational Review, 59*(3), 297–324.

Fingeret, A., & Jurmo, P. J. (1989). *Participatory literacy education*. San Francisco: Jossey-Bass.

Fingeret, H. A. (1983). Social network: A new perspective on independence and illiterate adults. *Adult Education Quarterly, 33*, 133–146.

Giroux, H. A. (1983). *Theory and resistance in education: A pedagogy for the opposition*. New York: Bergin and Garvey.

Goldgrab, S. (1991). Active student participation. In J. A. Draper, M. C. Taylor, & S. Goldgrab (Eds.), *Issues in adult literacy and basic education: Canada* (pp. 216–224). Toronto, Canada: OISE Press.

Hooks, B. (1988). *Talking back: Thinking feminist, thinking black*. Toronto, Canada: Between the lines.

Horsman, J. (1988). *"Something in my mind besides the everyday": Il/literacy in women's lives in a Nova Scotian county.* Unpublished doctoral dissertation, University of Toronto, Toronto, Canada.

Horton, M., & Freire, P. (1990). *We make the road by walking: Conversations on education and social change.* Philadelphia: Temple University Press.

Horton, M., Kohl, J., & Kohl, H. (1990). *The long haul: An autobiography.* New York: Doubleday.

Jurmo, P. J. (1987). *Learner participation practices in adult literacy efforts in the United States.* Unpublished doctoral dissertation, University of Massachusetts, Amherst.

Krotz, L., Martin, E., & Fernandez, P. (1999). *Frontier college letters: One hundred years of teaching, learning and nation building.* Toronto, Canada: Frontier College.

Laidlaw, A. F. (1961). *The campus and the community: The global impact of the antigonish movement.* Montreal, Canada: Harvest House Limited.

Lewis, M. (1990). Interrupting patriarchy: Politics, resistance, and transformation in the feminist classroom. *Harvard Educational Review, 60*(4), 467–488.

Lewis, M., & Simon, R. I. (1986). A discourse not intended for her: Learning and teaching within patriarchy. *Harvard Educational Review, 56*(4), 457–472.

Narayan, U. (1988). Working together across difference: Some considerations on emotions and political practice. *Hypatia, 3*(2), 31–47.

Norton, M., & Campbell, P. (1998). *Learning for our health: A resource for participatory literacy and health education.* Edmonton, Canada: The Learning Centre Literacy Association.

Sauvé, V. L. (1987). *From one educator to another: A window on participatory education.* Edmonton, Canada: Grant MacEwan Community College.

Toroshenko, N. (1998). The women's group on health: A study in participatory education. Unpublished master's project, University of Alberta, Edmonton, Canada.

Weiler, K. (1991). Freire and a feminist pedagogy of difference. *Harvard Educational Review, 61*(4), 449–474.

REFLECTIONS ON FOUNDATIONS

1

A Personal Journey Into Participatory Education

Virginia L. Sauvé
Portals: Educational Consulting Services, Inc.

BEGINNINGS

I think I know when I began to consciously name an approach to education for which I had long intuited the need, namely, participatory education. It would have been in 1986 when I was invited to do some minor editorial work for the local community college. They had been gathering information and resources for low-income women around budgeting and consumerism and were looking for someone to rewrite their materials at a Grade 3/4 level. Someone had given them my name; would I do it? As I asked the caller who the intended audience was, my heart weakened. (I need to interject for a moment to explain that I had just finished a year of graduate studies with a teaching assistantship and scholarship. With four children and a mortgage, I was desperate for some spring session employment.) I knew from the caller's description that the intended audience for the materials—women living in low-income housing, many of whom had never completed junior high—would not read the materials regardless of what level they were written at. The majority of such women did not respond to print; it went from the mailbox directly into the waste basket unless it looked like a check or a coupon. I told the person from the college as much, with visions of winged dollar bills gliding by, grinning wickedly at me.

Somewhat put out, the caller challenged me, saying, "Well, what would you do to get this information to these women?" I said, "I would work with them in a participatory education project." I swear I do not know where these words came from. For the next 45 minutes, I outlined to her a year-long project that combined education, community development, and childcare. When I was finished, still stunned with where these ideas had come from, she said basically that the money had to be spent by the end of June and not to call them as they would call me. I hung up laughing at my seeming folly but feeling at least in integrity with my values and considerably fascinated with the ideas that had emanated from my mouth. I said to my children, "So much for that job."

The next day she called and invited me for an interview for the job she had originally offered me. Having nothing else to do, and feeling that I had done my best to convince them of the uselessness of that task, I said, "Sure." The next day, I said to two people essentially what I had said to the original caller and on Monday they had found funding for a year-long position and invited me to do it. A new project had been born with women on social assistance in a housing development. The women who emerged in response to our advertising to take part in the project presented a variety of challenges to their living and learning, but they were curious and, if nothing else, valued a day out of their usual routine with care provided for their children.

PARTICIPATORY EDUCATION: THE CONCEPT

I had heard of the Participatory Research Group in Toronto and read much of their material, and I had read Paulo Freire, but nowhere had I heard, at that time, the term *participatory education* per se. I need to define for you my understandings as they have developed over time. My apologies if, in my fumbling experience, I have "discovered" ideas that have been written about by others. I have never been very good at researching other people's ideas and adding to them, which is of course what any good academic is expected to do. I have a preference for diving in and learning to swim out of the sheer need to survive. What I write are my learnings that have no doubt been heavily influenced by Freire and Barndt and other critical colleagues and friends I have come to know through the years. Although participatory research was appealing to me and was obviously an educational endeavor, there were aspects of it that did not seem to fit into the institutional settings in which I had worked up to then. I needed a concept that took the best of those ideas and put them into existing frameworks that would allow them to work.

I would like to start with what participatory education, as I understand it, is not. It is not a methodology or a technique, and it cannot be successfully done by those who lack at least the will to let go of unconscious values and understandings that have quietly invaded and shaped their worldview since the day they were born. It is not comfortable. It is not easy. And it is not to be rushed. It flies in the face of the language we use to talk about education (e.g., program delivery, target audience, etc.) and indeed the English language itself, laden as it is with racist and sexist words and expressions.

Lest that sound discouraging, let me assure you that it is also the most exciting, liberating, and fulfilling approach to learning that I have experienced in my long career.

Participatory education, from the perspective of an educator, is the enabling of a group of people to name *their* world, recognize their potential to create experience, and begin working to fulfill that potential, as individuals and communities. It is learning to see new, more life-giving choices and developing the confidence and skills to act on them.

FOUNDATION PRINCIPLES

I have come to articulate for my own work a set of principles that guide me in my explorations and that I offer to others as appropriate in various contexts to enable them to learn together, to work together, and to create together. In reflecting on these principles for this writing, I have tenuously separated them into two groups, the first of which I have called *foundation principles* because they seem to ground the work, and the second of which I have called *working principles* because they seem more related to the ongoing groupwork. It is not that either group is more important than the other, but the foundation principles seem to be the ground on which all else is made possible.

Participatory education is based first and foremost on profound *respect* for the human spirit and its ability to conquer all the failures, challenges, and woundedness of our pasts. The human spirit resides in every person, no matter how battered.

It is based on *hope* and *faith*—those two principles that serve to lift us above the muck of our lives and draw us into the light, without looking back. Hope is the energy that calls us forth into newness; faith is the energy that holds us fast when despair threatens. Faith steps in where knowledge stops. Hope springs out of that faith when least we expect it. Respect, hope, and faith are the first three foundation stones.

The fourth is *compassion*. Compassion is that which sees the other even as ourself and knows that, at some point, my well-being depends on the well-being of the other. Compassion rises above that which is convenient and even at times impossible and simply does what needs to be done because it needs to be done. It feels the pain of the other and reaches out to assuage that pain, unconsciously healing itself at the same time as the other.

These are simplistic definitions, as you may already have noticed, but my intent is not so much to develop these ideas for you as it is to *invite* you to develop them for yourself as you seek to understand why participatory education might change not only the lives of learners, but your life as well.

PRELUDE TO THE WORKING PRINCIPLES

Our foundation firm beneath us, we now turn to the working principles, those owned ideas that guide the work, which in the beginning feels like stumbling around in the darkness when our lived experience and that of the learners are considerably different one from the other. As primarily mainstream educators working with nonmainstream individuals, we most often come from a world as unimaginable to the learner as is theirs to us. There are cultural differences and class differences. We have a formal education commensurate with both its explicit and implicit learnings. They have an education based on their experiences as individuals and communities, and many of those experiences may seem harsh to some of us. Our implicit learnings imprison us even as their lack of socially demanded knowledge imprisons them.

If we are to locate ourselves on a common ground with the learner, which I believe we must do in this work, we must be willing to seek out and break the bonds that have kept us from moving in a broader world of experience, bonds that have caused us all too easily to judge the other and assume we know what is best for them. Whatever problems the other has, she has survived. Her strategies for doing so may appear counterproductive to us, but in some manner they have served her in the past and we need to recognize this, as does she, if she is to move beyond that and claim her dignity in its fullness. The principles I will describe in just a few moments have helped me to find or establish this common ground and to break new ground with different learners in different contexts over time.

WHO ARE THE LEARNERS?

I need once again to interrupt myself. You may be wondering at my assumption that we are working with nonmainstream learners. In fact, I would be surprised if you were not wondering this, unless you are already a participatory educator in which case the question may not have occurred to you. I have implied the learners of whom I speak are nonmainstream, challenged, barriered, and wounded. First of all, we are all challenged, barriered, and wounded; it is simply much easier for people without power to acknowledge that fact. Those who lack power are conscious of that absence. They feel their woundedness, suffer their challenges, and daily bat their heads against one or several of the barriers that prevent them from enjoying a life of relative ease: poverty, racism, a language in which they do not comfortably reside, illiteracy, learning disabilities, abuse, physical and/or mental health problems, low levels of functioning intelligence, lack of support in their lives, and the list goes on.

These are the people who find light in participatory education and, in it, discover they have the personal power to transform their lives against the most unbelievable odds. Those of us in the mainstream are there because we have learned to cope with (and in spite of) patriarchal systems of power, analytical and technological priorities in learning systems, and employment situations that use our skills without acknowledging our spirits. When we accept these ways of the world as normal and natural, we are not motivated to change. We have no investment in struggle when we are comfortable. It is the uncomfortable who may see their interest in trying out new positions, new ways of being. In fact, in my experience the less mainstream society expects in the way of capacity from an individual, the more likely such an indvidual is to grasp these ideas (the principles) and run with them.

Freire, the famed critical educator from Brazil who loved his work with the peasants of that country, of Guinea-Bissau, and elsewhere, struggled with the invitations his notoriety brought him to teach educators in the western world. They wanted to hear *about* his work but they did not want to have him *do* it with them. That was not comfortable, and I have known many fine people who left his courses because it was not what they came to do; they had come to hear the great one lecture. Freire worked with people to create their own knowledge, not to sell his. He knew the secret that most of us have to struggle to learn, that we cannot *teach* anyone anything truly significant. What we can do is enable people to learn if we ourselves are open to learning and relearning, to letting go of that which we struggled to learn in the first place.

THE WORKING PRINCIPLES

The working principles are not only guidelines for us as facilitators of this work. They are powerful ideas that, once owned by the individual, can be applied to effect radical changes in our lives and the lives of those around us. I would reiterate that these principles have emerged for me as I have worked with learners in various contexts. It is important that the reader not take them as a methodology, but simply as an accounting of my personal discoveries. To own these, one almost has to "discover" them for oneself, to see value in holding them as working principles.

It was in many ways fortunate that I did not have a clear sense of what I was doing when I committed to working with the women in Abbotsfield many years ago. Why? Because I approached the women humbly. I knew I had much to learn from them and with them if I were to be of any use to them in seeing new choices in their lives. My colleague and I listened to the women's stories, shared their pain, marvelled at their endurance, wept at the duplicity out of which some felt necessary to live, celebrated their strengths, and learned with them. Three principles emerged fairly early in that project: participation, community, and commitment.

Participation

As we worked together, we could see that those who dared to participate, to risk appearing ignorant or foolish, to ask questions, to answer questions, to give their opinions, these were the women who seemed to get the most out of the group. So, we named that as a working principle and acknowledged those members of the group who practiced it, which in their own ways, everyone did. We could all see there seemed to be a fairly obvious direct relation between the degree of participation and the energy one drew from the group.

Community

The second working principle we saw clearly was a need for the practice of community. I have always been fascinated by the difference between the poor in other countries and the poor in Canada in this regard. People I have been fortunate enough to meet in developing countries who were very poor were very strong in community. What little they had, they shared, willingly, with one another. They seemed to see their connectedness clearly. In Canada, the poor seem to be isolated from one another. There is mistrust and violence that one does not see in poverty situations elsewhere I have been. We could see it would take a lot of time for people to learn to trust one another but when they did, they could support one another in ways that would lighten all their loads and create new possibilities for them.

Each woman in that group, including the two of us, struggled with her own form of loneliness. That experience was, for the women in the housing development, accentuated by the degree of neediness each experienced that made others fearful of getting too close, and by the welfare system itself that drove people to lie and keep secrets to survive.

I think I learned the most about community from the participant least likely to be seen by any of us as a teacher, a woman who appeared to the world as odd at best, crazy at worst. She had no formal education, virtually no social skills of the most basic kind, and brought a doll to class that she variously treated with great love or great violence depending on her mood. She rarely spoke in the group and would dramatically fall out of her chair if anyone touched her. On the telephone, however, she was a skilled conversationalist. No one could be absent from the group without getting a call from N. . . . She would inquire as to their health, tell them that we missed them, and relate to them what we had done that week. She would express our hope that they would be there the next week. Whenever she saw my car or that of my colleague in the parking lot at the community college, where she would frequently visit the library, she would print a short note invariably signed, "your best friend, N. . . ."

One day she brought me a poem from a publication about personal growth. It expressed a kind of deep wisdom that threw me into chaos, challenging as it did all my perceptions of this woman. While she struggled with the most mundane aspects of her daily life, she manifested a strength that has continued to amaze all who meet her. (In the course of a program, she made the transition from a group home to independent living, a move that, although frightening in many ways, enabled her to grow in new directions that gave her much happiness.)

In spite of her bizarre behavior, she obviously had a lot of intelligence. She had taught herself to read and write by watching Sesame Street. She survived constant harassment from store clerks and the police because of her tendency to look furtive in public places. And she resisted any attempts to connect her with people as unusual as herself, for purposes of learning or socializing. In short, she had exceptional survival skills. Easily the most frustrating person in the group to understand or communicate with, she was also one of our greatest teachers. And what was truly beautiful to me was the casual way in which the whole group, to a woman, accepted her presence, another lesson in humility for us.

Commitment

Our most difficult challenge lay in figuring out how to move the women beyond their stories. Telling stories allows one to vent bottled up emotions, to name negative (and positive) events, and to position oneself in relation to those events. However, if one is to rise above the woundedness of one's past and the traps of the present, one has to move beyond the stories. One needs to develop clarity as to what one wants, believe one can achieve it, develop a plan of action, and, most of all, commit to getting there.

As a group, the women identified a need to clean up the grounds of their housing development for the health and safety of their children who played among broken beer bottles, used hypodermic syringes, and polluted puddles that backed up from the sewers whenever it rained. My colleague found some funding from National Health and Welfare that would pay the women a small honorarium and provided some capital costs to address these problems. With excitement, and disbelief, the women worked together to prepare a proposal that would pay them a small honorarium, not big enough to effect their welfare checks, and provide the money for a nice playground. My colleague and I were ecstatic when the proposal was approved. We could not wait to tell the women and when we did, they smiled but were nowhere near as excited as we were. We wondered why. Then, no one (other than N . . .) came to the group for the next two weeks. So, we went calling.

The women were terrified. In spite of our assurance that $100 per month additional income for each of them would not effect their welfare, they were afraid they would get cut off and dreaded the thought of trying to get back on. They knew they could cope with their lives as they were. They did not know if they could cope with their lives if they changed, if they had more money and more power. They feared the consequences of cleaning up the neighborhood. Someone might be angry. Already, break-ins were common. What would happen when they started to confront the social problems in their area? They were just plain afraid. We asked them if they would like us to withdraw the proposal and with great relief, they said yes. The next week, everyone came back.

It takes a great deal of trust, commitment, and support to overcome the fear of change.

Two other principles that have emerged over the years as important are vision and action–reflection, or praxis, as the Greeks called it. *Vision* is the ability to see what it is you want to create as an alternative to what you have already experienced. I have discovered to my surprise that not everyone is easily able to envision, whereas it has for the most part come naturally to me. Vision requires great detail and clarity. It is a giving of full rein to the imagination, a return to the joys of being childlike in one's sense of wonder and belief in possibility. Without vision, one returns to the void. We do not create peace by stopping war. We create peace by understanding and seeing what it is that peace is, not what it is not. We do not create happiness by drying up the tears; we create happiness by recognizing it in the moments it is upon us and celebrating those moments with gratitude. The experience of collective envisioning can be exciting, but it is not easy for everyone. Collective envisioning enables us to know one another differently from how we have in our contexts up to that moment. It brings out the gifts in each one that had not been seen before, sometimes even by the one who had them. By sharing the best of our gifts in this process of envisioning, we create new possibilities that had not existed before, and, what is best is that once we see them, we have already begun the long journey into creating them.

Action–reflection, or *praxis*, is the union of two notions that we have previously thought to be separate although related. We know it is not enough to have an idea; we have to take action. We know action without reflection is probably ill conceived. What we have not recognized historically is that the deliberation of reflection is itself an action that sets off a series of consequences, and that, in reflective action, we are, though in motion, evaluating what we are doing and changing it as we go. To see them as the linear circle—first this, then that, then this again—is limiting. To see it as one movement, as did the Greeks in their word praxis, the highest form of action, is to create new possibilities for ourselves.

CONCURRENT PRINCIPLES

Other principles emerged from the first three previous working principles and seemed to be connected to them in one big circle. *Risk, trust and trustworthiness, honesty,* and *acknowledgment* were all involved in the other working principles. One could not participate or be in community without taking a risk. To commit to something was also a risk because we do not feel in total control of the outcomes.

Honesty and trust and trustworthiness were also hooked into these other working principles. Honesty was huge problem for some of the women. They had been so accustomed to feeling the need to lie to get what they needed that it had become an inescapable labyrinth from which they did not know how to disentangle themselves. One woman seemed to have lost the ability to discern for herself what was true and what was not. Once you catch someone in an outright lie, it becomes hard to trust that person again, or so it was for me. For the others, I think they were so used to it that they did not expect truth to begin with. Acknowledgment was easy and important. We cheered and clapped when one of the women told us of any achievement she had made or when she contributed anything to the work of the group. They loved it and so did we. Acknowledgment created an atmosphere of happiness in the group and it was something everyone could participate in.

MOVING ON

After one year, the project funding was completed and I was moving in new directions. The women formed a new group called Candora about a year later; this group has just celebrated its 10th anniversary. The original objectives remain reasonably intact and they have achieved many positive changes in their community.

In 1987, I opened English Language Professionals, Inc., a private school for adult immigrant learners that offered ESL and job training programs as well as English in the Workplace. Our first job training program was the Bilingual Community Worker program, which was intended to train immigrant women to become settlement workers and to work in other multicultural settings. I immediately saw the value of building the principle work into our curriculum, and eventually saw the need for additional principles.

Employers talk a lot about attitude. They are looking for a good attitude. What is that? I suppose one could find many definitions for this, but for me it is about *accountability*. This is not the kind of accountability we are held to by someone else, but the kind in which I choose to account for my own experience in a way that gives me the power to make it better. The opposite of this kind of accountability is blame, and no one likes to work with someone who is always blaming others for his or her problems. Accountability is a choice we make in relation to the events of our lives. When I choose to be accountable, I take credit for my successes and my failures, which I regard as learning experiences. When I am choosing to be accountable, I ask myself, "Hmm, what was going on when I allowed this to happen?" This kind of accountability is the single most important idea I have identified in my own life and in the lives of learners with whom I have worked. When angry people, for example, are able to shift that energy into accountable action, the results are dramatic.

For the past several months, I have been working with environmental service workers (housekeepers) at six Edmonton hospitals. Just as the dishwasher in a hotel kitchen is at the bottom of the hierarchy and takes everyone's guff, so the housekeeper in a hospital most often feels invisible to some healthcare workers who take her work for granted and think nothing of dragging furniture across newly waxed floors, leaving hypodermics in the bed linens, or verbally abusing these hard-working men and women.

Project Worksafe Plus, as the program is called, consists of 3- and 4-day workshops (4 if English is your second language or you struggle with literacy). The first day is primarily spent listening to everyone and getting to know one another. I find it both interesting and disturbing that in every successive group, the same issues and problems arise: verbal abuse, lack of respect for their work or their being, no privacy, inadequate health and safety training, no professional development until now, unreasonable caseloads, fear of privatization, and the list goes on. At the same time, these men and women are extremely proud of their work and particularly enjoy working with the patients, who give them more acknowledgment than the staff do, as a rule. I am in awe of the jobs they do: the volume of work; the quality of results; the care I see extended to patients (which is not in their job description); the dangerous chemicals they handle everyday; and, in many cases, the degradation they bear in silence.

Because of their position at the bottom of a complex and currently chaotic hierarchy, they feel powerless to voice their fears or concerns or to in-sist on their rights. I believe I am allowed to do this project because I teach accountability. I teach people to ask themselves what they personally and collectively can do to improve their working environment for themselves and for others. Management likes to see workers taking more accountability and the workers are thrilled to discover that, in fact, they can take accountability and the roof will not fall in when they do so in appropriate ways.

One activity I do with this group on the last day of the workshop is invite them to compose a group Declaration of Rights. The only rules I impose are that no one could take exception to any of their "rights," that is, that they appear logical and reasonable to anyone working in the system. They have no problem with this. I also ask that they not list things they feel are already well in place because I know that if they do so, other staff would feel defensive. So, they write, "I have the right to working conditions which respect my need to be healthy and safe. I have the right to receive training in the use of any new chemicals or equipment which are part of my job. I have the right to be respected, to be listened to, to be consulted in decisions which affect me," and many more. The 3-day workshop generally generates 15 to 20 rights, and the 4-day (ESL) workshop generally generates about a dozen rights, but they are similar. What is wonderful is that the workers often take these back and post them in their staff rooms or on their locker doors. They are taking accountability for their experience and enjoying it.

Alongside accountability is *responsibility*. Again, I do not mean the kind of responsibility that means duty but rather response-ability. Whereas with accountability I refer to the individual or collective choice to account for one's experience in a way that gives one power over that choice, with responsibility I refer to the outward movement of choosing to respond from one's abundance to the needs of another. When I have completed my work and you are struggling with yours, I can choose to help you. When I have enough money and you are suddenly lacking, I can choose to share. When I have knowledge you need, I can choose to tell you what I know. In being accountable, we take care of ourselves. In being responsible, we share from our abundance with those who need what we have, be it time, money, or knowledge.

Two last principles, the most recently added to the list, are *celebration* and *self-care*. Celebration is important when we get so caught up in our sense of "work," whatever we understand that to be, that we become burdened. Celebration recharges our energy and returns us to the state I believe we were intended to enjoy, that of creatures gifted with much. Celebration takes a position of gratitude for the good things and freedom to enjoy life, no matter what. Self-care was added to the list after I got to know the first two groups of environmental service workers and saw how they were so busy taking care of everyone else that they had neglected to take care of themselves. These two are, like all the other principles, related. How can we celebrate without taking care of ourselves? How can we find the energy to be present to others when we have allowed all of our own energy to be drained away? Self-care is physical, mental, emotional, and spiritual. We take care of our bodies, nourish our minds, protect our emotional beings from that which we cannot understand but experience as destructive, and nurture our spirits by recognizing and participating in the vastness of the meaning of life and existence.

RESULTS

Although fewer than 8% of the workers in Project Worksafe Plus have completed the training, already we are hearing about changes in the workplace. One manager said, "No one used to have anything to say at staff meetings; now, I can't shut them up. It's great!" (And he had been a hard sell in the beginning because he did not believe in wasting money on "soft" skills.) Another manager is so pleased with the program that he did not wait for us to come up with funding for the next group; he took it out of his supply budget for the year saying, "Which is more important: people or mops?" In fact, the feedback has been so positive that a board consisting of union and management that is winding down its operations in another program voted unanimously to give their remaining funds to this project, which is sufficient to offer the program to more than 500 workers, namely everyone in that occupation. When union and management are of one mind on a program, you know you are doing something right.

Is it all wonderful? Not by a longshot. I celebrate the successes—they keep me going—but I would be less than honest if I did not also confide the seeming failures. Risk means sometimes we win and sometimes we lose. Whereas I had had only positive feedback on this most recent project from participants and managers alike, I got a phone call on Friday that sent me into the depths of despair momentarily. Two participants scheduled to come next week backed out saying they had heard from a colleague that the workshops were just socializing and were a waste of time. I could not believe my ears. Once over the shock however, I considered how they might have heard that, and I realized the woman who works with them who had been to the workshops had been frustrated by our use of print materials. She is an older woman and not willing to confront her own needs in literacy. She said to me what she thought I wanted to hear, but she struggled with the pain of dependency in silence. There are many like her coming as participants and I have to address this need. I have to find ways of facilitating highly literate and illiterate people together around their common ground: the work of the hospitals. I want them to go away all feeling like they drew something of benefit. If even one does not feel this way, I have failed in my own eyes. And yet my intellect recognizes that we all have choices, and, whereas I can no doubt continue to find better ways to work the workshops, ultimately, the individual always has the choice to open and receive or to stay closed and "get nothing out of it."

And so, I continue to become a participatory educator, listening, being as authentic as I know how to be, identifying principles that work, respecting and learning from one and all, celebrating successes small and large, and learning from my mistakes. And I rejoice in the discoveries of participants. I would like the last word to go to a participant in the most recent group completed in Worksafe Plus, an older Vietnamese man who seemed skeptically tolerant throughout the bulk of the course. On the last day, he argued with the rest of the group when, in a problem-posing exercise, they said the housekeeper would have to confront the nurse on her behavior. He said, "No, that takes too much courage." They argued and he finally conceded. A few moments later, he sent me a note. It read, "I wants to thanks you for this wonderful program. I will never be a powerless man again." May it be so.

ADULT BASIC EDUCATION, ESL, AND LITERACY

2

Naming, Making, and Connecting— Reclaiming Lost Arts: The Pedagogical Possibilities of Photo-Story Production

Deborah Barndt
York University

WHAT'S WRONG WITH THIS PICTURE?

Imagine a typical day in your life. If you have a job outside the home or go to school, you may rush out the door and grab a bus, enter a subway, or jump into your car; or perhaps you just walk down the street to a neighborhood store or to see a friend. Wherever you are going, one thing is pretty certain: Your visual environment, filled with images that bombard you constantly as you move through the day, has been defined for you. One day try counting the number of advertising images you encounter: television commercials and flyers on your doorstep; signs on telephone poles and billboards on the expressway; illuminated ads in the subways and painted ads covering buses and in bus shelters; ads on the placemats at fast food restaurants, in banks, in shopping malls, in the morning newspaper you read, and, in the case of York University where I teach, even inside the bathroom stalls!

This environment of images is taken for granted; it has become normalized. If it weren't there, we would feel that something was missing. When I worked in Nicaragua in the early 1980s, the Sandinistas had banned the use of women's bodies in advertising. I was struck by their absence, which made me realize how common their presence had become in North America, and how most of us have stopped even questioning it. Or if we did, we felt powerless to change it. And why? Because we have a sense of someone with more power than us making those decisions, creating those images, not even bothering to ask us if we want to digest them as daily fare.

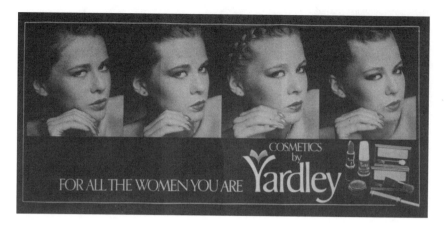

FIG. 2.1. Yardley advertisement: All the women you are.

What does this visual environment have to do with adult education? For one thing, it is part of the ideological landscape that surrounds us and forms us, and within which we work. It is also a resource for critical and creative educational practice. When I was teaching ESL in the late 1970s and early 1980s in garment factories in downtown Toronto, we often brought bus or subway ads into the classroom, first to reinforce language practice in reading the few words they bore (and that could be practiced on the way to and from work), and second to use the photos as catalysts for deeper discussion. The Yardley ad (Photo 2.1) generated tremendous response. "For all the women you are," it proclaimed. "It doesn't say anything about OUR lives," was the critical response of the immigrant women in the class. And so they proceeded to alter the title (inserting words to read "For all the women we REALLY are NOT!") as well as the image (plastering the idealized face of western beauty with their own photos reflecting a multiplicity of origins and colors and moods.[1]

The following year, a group of middle-class community educators at an international women and media conference also had their hand at reconstructing the Yardley ad. They noted that only a small corner of the ad revealed the product being promoted, whereas most of it promoted an ideal notion of beauty and a particular lifestyle. Then they asked, as the factory workers might have, where are the workers that made this product? It did not suddenly appear out of nowhere. In probing "what was behind it all,"

---

[1]At that time, almost 20 years ago, deconstructionism had not yet become vogue, and the fine art of "ad busting" was yet to be born. These days there is even a monthly magazine, *Adbusters*, put out by the Media Foundation in Vancouver, that features creative and critical reconstructions of ads as part of a deeper critique of consumer culture. For a good chuckle and a new critical tool, check them out on the Internet at adbusters@adbusters.org.

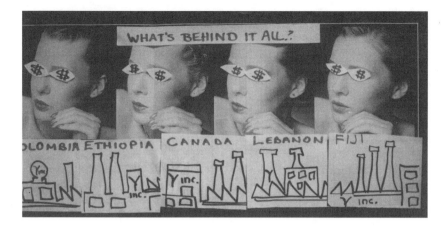

FIG. 2.2. Doctored Yardley advertisement: "Really are Not" and "What's behind it all?"

they developed a collective analysis of the multinational production and promotion of cosmetics. In the process, they discovered that Yardley had branch plants in each of the countries they represented, and so they turned the ad over and revealed the global production of goods that the original image obscured.

This ad and the critical and creative doctoring it received at the hands of immigrant workers and women educators reflect some important aspects of the cultural terrain that shapes our pedagogical work. The ad, like most, reveals one of the ways people, and in this case women, get officially "named," and how a homogenous ideal gets perpetuated, denying or devaluing the existence and daily reality not only of marginalized groups but of most of us who do not fit this market-driven ideal. The obscuring of the product as well as the invisibility of the producers and of the production process keeps us as consumers unaware of how what we consume is made, by whom, and under what conditions. In the same way, the image itself has magically appeared in our visual landscape; there is another factory somewhere for "ideological image production" where someone decides what we will see, and by extension, influences how we think about ourselves and the world. Both processes disconnect us: from the material and natural world, from the relations of production, from *naming* and *making*. In effect, such images, which by excluding us negate the value of our lives, also *disconnect* us from ourselves.

Yet when we critically and actively engage these images we can uncover the deeper processes behind them. We can begin to name, to make, and to connect parts of our lives in ways that make us more whole and that build a sense of community. Beyond these images, we can make our own; beyond these stories, we have our own to tell. Building community does not mean obliterating our differences either; telling our stories may uncover conflicting interests just as it may help us find common ground. But the process of imaging and writing our own diverse histories counters any homogenous representation of community and feeds new ways of connecting.

In this chapter,[2] I share some of the ways I have been involved over the past 25 years in collective photo-story production, in various community education contexts in both Latin America and North America. What I hope to emphasize in this revisiting is the pedagogical potential of the processes of production, and how they can be part of a reclaiming of what I call the lost arts of *naming, making,* and *connecting.*

PHOTO-STORIES OR FOTO-NOVELAS: BORROWING FROM THE SOUTH

Just as many North American educators have been inspired in the past two decades by the creative practice and highly developed theory of "popular education" growing out of social movements in Latin America,[3] so too have we learned from the related evolution in that region of "popular communications." As Riaño (1994) elaborated, this field includes multiple forms of cultural expression: from more traditional practices of poetry, textile work, silk screen, cartoons, music, and popular theater to more technologized forms of communications such as community radio, photography, video, and, now, the Internet. What distinguishes popular communications (from the official media and even some alternative media) is the stance it takes with marginalized populations (the word *popular* in Spanish refers to "the people," with a clear class connotation). It is also different from mainstream media in its emphasis on the involvement of people not only in producing their own art and media but in producing their own meanings through this process.

Popular communications is a tool for popular education, especially when it promotes collective and creative processes, countering the more individ-

[2]I would like to acknowledge the contributions not only of all the coworkers and participants in workshops and productions described here, but also of current coworkers and students at the Faculty of Environmental Studies, particularly those involved in the Cultural Production Workshop, the Focus on Food project, and the "Roots and Routes" media festival. Special thanks to those who have offered useful critical feedback on this chapter: Stephanie Conway, Mark Haslam, Zabe MacEachren, Robert Mound, and Julia Winkler.

[3]Although Freire (1970, 1993) may be the best known of the theoreticians (*Pedagogy of the Oppressed*), popular educators in networks such as CEAAL (Latin American Adult Education Council) and ALFORJA (a consortium of Central American popular education centers) have been prolific in collectively developing and systematizing their methodology.

ualized, competitive, passive, fragmented, and text-based pedagogical practices of most hegemonic educational institutions. Vancouver-based popular educator Nadeau (1996) has delineated the following characteristics of popular communications: It is concrete (not abstract); it's hot (starts from the heart, not the head); it starts from the local moving to the national and global; it often uses stories and metaphors; it is intersectoral, linking the realities of different groups; it takes a stand; it includes humor, celebration, and joy; it is always part of a broader ongoing process, linked to critical education and collective organizing for change.

I first became exposed to popular communications while working with a literacy program in Lima, Peru, in the mid-1970s (Barndt, 1980), which was applying a methodology of *conscientization* developed by Brazilian educator Freire (1970, 1993). As we sought appropriate cultural forms for teaching literacy to rural migrants forced off their land into the burgeoning cities, we came upon the "foto-novela." Found on newsstands throughout Latin America, photo-novels are a kind of soap opera in comic book form, using photographs instead of cartoons to illustrate an unfolding melodrama of intrigue and passion. They were particularly popular among illiterates in Peru, who would sit on street corners engrossed in the visual dramas, able to "read" them through the actions and expressions in the photos. In deciding that foto-novelas had great potential as a teaching tool, we borrowed only the form, consciously transforming the content and, ultimately, their use as well as the processes through which they are produced (Barndt, 1982).

Those first attempts at producing socially critical photo-novels resulted in some interesting lessons. Working with a group of literacy teachers we "constructed" two stories to illustrate traditional and transformative approaches to teaching literacy. Whereas the adult participants in the literacy program were good natured about acting out our story, they also let us know they would have constructed it differently. First, they noted, we had an indigenous teacher playing the role of the authoritarian literacy worker and an outsider playing the role of the teacher committed to participatory learning. No matter the method, they preferred to be with "one of their own," in this case the (more oppressive) indigenous teacher. And so our casting had failed miserably. Second, the dialogue was definitely not theirs; it was ours. Finally, the story was ultimately BOR-ING: "This isn't a foto-novela," they chided us, "Where's the drama, the intrigue, the love?"

Since that first attempt more than 20 years ago, I have been involved in facilitating collective productions of more than 50 photo-stories,[4] from stories of immigrant women in Toronto looking for work (for use in ESL classes) to tales of Nicaraguans evacuating the mountains during the con-

---

[4]See Barndt (1980); photo-stories in Barndt (1986–1991); Barndt et al. (1986); Barndt et al. (1983); Barndt & marino (1983).

tra war (for teaching literacy), from a musical photo-story (in images and song) produced at Tennessee's Highlander Center to a tool kit of photos produced for workplace classes in Toronto and Syracuse (Barndt, Belfiore, & Handscombe, 1984). In the early 1980s, we[5] facilitated workshops across Canada that involved community activists in making Polaroid photo-stories on the spot, on social issues ranging from unemployment in Newfoundland to the role of Native Friendship Centres in Montreal, from exploitative advertising in Calgary to househusbanding in Victoria (Barndt & Caselli, 1983). Between 1986 and 1992, we integrated into every issue of the Jesuit Centre publication, *The Moment*, a double-page photo-story on a conjunctural issue, each one coproduced with a community group working on that issue. Through three editions a year over seven years, we explored issues ranging from free trade and native self-government to environmental health and peace in Central America.

Finally, a course we offered from 1989 to 1993 at the Jesuit Centre on "Photography for Social Change" trained community workers in collective processes to produce their own stories with photos. Today I continue to be engaged in photo-story production as part of a research project uncovering the experiences of women workers in the food system: In Mexico, a tomato field worker tells her story,[6] and in Toronto, a supermarket cashier tells her story at the other end of the food chain. And as a counterpoint to these stories of globalized food production, a group of women on social assistance

---

[5]Throughout this historical review, I use "we" not in the "royal we" sense, but to indicate that I was usually codesigning and cofacilitating these participatory production processes. My coworkers, however, shifted from one project to another: I taught English in the workplace with dian marino and May Ann Kainola, and produced *English at Work: a Tool Kit for Teachers* with Mary Ellen Belfiore and Jean Handscombe, with the involvement of more than 20 ESL teachers. The *Getting There* photo-stories involved collaboration between the Development Education Centre (Ferne Cristall and Anita Martin) and the Participatory Research Group (dian marino and myself). The Nicaraguan and cross-Canada photo-story workshops were coordinated with my former husband, Daniel Caselli. The *Moment* photo-stories were eventually coordinated by Christine Almeida and involved myriad coproducers from community groups. I cotaught the Photography for Social Change course with Amy Gottlieb. Other coproducers over the years have included photographers David Smiley, Kathleen Flanagan, and Vince Pietropaolo. More recently, it's popular educators in Mexico, food activists in Toronto, and graduate students from the Faculty of Environmental Studies at York University that are working with me to shape these processes and products. Without diminishing my own initiative and leadership, I want to emphasize the collaborative way in which I have always worked, my own creativity fed by the synergy of an interactive process, not only in codesigning and cofacilitating workshops with colleagues but in engaging participants in their own productions. This dynamic was captured well by Daphne Uras (1996) in her Master's thesis at Carleton University, *A Certain Richness: Dialogues With and Within the Use of Photography of Popular Educator Deborah Barndt*. I am deeply grateful to her for giving me back a clearer sense of my own process.

[6]For a deeper analysis of some of the problematics of being a northern gringa researcher and photographer making photo-stories of poor Mexican women field workers, as well as a full version of the photo-story, *Teresa, Food Producer—At Work At Home* (see Barndt, 1997).

examine the "roots and routes" of their food histories, illustrating recipes with photo-stories of their lives.

Although we've come a long way since the first foto-novela in Peru in the 1970s, this process continues to be influenced by a cross-fertilization of ideas and practices in exchange with popular educators in Latin America and in North America. And, no matter the content, or whether the story is melodramatic or didactic, it is the *collective production process* itself that offers the richest moments for transformative learning, and the greatest possibilities for reclaiming the powers to name, to make, and to connect. It is time to explore what those processes are about, how they have been distorted or stolen from us, and how they might be reintegrated into our educational practice.

NAMING

> To exist humanly is to name the world, to change it.
>
> —Freire (1970, 1993, p. 76)

In a documentary film released in 1997, *Shooting Indians*, Ali Kazimi, Canadian filmmaker born in India, explores with his subject, native Canadian photographer Jeffrey Thomas, what it means be called "Indian," a label they both share, albeit with different cultural histories and meanings. Kazimi admits that his own stereotypes of North American Indians were shaped by the images of American popular culture permeating India that continued to *name* the reality of First Nations people through a colonizer's frame, starting with the cowboys and Indians of childhood games and movies. The film peels away the layers of this "official" naming process and reveals its effects on how we see ourselves and others. Not only people but places were named by the colonizing powers, so, for example, aboriginal territory off the coast of British Columbia bears the name of a dead British queen. And this naming process is not merely a thing of the past; we are constantly being named and renamed by others. Consider the evolution over recent decades of state-constructed categories for new immigrants, from alien and foreign to Third World and visible minority. At the same time that an increasingly globalized and homogenized mass media culture (as in the Yardley ad analyzed earlier) names us mainly as consumers and labels us with less valuing of our differences, identity politics[7] (in trying to address who names whom) often perpetuates a naming process that limits us to one

---

[7]The "politics of identity" became a strong theme in Canadian social movements in the 1980s, particularly because the naming of sexism and racism promoted a process whereby people examined more closely their own historical and cultural identities, and the ways they carried experiences of both privilege and oppression (see Giroux, 1994).

category, denying our multiple and mixed identities, and obscuring the more complex struggles of our daily lives.

Naming ourselves and our world is a basic power, essential to our capacity to be subjects of history and not objects or victims. Freire (1970, 1993) said, "We cannot enter the struggle as objects in order later to become subjects." For hooks (1994), Freire "affirmed my right as a subject in resistance to define my reality." Yet so much has mitigated against our being able to name our world, to tell our own stories. Rich (1979) talked about the importance of breaking this silence: "Where language and naming are power, silence is oppression, is violence." When we speak our story, we make meaning of our lives, and we find connection with other stories. Griffin (1992) described the power of this connection:

> I am beginning to believe that we know everything, that all history, including the history of each family is part of us ... and when we hear any secret revealed ... our lives are suddenly clearer to us. For perhaps we are like stones; our own history and the history of the world embedded in us, we hold a sorrow deep within and cannot weep until that history is sung. ... For deep in the mind we know everything. And wish to have everything told, to have our images and our words reflect the truth. (pp. 8, 16)

The "truths" are, of course, subjective and shifting, and there are no assurances that our own telling is more accurate or truthful than another's telling, but to engage in naming and telling (whether visually or verbally), and even in the contradictions of that act, is in itself a process filled with pedagogical potential. Lippard (1990), in *Mixed Blessings: New Art in Multicultural America*, titled her chapters around processes of what I see as reclaiming our power to create and connect (Barndt, 1995). The first three processes that she calls "mapping, naming, and telling" are intimately related: Naming ourselves in the world involves a mapping, locating ourselves in time and space, in a historical and cultural context, putting ourselves in a bigger picture, seeing ourselves as part of a longer journey. Naming also invokes telling: To name is not only to declare who we are but to make sense of our lives. Telling our own stories affirms our power to write our own histories and our participation in making our history.

So how does photo-story production stimulate these mapping and naming and telling processes? In most of the productions I have been involved in for more than 25 years, there has been a collective process where people with some common interest have had an opportunity to tell their stories, in many cases breaking a silence in that act of naming. And the use of photos also made visible what had until that point been invisible. There is a tremendous energy released at these moments when people recognize themselves and their complex histories. The experience integrates pain, joy, and connection.

One of the first experiences in the early 1980s involved immigrant women from an English in the Workplace program sharing their stories of looking for work and "just getting there." Managing the urban transport system or getting to the first job interview were actions deeply symbolic of what it meant for these women to believe they could make their way in this new country and into the work world. The process itself (Barndt, Cristall, & marino, 1983) brought women together in living rooms on Sunday afternoons to share their tales of looking for work and eventually to re-enact those tales with photos. The way they "named" and told their tales was intensely personal and revealed an inner dialogue with themselves. Climbing the wooden stairs of a railroad bridge, for example, became a metaphor for developing the confidence to enter an alien world. We tried to recreate through the camera lens the emotional as well as the physical perspective of the woman talking herself into taking the first step—up the stairs and toward work outside the home in a new country. This view of women's internal struggles was never revealed in the more official dominant media images.

FIG. 2.3. Aurora climbing stairs of railroad bridge.

FIG. 2.4. Aurora looking at image of a western woman.

The photo-story production, although affirming the common experiences and feelings of immigrant women seeking work, was not without its own contradictions. As middle-class educators and editors, with more time to spend on the project and with an interest in publishing the stories, we made many of the decisions about what would stay and what would go in constructing the final product. In looking back on this process, coauthor marino (1997) suggested that we "cleaned up the text," taking out the racism, sexism, and classism. At the same time that we juxtaposed their images with advertising images of women they confronted on their journeys, we had "turned out a whiter than white narrative, inadvertently silencing conflict and affirmation" (marino, 1997, p. 114). Here we failed to name and deal with our differences, and we ran the risk of reproducing what we were critiquing: naming these women through our own critical frames. This is always a danger in the process of collective photo-story production, especially when the editing is done by a select few. There are probably no perfect ways to approach these limitations and differences, but it is important to acknowledge and engage them.

In another experience, a decade later, we chose as facilitators to participate in the naming and telling processes, putting ourselves into the picture, revealing ourselves just as we asked participants to do. In a year-long photography course built around the theme of "Lifelines: Recovering Family and Community Histories," we started with family album photos, which evoked deep memories and generated storytelling immediately. Building on those first photo-storying processes, our personal projects engaged us in selecting aspects of our histories that we wanted to explore visually and verbally. Gathering oral histories was, in fact, an important part of the process.

During the first months of the course, we used an exercise called "Power Flower,"[8] which asked each of us to identify different aspects of our social identity, related to power relations based on gender, race, class, sexual orientation, religion, political perspective, and so on. The activity required that we name what we thought was the dominant group in each category and indicate how we would name ourselves. It is always interesting to see how easily we fall into using the labels we have been given. In the past several years the categories that seem to be the most fluid and contested are "religion/spirituality" and "political perspective," indicating people are struggling (individually and collectively) to define and name themselves in new ways around these dynamic aspects of culture. When we were really able to move beyond identity politics was when we began to dig into and share our own histories. Then our stories reflected the complexity and messiness that could not be edited out or placed into neat petals of a flower. By grounding ourselves in our own cultural contexts, unearthing our own histories while others were unearthing theirs, we were better able to acknowledge and deal with our differences.

Naming, then, is not a simple process, for it calls for us to be fully alive, reflecting on where we've come from and where we're going. Yet, if we see ourselves not only as receivers of history but as makers of history, we can reclaim our capacity to name and rename ourselves. Photographs and photo-story production can be tools in this process, reflecting back to us, like a mirror, and framing our presence in the world, like a window. The struggle to name is not only individually affirming but also contributes to a deeper connection among people.

MAKING

Through the separation of matter and spirit, ordinary life has lost its significance.
—Griffin (1995, p. 121)

I have long been fascinated with the creative energies released when people come together to make something, using their minds and hearts as well as directly engaging their bodies in a production, whether it be a theater

---

[8]See Arnold, Burke, James, Martin, and Thomas (1991, pp. 13–15) for a more thorough discussion of this tool and its uses.

piece, a quilt or banner, or, in this case, a photo-story. In the 1970s, with other members of the Participatory Research Group, we formed a Popular Art and Media Cooperative, attempting to counter the notion that only certain people could make art and produce media. We drew from a Marxist analysis that work within capitalist industrialization had alienated workers from the sources and processes of production, from any connection to the whole product (which, in contrast, the craftsperson experienced). In the same light, we suggested that artistic and media production, too, had become commodified and specialized, alienating most of us from any sense of being producers or makers of culture or cultural expression.

How is it that we have become separated from our "bodies," in such a way that we speak of them as though they were outside of us, separate from our "minds"? The epistemological roots of this mind–body split lie in the emergence of western science in the 18th century based on a mechanistic rather than a holistic paradigm. The philosopher Descartes ("I think, therefore I am") articulated the divorce of the human mind from the human body, of human from nonhuman nature, of cerebral thinking from the emotions. Still with us today, this dualism is reflected in western education systems that divide knowledge into subjects and disciplines, that privilege so-called intellectual over manual labor.

To reclaim making as a valid and dynamic pedagogical process is also to value the process of engaging directly with material reality and in the social relations of production. To see the transformation of a story into a photo-story, for example, is a rich educational process that is both manual and intellectual. Through an engagement that is visceral, it affirms body knowledge and "flesh knowing" (Heath, 1995). One of the things I have loved over the years about my involvement with photography as a tool is the many ways it calls me to engage with both material and symbolic reality: from manipulating camera and film, light and shadow (mediating my experience with the subject) to processing and printing, designing and laying out a story with photos and text (representing that experience). It engages me with matter as well as with spirit.

Although a hegemonic practice of photography is usually individualized, the participatory production of photo-stories in an adult education context is consciously a collective process. We have not only reclaimed the production process (i.e., rather than digesting someone else's texts, we are making our own), but we have attempted to democratize that process. There are several points at which the process can be participatory: in deciding what themes to focus on, in sharing stories that become the core of a text, in taking the photos, in making them in the darkroom (and for those with access, on the computer with photoshop software), in laying them out, in integrating text and photos, in celebrating a finished product, and in using it collectively and critically in a new context.

A couple of examples illustrate this engagement in the *making* process that serves to demystify the technologies and reskill (rather than deskill) us as producers of goods as well as producers of meaning. In training literacy teachers in Nicaragua in the early 1980s to become what we called "popular photojournalists" (Barndt, 1990), I was amazed at how collectively they approached the process of production. After gathering oral histories and photographing in the community around a theme, we would crowd into our makeshift darkroom. Whereas my experience of making photos in a darkroom had been always a personal experience (bordering on the meditative and mystical), the Nicaraguans entered into the process with a collective energy I had never before witnessed: deciding among themselves the correct exposure and appropriate cropping, sharing the tasks of manipulating the enlarger, running the print through the chemical baths, and washing and drying the finished product. It was, in fact, a wonderful social activity, filled with laughter and creative fusion. A similar dynamic reigned in the construction of the final story as photos were integrated with text.

Whereas in the north we are so removed from production processes we most likely consider collective darkroom work as out of the question, there are other simpler ways we can engage groups in production. During a cross-Canada tour with a photo exhibit on Nicaragua in the early 1980s

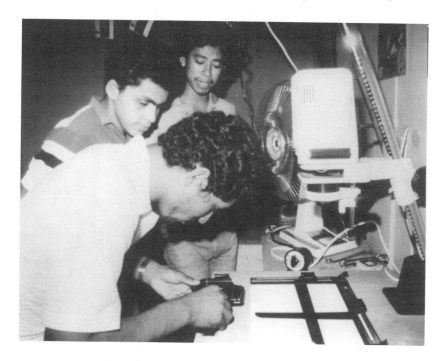

FIG. 2.5. Nicaraguans working in darkroom together.

(Barndt & Caselli, 1983), we offered 23 photo-story workshops for educators and community workers in cities across the country. Using a slide show on photo-story production made by the Nicaraguan literacy teachers, we proposed using Polaroid cameras to speed up production during these one-shot workshops that lasted either 3 hours or 6 hours (a shorter and a longer version). Participants were surprised by their capacity to engage with the technology and with the world outside the workshop space. With a limited amount of time and working in small groups, they collectively selected themes, gathered images, laid them out with text in a scrapbook form, and shared them with other groups. I am convinced that part of what made this process so dynamic and empowering was the synergy that emerged from what was, in fact, a physical process: going out with a camera (or constructing sociodramas to photograph inside), playing with the order and design of the images, and presenting a product to the plenary. Although the product itself was deemphasized for a focus on the process, it was nonetheless a source of great pride to see and touch and pass around something they had made so quickly and yet so creatively.

The physical synergy stimulated an intellectual synergy (just as the kinetic experience of walking can generate creative thinking), and the discussions and debates that accompanied the decision-making processes (what issue will we address? how will we frame this image? where will this photo

FIG. 2.6. Halifax group: hands putting Polaroid photos in order; Winnipeg group sharing finished photo stories.

go? what words will embellish it?) were active forms of collective analysis. First the camera and then the photos mediated the discussion, generated interaction, and sparked creative thought that I am certain would not have emerged if we had merely discussed the issues rather than produced images that represented them. The speeded up production processes, of course, were not conflict free, and part of the struggle was the common one of working together as a group, honoring individual interventions while coming up with something they could collectively own. No easy task. But the energy that filled the room was contagious, and, in part, I believe the participants' pride came from being directly involved in making something—hands, heart, head all working together, one stimulating the other, the artificial division between them dissolved.

CONNECTING

Because we think in a fragmentary way, we see fragments. And this way of seeing leads us to make actual fragments of the world.
                                                                —Griffin (1995, p. 61)

We have been denied opportunities to name our world and ourselves, and production and consumption have become commodified so that we no longer see ourselves as makers—of our food and shelter, of our artistic and cultural expression. In this loss of the power to *name* and to *make*, we have become disconnected: culture from nature, mind from body, ourselves from each other, from our roots, from our communities. Many of us, especially in the west, have become in certain ways refugees, homeless people, fragmented, postmodern persons. As people are beginning to name this schism and to address it, there are efforts to reconnect what has seemingly become disconnected. Indeed, reconnecting—body and mind, spirit and matter, human and nonhuman nature—is essential to our survival and the survival of the planet. Griffin (1995) spoke poignantly about this connection:

> Of course, the body and the mind are not separate. Consciousness cannot exclude bodily knowledge. We are inseparable from nature, dependent on the biosphere, vulnerable to the processes of natural law. We cannot destroy the air we breathe without destroying ourselves. (p. 226)

This may seem like a tall order for adult education, but I believe that as educators we must see every learning event as a moment for nurturing these connections and countering the fragmentation that permeates our culture and many of our daily interactions with it. I am using "connecting," then, in several ways that in fact incorporate the acts of naming and making discussed earlier. Participatory photo-story production connects us individually with our own histories, encouraging us to name and to tell, valuing our stories as the central content for our learning, whether it's language training or community development or cultural work that is the context. Engagement with words and images, the production of learning materials, connects us as whole persons—body and mind, reason and emotion, intellectual and manual—challenging these dichotomies (and their implicit hierarchies) that have been perpetuated by one-sided educational practices. The physical engagement with cameras, photos, bookmaking, connects us with the material world, and, ironically, this creative process (transforming matter) nurtures our spirit.

The collective-production process illustrated in the examples offered thus far also connects us with one another: Personal stories are shared for their common elements; the construction of composite stories links both people and issues; the group creations draw on the varied skills of diverse group members; the finished product is not only an individual but also a collective achievement. Photo-story-production processes, which nurture both critical thinking and creative action, help to build a sense of community (hopefully honoring diversity and differences) among the namers, makers, and connectors. Again, this approach is in contrast to dominant educational practices that emphasize individuality, rationality, competition, conformity, and ultimately isolation and fragmentation.

I draw from two examples to illustrate the different kinds of connecting that photo-story production can engender. In 1986, we at the Jesuit Centre produced an issue of *The Moment* on native self-government to feed the public discussions generated by a series of First Ministers Conferences on the subject. The photo-story that served as a centrepiece for the issue was coproduced with a local First Nations School and the Riverdale Immigrant Women's Centre, both located in the lower eastside Toronto neighborhood where we worked. In the process of sharing stories, first between adults and children at the school and later between native people and new Canadians, we uncovered the connections between the mercury poisoning of a lake in a northern Ontario native community and the poisoning of the soil and the Don River in South Riverdale by a local smelter spouting lead into the air. The native children shared the perspective they had gained from their elders with the immigrant children as they explored the smelter and the river: "If you hurt her (Mother Earth), it's like hurting your own skin."

Thus, the content of the story that resulted from this cross-cultural dialogue connected political-economic and ecological issues, and connected communities affected by them, and connected all of us with the earth that feeds us even as we sometimes threaten to destroy it. The production process brought together two communities that rarely see the common ground on which they stand. The published story was to link the struggle for self-government with the broader struggle to protect the environment, connect-

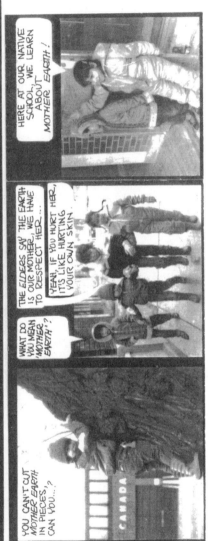

FIG. 2.7. From photo-story "Who Owns Mother Earth?"

ing the nature–culture divide perpetuated by industries and governments that deny human complicity and the reality that we are all part of nature.

In my research on the journey of the tomato from the Mexican field to the Canadian table (Barndt, 1997), I also challenged the fragmentation wrought by a globalized food system that has disconnected most of us from the sources of food we eat. Photo-stories of Tomasa, a Mexican field worker picking tomatoes, and of Marisa, a Canadian cashier scanning tomatoes at the supermarket counter, each help to reveal the processes of production, distribution, and consumption that bring food to our table. As these stories are shared across borders and among women workers, they also are able to connect themselves to this broader process and to join in the analysis of our disconnection from the earth, from agriculture, and from food (Barndt, 1997). Marisa, for example, read Tomasa's story and became interested in the working and living conditions of the Mexican fieldworkers who pick the tomatoes she sells in Toronto. She learned from Tomasa about what's happening to the land because of monocultural cash crop production and the vicious cycle of ever-changing hybrid seeds and agrochemical use, and she wondered about its effect on the health of northern consumers. There are indeed many levels and layers of connections to be made.

The project also explored alternatives to this global process and involved a group of (mostly) immigrant women participating in a training program in downtown Toronto in naming and making their own food stories. In a collaborative project between the Focus on Food program of Metro Toronto FoodShare and the Faculty of Environmental Studies at York University, we explored our diverse relationships to food under the theme "Roots and Routes: Nourishing Connections from Land to Table." The initial storytelling was catalyzed by sharing favorite recipes that revealed something about our personal and cultural histories. Tracing the origins of these recipes and their ingredients, and the equally twisty journeys of our own lives moving from one continent to another, we produced photo-stories that unearthed the tales hidden in the dishes we eat or in the ground of our often invisible histories.

Although the naming of the recipes and their "roots and routes" proved empowering, it was the making process that taught me new things about reconnecting with our histories and our creativity. By accident, we found ourselves working one day on the stories, while Maeza, an Eritrean, rushed back and forth to the kitchen to monitor a traditional stew she was making. Finally, we followed her and the aromas to the kitchen to taste the product of her culinary creativity. There, with her hands on the bread or stirring the stew, the stories really started to flow, and as we tasted her work and queried her process, a collective learning process emerged that was palpable. Cameras were there to capture some of it, and the photos proved lively additions to the photo-stories. We realized that the more visceral processes of

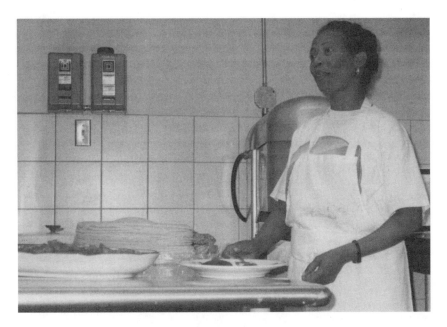

FIG. 2.8. Maeza in the kitchen.

cooking and eating really tapped her (as well as our) embodied knowing, and this was a much more dynamic way to work on our photo-stories. Thus, for the next 7 weeks, each week with a new person at the stove, we worked collectively on the individual stories that reconnected us to our own histories while connecting us across continents and centuries, bodies and spirits, land and table.

ENGAGING CREATIVE TENSIONS: IT'S NOT ALL SO SMOOTH (NOR IS IT MEANT TO BE)

I don't mean to paint a picture of a seamless process, methodically planned and executed, conflict free and deeply meaningful. In fact, just as the above story illustrates, these processes emerge often serendipitously, unlike what we might have planned, and it requires the ability to recognize the moments, pregnant with pedagogical possibility, that are to be grabbed, used, and deepened. Photo-story production, just like any other form of popular communications applied to contexts of popular education, must engage certain creative tensions. These tensions may make us uncomfortable but they can also challenge us, I have come to believe.

FIG. 2.9.

In my teaching I use a framework that suggests we pay attention to five aspects of popular communications: the *context* within which we are working and creating (which offers both constraints and possibilities), the *content* of our product (the message or story we want to tell), the particularities of the *form* (media technologies, their evolution, and how they have shaped the process of telling), the processes related to *production* (what has been emphasized here), and its *use* (from the dominant function of selling goods and a way of life that predominates the use of mainstream media images, for example, to the pedagogical and political uses suggested here for images we find or make). Under each of these elements, I've identified tensions that are engaged through counterhegemonic media production, which is where I locate the participatory photo-story production. The framework is as follows:

Content
Personal versus political
Didactic versus problem posing

Form
Technical or artistic quality versus relevant content

Artist versus animator

Production
Process versus product
Individual versus collective

Use
Private versus public
Education versus organizing

I name these tensions not as dichotomies to be resolved but as contradictions to be engaged. And it is the overarching factor of context that usually determines how we work or play with each of them. When I'm training a group of students or a community group in participatory photo-story production, for example, but we have a deadline for a publication or an exhibit, I inevitably must confront the tension of process versus product. If it is important that the product see the light of day, and there are real time constraints, this may shape the process, making it less than ideal. There are judgment calls all along the way. Do I want to offer a clear statement of my own message in the content of my story or do I want to pose some questions and ambiguities that engage the viewers and readers in the issue, compelling them to develop their own positions? How can we honor the unique experiences of individuals within a group while finding common ground that gets expressed in a collective production? Is our photo-story mainly to raise awareness about an issue or to stimulate people to act? These are not simple questions, nor are the answers necessarily straightforward. Sometimes these seeming contradictions are not resolved with an "either–or" framing but rather with a "both–and" response. My motto is ultimately: "Embrace the contradictions" and find within them the possibilities for moving forward.

Other tensions inevitable in the kind of production process promoted here arise out of the differences in power among participants. As suggested earlier, these are not always easy to articulate, as each of us embodies both privilege and oppression in our multiple social identities. As a white teacher in an ESL class of immigrant women of color, for example, although we share the experience of gender discrimination, I have to be conscious of how my skin color privilege, my class privilege, and my educational and occupational privileges shape our interactions. We had this difference brought home to us only too poignantly, when we did a story in a factory-based English class on the dangers workers faced in crossing a busy highway to catch the bus after work. Although we supported their organizing a petition to request a crosswalk from the city, officials responded by fining them $28 for jay walking, consuming their daily wage and angering management. In a painful reflection on this process, they reminded us that we could leave the factory, while they had to live with the consequences of any political action we might engender in the class.

As educators, we have responsibilities to our students, and these must guide our production and use of any stories that are drawn from their daily lives and struggles. Razack (1993) warned about the dangers of "storytelling for social change" and suggested we develop an ethical vision based on our differences. Even in mixed-sex and mixed-race groupings where there is a commitment to social change, "our various histories are not left at the door when we enter a classroom to critically reflect" (p. 90). She invoked Ellsworth's (1992) suggestion that we critically examine what we share and don't share. Narayan (1988) also explored strategies educators might apply: "If 'working together across difference' is to at all be possible, we must learn to analogize from situations of oppression in which we have been 'insiders' to those in which we are 'outsiders.'" Photo-story-production processes, then, can generate rich (and sometimes tense) discussions about our differences, as stories are told, interpreted, compared, and represented. Again an educator's sensitivity and skill are as important tools as the camera.

CRITICAL CONDITIONS LAY THE GROUND

I have resisted offering any formulaic outline of the principles or steps of participatory photo-story production because I believe these tensions and questions have to be confronted *in the process* and *in the context* and *with the people* whose lives are implicated and whose critical and creative capacities are engaged. But I do think there are certain critical conditions for these kinds of processes to unfold. The first is a basic and deep *respect for the people involved*; no matter how careful the planning or creative the tools, without this, the process will fail. Second, a *climate of trust* must be nurtured that affirms participants' diverse histories and their capacities to tell them in a variety of ways (as well as their right not to tell them at all). Trust takes time to develop and has to be constantly nurtured, and sometimes regained and renegotiated.

A *commitment to learning and growing*, and the willingness to learn from mistakes (which includes recognizing our own racism or sexism, for example), is also essential. Almost any daily situation can become an educable moment with this attitude. A *spirit of adventure and playfulness* is also important in this very "serious" work. It is risky to try new things with many voices saying you're not able, it's not appropriate, it's not good enough. With all of this comes the belief that the sources of *knowledge and creativity are within us and among us* that we know more than we think we do, and if we don't, perhaps someone else in the group can fill in or pick up where we left off.

A final condition is the ability to *embrace the contradictions* named here and the inevitable contradictions within our own personal lives and ways of being. Granted, these conditions are not easily created, so we have to forgive ourselves for not reaching them all, and nonetheless jump in and try. The rewards ultimately, I believe, are in the energy and strength we gain as we reclaim our own power to name ourselves; to make our stories visible; and to connect, challenging the dichotomies of body–mind, private–public, personal–political, individual–collective, critical–creative, and nature–culture. Perhaps it's a radical notion, but as *radical* means "going to the roots," promoting participatory photo-story production in adult education can address the roots of our alienation and fragmentation, and reclaim the lost arts of naming, making, and connecting. As educators, can we aim for anything less? Not only our learning, but our survival depends upon it.

REFERENCES

Arnold, R., Burke, B., James, C., Martin, D., & Thomas, B. (1991). *Educating for a change*. Toronto, Canada: Between the Lines and the Doris Marshall Institute.

Barndt, D. (1980). *Education and social change: A photographic study of Peru*. Dubuque, IA: Kendall-Hunt.

Barndt, D. (1982). *Just getting there: Creating visual tools for collective analysis in Freirean education programmes for migrant women in Peru and Canada. Working Paper No. 7*. Toronto, Canada: Participatory Research Group.

Barndt, D. (Ed.). (1986–1991). *The Moment*, quarterly educational resource. Toronto: Jesuit Centre for Social Faith and Justice. Photo-stories referred to in the text: Who owns Mother Earth?, *1*(1), Winter 1987. Digging deeper, *1*(3), Autumn 1987. Beware the summer of '88, *2*(1), Winter 1987–88. An intimate connection, *2*(2), Spring 1988.

Barndt, D. (1990). *To change this house: Popular education under the Sandinistas*. Toronto, Canada: Between the Lines.

Barndt, D. (1995). Cultural work: Reclaiming the power to create. *Arts, 7*(2), 23–28.

Barndt, D. (1997). Zooming out/zooming in: Visualizing globalization. *Visual Sociology, 12* (2), 5–32.

Barndt, D., Belfiore, M. E., & Handscombe, J. (1984). *English at work: A tool kit for teachers*. North York, Canada: CORE Foundation.

Barndt, D., & Caselli, D. (1983). *Crossing Canada for solidarity*. Toronto, Canada: Canadian Action for Nicaragua.

Barndt, D., Cristall, F., & marino, d. (1983). *Getting there: Producing photo-stories with immigrant women*. Toronto, Canada: Between the Lines.

Barndt, D., & marino, d. (1983). *Immigrants speak out*. North York, Canada: North York Board of Education.

Ellsworth, E. (1992). Why doesn't this feel empowering? Working through the repressive myths of critical pedagogy. In C. Luke & J. Gore (Eds.), *Feminisms and critical pedagogy* (pp. 90–119). New York: Routledge.

Freire, P. (1970, 1993). *Pedagogy of the oppressed*. New York: Continuum.

Giroux, H. (1994). Living dangerously: Identity politics and the new cultural racism. In H. Giroux & P. McLaren (Eds.), *Between borders: Pedagogy and the politics of cultural studies* (pp. 29–55). New York: Routledge.

Griffin, S. (1992). *A chorus of stones: The private life of war.* New York: Doubleday.

Griffin, S. (1995). *The eros of everyday life: Essays on ecology, gender, and society.* New York: Doubleday.

Heath, F. (1995). *Home etc.* Unpublished manuscript, York University at Toronto, Canada.

hooks, b. (1994). *Teaching to transgress: Education as a practice of freedom.* New York: Routledge.

Lippard, L. (1990). *Mixed blessings: New art in multicultural America.* New York: Pantheon.

marino, d. (1997). *Wild garden: Art, education, and the culture of resistance.* Toronto, Canada: Between the Lines.

McIntosh, P. (1992). White privilege and male privilege. In M. Anderson & P. Collins (Eds), *Race, class and gender: An anthology* (pp. 70–81). Belmont, CA: Wadsworth Publishing.

Nadeau, D. (1996). *Counting our victories: Popular education and organizing.* Vancouver, Canada: Repeal the Deal Productions.

Narayan, U. (1988). Working together across difference: Some considerations on emotions and political practice. *Hypatia, 3*(2), 31–47.

Razack, S. (1993). Storytelling for social change. In H. Bannerji (Ed.), *Returning the gaze: Essays on racism, feminism, and politics* (pp. 83–100). Toronto, Canada: SisterVision Press.

Riaño, P. (1994). *Women and grassroots communications.* Thousand Oaks, CA: Sage.

Rich, A. (1979). *On lies, secrets, and silence: Selected prose, 1966–78.* New York: Norton.

Uras, D. (1996). *A certain richness: Dialogues with and within the use of photography in the work of popular educator, Deborah Barndt.* Unpublished master's thesis, Carleton University, Ottawa, Canada.

3

Participatory Literacy Practices: Exploring Pedagogy

Pat Campbell
Centre for Research on Literacy
University of Alberta

During the 1990s, literacy workers across Canada began to encourage adult literacy students to get more involved in literacy programs and activities. In 1994, I explored participatory literacy practices with students and educators from five adult literacy programs. Throughout this study, the educators questioned their pedagogical approach with students as they tried to move toward a more participatory model. The students, who adopted leadership positions, struggled with their new roles and responsibilities. This chapter explores the tensions inherent in a participatory approach.

THE DESIGN

The main purpose of this research was to study participatory literacy practices or the active involvement of students in the operation of one or more components of their adult literacy program. The study was guided by the following two questions:

1. What are the individual and group experiences of students and literacy workers who are involved in participatory literacy practices?
2. What changes do students and literacy workers see in themselves and in their programs as they become involved in participatory literacy practices?

55

This study examined participatory literacy practices in one urban and four rural literacy programs in Alberta. As a reference point, the growth and development of student groups within these adult literacy programs were followed. These groups were viewed as a venue for students to represent their interests and needs in relation to their literacy programs.

The study was conducted within the naturalistic research paradigm (Lincoln & Guba, 1985) and the data regarding the two research questions were collected through 28 individual and 5 group interviews, journals, fieldnotes, photostories,[1] document analysis, and a questionnaire. Photo-stories were used to generate knowledge and record information about participatory practices. Photo-stories were used because they involve a group experience that employs visual and verbal modes of communication appropriate for adults with low literacy skills. As well, photo-stories are a fluid process that created a safe place for students to express desire(s) for change.

THE PROGRAMS

Five programs were involved in this study: (a) ALFA, a rural southern Alberta literacy program whose primary mode of instruction was one-to-one tutoring; (b) Action Read, an urban Alberta literacy program, which also followed the one-to-one tutoring model; and (c) The Literacy Network, an educational institution that sponsored three full-time literacy programs in the northern rural communities of Creston, Haines Junction, and Virden.[2]

ALFA, which is staffed by one part-time literacy worker, serves approximately 50 students from five rural communities on an annual basis. At any one time, approximately 30 to 40 students are working with volunteer tutors. At the time of this study, 39% of the registered students were male and 61% were female. English was the mother tongue for 67% of the students, and English was a second language for the remaining students. Action Read, with a staff of three full-time literacy workers, serves approximately 170 to 200 students every year. At any one time, there are usually 90 to 100 students matched with volunteer tutors. During the time of this study, 47% of the registered students were male and 53% were female. English was the

---

[1]A photo-story or photo-novella is usually a book that combines photographs with text. "The goal of photonovella is to use people's photographic documentation of their everyday lives as an educational tool to record and to reflect their needs, promote dialogue, encourage action and inform policy" (Wang & Burris, 1994, p. 171). In this study, each student group narrated their story about participatory practices. One photo-story dealt with a critical issue centering on staff–student relations, another dealt with the benefits of student groups, and another focused on the difficulties in forming a student group.

[2]Pseudonyms are used for these literacy programs and their geographical locations as well as for the students and literacy workers who participated in the study.

mother tongue for 69% of the students, and English was the second language for the remaining students. Finally, the Literacy Network, which is coordinated by one full-time staff member, sponsors three literacy programs, each of which is staffed by one paid tutor for every four students. The 13 female and 6 male students enrolled in the Creston program were from the Mennonite culture, with English being their second language. Of the 6 female and 3 male students in the Haines Junction program, 7 spoke English as their second language. The 6 male and 5 female students registered with the Virden program were Native and spoke English as a second language.

THE FINDINGS

The findings pertaining to pedagogies are presented and discussed under the following three themes: (a) to be versus to do, (b) top-down versus bottom-up, and (c) leadership.

Pedagogies

To Be Versus to Do. Pedagogy attends to the practices of teaching and learning and the knowledge that educators and students produce within a given time and space. Within this time and space, the question "What are we going to do?" underscores the practices of teaching and learning and tends to surface more than the question "How should this class be?" According to Shor (1980), this emphasis on doing sometimes results in a "liquidation of autonomous time and space" where students and educators can engage in free discussion, exchange of ideas, and collective exploration of experiences (p. 8).

In this study the literacy workers were working with student support groups and student associations. Consequently, the focus was not on teaching and learning per se, but, nonetheless, there was still an emphasis on "doing." The following excerpts illustrate how Shelley, an Action Read staff member, and Liz, the Literacy Network coordinator, focused on the need "to do":

> I realized I was concerned that are they really *doing* something, the students, sort of in their student associations or their groups, like are they really doing anything, you know sort of concrete and very formal. . . . And what's happening when they're meeting? Are they *just* talking that type of thing? But then I learned well maybe that's what for me *I* would need, that if I was a student maybe and I was involved more in an association. (Liz)

> I guess because I'm really task oriented, I always think you meet, you have plans and goals and you *do* things and you keep meeting until they're *done*. And it's a very linear kind of thought process. And I realize that that's really

not what's happening. Different people coming to different meetings, having different expectations. And I'm sort of trying to see where it all will lead.

And then, I ask myself questions, what kind of group would it take to get something *done*. And you know, why are they not really interested? (Shelley)

Shelley and Liz described their preference for doing as an individual trait. However, I would like to argue that their orientation toward task is not just an individual trait, but part of the structure of their literacy programs in which they are positioned. Their programs are very production oriented, an orientation that mirrors today's society. Consequently, programs and staff who produce products and results are praised and supported. According to Sauvé (1987), "In our society there is a tremendous value placed upon the doing of something. We may indeed be driven to the point of feeling guilty if we cannot readily tell someone what it is that we are doing. Yet education is, in the classic sense, more concerned with being than doing" (p. 47). Sauvé argued that the present educational system is based on a delivery-based model that reflects society's orientation towards production.

In rereading the interview questions that I posed to students and educators, I can see that, like Shelley and Liz, I was also caught up in the framework of doing. For instance, the question "What are the group's goals?" indicates an emphasis on doing. When I posed this questions to Barb, the ALFA literacy coordinator, she framed her response around the need to be, rather than the need to do. She told me "that they're still groping. We're trying to find out who we are." Barb was the only literacy worker who was not overly concerned that the student group had not formulated goals; she recognized that the student group needed time to be.

The text of the ALFA photo-story suggested that being is a prerequisite to doing. It was only once the group had time to "be," that they were ready to move on to "do." The text reads:

We enjoy student meetings because we make new friends. We feel comfortable about sharing our feelings and ideas. You feel as if you are not alone. You don't feel like you are the only one in this position. We feel more confident. Some of us used to be so shy we could not even speak to people. Now that we have more confidence, we are doing more things by ourselves and with the group.

In the early stages of the ALFA student group's formation, they spent time talking and sharing. When asked why she attended the meetings, Heidi, one of the ALFA students, responded, "I think just to be with them and just to talk how they feel here . . . and you can share some feelings that other people don't understand." As well, Peggy, president of ALFA's student group, accentuated the importance of "being" in the following statement:

"I've really learned how important it is *to be* with other students." Shor (1980) located discussion within a socioeconomic context and believed that "discussion is a privilege, not a democratically distributed right" (p. 73). In other words, those who are in positions of power and privilege have more time and opportunity to engage in discussion, whereas working class people are often employed in labor-intensive and service-oriented jobs where one is not rewarded for discussing ideas.

The findings suggest that the students in Action Read and the Literacy Network also wanted to be engaged in a mutually reinforcing process of being and doing. In the following dialogue, Maria, an Action Read student, responded to my question about the purpose of the student group:

Maria: Everybody had different ideas about starting [the group] you know.

Pat: About what it should do?

Maria: What it should do, what student group should be.

If we juxtapose Maria and Shelley's vision of the student group, we can see a striking difference. Whereas Shelley, the literacy worker, wanted the student group to have plans and goals, Maria, the student, wanted the group to engage in being *and* doing.

In examining the written purpose and objectives of Virden's student association, I saw how the group was trying to resist society's dominant discourse that values doing over being. Although half of the objectives related to doing and were production oriented, the other half were related to being. Objectives that came under the rubric of being were items such as giving everybody a chance to speak, discussing ideas, supporting other ideas, and involving everybody. Objectives that came under the rubric of doing were items such as going on field trips and buying books for beginning readers. When I initially saw that the student group had slotted discussing ideas and giving everybody a chance to speak under the heading "objectives," I thought to myself, "These ones don't fit." Now, I realize that although the being objectives did not fit my schema that emphasized doing, they did fit a schema that emphasized being and doing.

Why do we, as educators, place such importance on doing, when students seem to clearly speak for a balance between being and doing? I think that, as educators, we are positioned within a product-oriented discourse that is governed by a set of discursive practices. For instance, programs, projects, and proposals that receive recognition and government funding are those that are time bound and tied to products and results. And increasingly, within the conservative climate of Alberta, it appears that if we don't do, they won't allow us to be.

Top-Down Versus Bottom-Up. Bottom-up, top-down—educators use these words to describe the pedagogical process.[3] Bottom-up refers to a process where students are participants in setting the agenda of their learning experience; they are active subjects of their learning. Top-down, on the other hand, refers to a process where students are passive recipients of a predefined agenda; they are objects of their learning. Within the literature, top-down and bottom-up usually relate to educators' negotiation of the classroom experience. In this study, top-down and bottom-up refer to the literacy workers' approach to working with the student group.

In the initial stages of this study, Jody, the Action Read coordinator, Shelley, and Liz held beliefs based on the assumption that students have the skills, knowledge, and experience to act in their own interests. Therefore, in terms of pedagogy, the bottom-up approach was favored. It is interesting that these literacy workers employed a top-down approach in their decision to engage in a bottom-up pedagogical process. That is, the staff made the final decision about which approach to use without collaborating with the students. In a more participatory approach, the staff might have broached the question of top-down versus bottom-up with the student group. For instance, the staff could have asked the group, "What are your expectations of me?" or "What kind of role would you like me to take with this group?"

According to Youngman (1986), "Many adult educators who oppose the authoritarianism of traditional capitalist pedagogy have adopted forms of 'student-centred' pedagogy" (p. 206). Yet, most students in this study possessed minimal skills and knowledge in working with groups because of a lack of opportunities and experience. Therefore, these students would probably have benefited from the literacy workers' expertise. Barb immediately recognized the student group was "new to them." In other words, the students would initially require some structure, support, and direction. Consequently, she fluctuated between using top-down and bottom-up approaches with the group. Youngman (1986) advocated this dynamic approach and believed the educator should "take responsibility for making their expertise available in a way that will further the learners' interests" (p. 207). Barb hoped that, as time passed, the students would gain the skills and confidence and become less dependent on her expertise.

In listening to Liz, Shelley, and Jody, I assumed their verbal support for a bottom-up approach would result in their employment of a bottom-up approach. However, this was not the case in one program; a contradiction existed between the literacy worker's words and actions. I have chosen to highlight this contradiction because it illustrates how, as educators, we can be unconscious of contradictions between what we say and what we do. Also, rather than being critical of the contradictions of ourselves and oth-

---

[3]Bottom-up and top-down are terms found in the liberal educational discourse.

ers, we need to unpeel the layers in an effort to explore what lies beneath these contradictions.

The Action Read staff advocated a bottom-up approach with the student group. At the first group meeting, Shelley informed the students that "this is a group based on what you women or men think and it's going to go where you take it. And I'm really not going to decide what to do or what to think." Toward the end of the study, Shelley told me that literacy workers must "be prepared to really *listen* to what [the students] have to say." Jody, Shelley's supervisor, also stressed the importance of "really *listen[ing]* to what the students have to say." The identical wording of their statements suggested Jody and Shelley had discussed and were in agreement about the importance of listening in a bottom-up approach.

Rockhill (1991) stated that "unless [students] can bring their experiences into the classrooms and we can truly learn to *listen*—to hear their stories—to learn what they know, that they know, and *how* they have come to know what they know, I don't see how we can talk of critical literacy" (p. 23). Rockhill believed in the necessity of listening to students' personal narratives. After the first Action Read meeting, it was clear that some of the students wanted to talk about their lives. After the third student meeting, I interviewed Shelley and read her journal. At that time, I became cognizant of her thoughts about listening to *personal narratives* within the context of the student group.

In her journal, Shelley recorded that "even though the first hour of the student group was spent talking about students' lives, their failures, successes and experiences in general, I felt this was an important step in building trust and group cohesion." The words "even though" provides the first hint that although Shelley recognized the importance of building trust and group cohesion, she did not want to "make the focus of the group a complaint session." After the second student meeting, Shelley wrote that she "took a more vocal role as facilitator this time with the intention of mobilizing them *to do* something instead of just complaining about how unfair life is to them." Later, Shelley verbally expressed her frustration with the group and how she "realized in the first two meetings that there was a lot of complaining happening and it was really important to say, 'Ok, we've had a chance to do that; now let's move on.'" Although the students wanted to talk about their lives, Shelley continually talked about her role in "shifting the conversation," "bringing them back on topic and moving them along," and how it was "difficult to get right to the point." Whose topic? Whose point? Listening to personal narratives was problematic for Shelley because of her need to move the group forward and an assumption that listening to personal narratives was a form of therapy. At a much later date, while engaged in "member checking" with Shelley, she also expressed a fear in focusing on the personal.

It should be noted that listening to personal narratives was also problematic for some of the students. According to Shelley, "Not all of the students were comfortable in discussing or sharing their experiences. Some students were interested in attending a student group for other reasons." Shelley was referring to Jacob and Ted. Although these two men did not verbally express their discomfort in listening to personal narratives with either Shelley or me, Shelley told me she had known these students for a long time and they held a positive outlook on life, even though they had experienced hardship. Consequently, Shelley perceived that Ted and Jacob were "turned off" by listening to students complain about their lives.

Ted and Jacob were the only students who had immigrated to Canada. In this respect, they shared a similar social identity that differed from the social identity of the other students. Perhaps the dominant discourse of being an immigrant had informed Ted and Jacob that if you are motivated and work hard, you will succeed. Within this discourse, there is little space for "complaining" about the injustices of life. It should be noted that Jacob was the only student who had experienced financial success; he owned a home and a recreational vehicle. Nonetheless, this difference in social identities created a tension for Shelley in her role as group facilitator; she was working with a group whose social identities affected their needs and interests.

Although the Action Read staff were in favor of initiating a student group and using a bottom-up approach, there was an underlying agenda with respect to the group's purpose. The staff wanted the student group to focus on program-related ideas and activities. In her journal, Shelley wrote that, at the first meeting, she stated that "students are equal members in the association and had every right to voice their concerns, make requests or present proposals to the board." As a researcher, I had also promoted the concept of using the student group as a forum to involve the students actively in program decision making. In a way, this preconceived agenda was contradictory to the bottom-up approach. According to Shor (1980), the "teacher needs to come to class with an agenda, but must be ready for anything, committed to letting go when the discussion is searching for an organic form" (p. 101). In other words, staff must be willing and ready to renavigate their route, if the winds of change blow their ship in a completely new direction, away from its original destination. As well, staff must always be listening for these winds of change, for sometimes they can be very quiet.

Although Shelley believed in a bottom-up approach, where one listened to the students and was not "orchestrating them," her actions contradicted her words. In the following conversation, I began to understand her reluctance toward talking about personal experiences within the student group:

Shelley: They talked about their experiences and their lives. . . . How hard their lives were and how hard done by they were and I be-

> lieve it and I'm sure it's true, but you know you don't want it to be a therapy session.

Pat: How come you didn't see it as being that?

Shelley: Well, if it's a therapy session, where do you go from there?

This exchange raises two important questions. First, why would a literacy worker express objections to a therapy session? I would like to put forward the argument that literacy workers who work within Alberta's volunteer adult literacy programs have been exposed to education and professional development that "trains" them to focus their attention on the individualized learner and her or his reading deficiencies rather than on social structures and practices that perpetuate illiteracy. Speaking for myself, I can remember a time, not long ago, when I was so obsessed with assessment, methodology, and remediation that I ignored gender, race, and class. I worked within the boundaries of education and the public sphere, and I did not think it was my "place" to cross these lines. After all, were there not counselors and psychologists better equipped to deal with the private lives of students? In effect, I was not working with the whole person, because my education had trapped me within an analytical, partialist framework of thinking. I viewed illiteracy as the student's principal source of oppression rather than their gender, race, or class. It is only through a combination of events—a questioning and readiness to change my views, an opportunity to study and reflect—that I have been able to see my work in a new dimension. Perhaps Shelley also believed that therapy should be kept outside the realm of education because she was operating within the dominant discourse that decontextualizes what "il/literacy" means to students in their day-to-day lives.

Shelley's words and actions suggested she was operating under the assumption that listening to personal narratives is a form of therapy. The reluctance to listen to the personal appears to originate in the dominant discourse to which Alberta's literacy workers have been subjected in their practice. In Alberta, the dominant discourse appears to be one that locks educators into a dualistic framework by creating boundaries between the personal and the political, as well as the private and the public, education and therapy, and at times, literacy and illiteracy. This discourse is reflected in the language, assumptions, and meanings that literacy workers ascribe to their experiences that, in turn, shape their social relations and practices. Critical (Freire & Macedo, 1987; Giroux, 1983; Giroux & Simon, 1988; Shor, 1980; Youngman, 1986) and feminist (Briskin, 1990; hooks, 1988; Horsman, 1990; Miles, 1990; Stanley & Wise, 1993) discourses, on the other hand, address the connections between the self and political reality; the personal is political.

Critical and feminist ideology often result in a pedagogy where the personal becomes the springboard for learning. According to Youngman

(1986), "The starting-point of this [pedagogical] process is unambiguously the experience of the students and the issues and problems of their every-day existence" (p. 202). As students examine the commonalities of their ex-periences, they may begin to look critically at the location of problems they encounter as personal and identify their systemic economic, political, and ideological roots. In other words, they will (ideally) be enabled to address the connections between the self and political reality so as "to understand how power is reproduced, mediated and resisted at the level of daily exis-tence" (Giroux, 1983, p. 238). To a large degree, such a practice could step out of the dominant discourse that locks us into a dualistic framework by creating boundaries between the personal and the political, the private and the public, and education and therapy.

In this study, I found that Shelley was not alone in her fear to focus on the personal. Liz also discussed how her staff would "cap" discussions about the personal. In Liz's case, this capping resulted from insecurities about how to deal with the personal. Liz shared why staff, including herself, would resist personal narratives:

> [Students] start talking in great anger about maybe being abused. Like, I think a lot of our staff would cap it because like me they likely would feel, I don't know, if I'd cap it, like, but like me in other instances, I would say, "I don't know how to deal with it, I don't know what to do, so I better not get into it."

Liz spoke of the staff's difficulties and uncertainties of moving from the familiar terrain of instruction and remediation to the unfamiliar terrain of personal narratives. Like Liz and her staff, Shelley expressed the need to develop her knowledge base so she would be "pedagogically ready" to deal with personal narratives.

The second question raised by Shelley in our previous exchange was "If it's a therapy session, where do you go from there?" Although Shelley's pedagogy seemed to fit within a liberal ideology, personal conversations with Shelley informed me she was sympathetic to political activism at the macro-level. Perhaps she was having difficulty transferring political activ-ism to the micro-level. Shelley appeared to be searching for a concrete an-swer to the question, "How does an educator facilitate a process that con-nects the personal to the political?" This question was posed to Shelley in a subsequent interview and she replied, "If they're stuck on their personal story, then perhaps lines such as, 'How do you think this relates to the other adult literacy students?' " Although Shelley realized the need for stu-dents to share the commonalities among their experiences, she did not go on to discuss the need to look critically at the location of these problems. Literacy workers in Alberta's volunteer literacy program who want to begin addressing personal narratives within the context of their student groups do not usually have the experience or education in teaching for social change.[4] Furthermore, these workers do not have experience in working with groups of literacy students, because their programs promote one-to-one learning situations. Therefore, it is not surprising that these workers may wonder about the pragmatics or what to do after students have shared their personal stories.

Educators who support a bottom-up approach must be constantly vigilant about the way they negotiate the agenda with students. So often we are not even aware that what we are saying contradicts what we are doing. Therefore, although we may create spaces for students to have a voice, we have to make certain we do not silence their voices when they do not say what we want to hear. Instead, we must truly listen to what they have to say.

Horsman (1993), in a keynote address to the 1993 Alberta Association for Adult Literacy's conference entitled "Voices and Visions," shed light on what it means to truly listen:

> We [literacy workers] don't have a lot of experience in how to listen well, listen supportively, listen challengingly. We struggle, I think, a lot in our literacy work with the whole concept of learner centred and we say we want to start from the voices of the learners. But I think we have to learn how to do that in ways that are challenging. It's not just 'learners speak the truth.' We all have many truths, and the truths are formed out of the experiences in our lives. We all need to be able to challenge each other.

Truly listening is more than listening to voices, especially those muted ones, that differ from ours. It is offering support while challenging the "truths" that have been formed out of our experiences.

Leadership. In this study, we have learned that the literacy workers, except for Barb, whose approach fluctuated from top-down to bottom-up, initially preferred and promoted a bottom-up approach. This being the case, it is not surprising to learn that the literacy workers did not want to act or be viewed as the leaders of the student group. Even Barb stated that although "they're looking to me for more than back-up, but more for being the leader, [I didn't] want to be the leader in their student group." All of the literacy workers wanted the students to assume a leadership role within the student groups, although none of the 18 students I interviewed had ever held a leadership position within a group or organization.

---

[4]For 3 years, part of my responsibilities as a literacy worker included the development and implementation of training for Alberta's literacy workers. I came to know their background and needs, so I think this is a fair statement to make. However, a deeper concern for me is that the participants seldom, if ever, identified education for social change as one of their needs.

This raises two questions: How do students, who have never held leadership positions, respond to their new role as leaders? How do staff approach the issue of working with students to foster leadership skills? Before responding to these two questions, I describe how student leaders were chosen in their respective programs.

Choosing a student to be the president was handled through an election process in four of the five programs. ALFA and two of the three programs with The Literacy Network (Haines Junction and Virden) formed student associations with elected officials. The remaining Literacy Network program (Creston) elected a student representative to serve on their literacy council that was affiliated with Laubach International.[5] In these four programs, Barb was the only coordinator who provided a rationale for wanting students to hold titled leadership positions. She told the students that "somebody always has to be in charge and I didn't want it to be me." Barb believed that electing student leaders was an effective strategy that would shine the spotlight on students, rather than on the literacy worker.

Action Read used a grassroots model for their student group, which meant there were no elected officials. Instead, Shelley facilitated group meetings. She recognized that the group "need[ed] a leader," yet the occasion never arose where the staff or students formally discussed the election of representatives. Shelley recognized that Daniel, a student, was "very much a natural leader," yet he was never approached by staff or students to head up the student group because, after the first student meeting, he began to pressure the program for material resources. Although Action Read was not a full-time program, Daniel wanted tutoring 5 days a week and started coming to the center on a daily basis. He would stay at the center for 3 to 4 hours, and during that time, he would photocopy books, tie up the telephone lines, and wander in and out of the learning center, disturbing other tutoring pairs. The staff found Daniel's daily visits a drain on their resources and decided to belatedly set some parameters. When Daniel was approached with their decision, Shelley told me he responded by stating, "You're just like every other program. You don't want to help. You really don't care about students."

Toward the end of the study, I asked Shelley if there were ways staff could foster leadership among the students. She replied that "I suppose they could vote. We could put it in a formal way or you could just observe who's coming and who seems to be really supportive and committed and say, you know, just approach them, and say, offer to them, would you be interested in heading up this committee."

---

[5]Laubach Literacy International is a nonprofit, educational corporation founded in 1955 by the late Dr. Frank Laubach. It is dedicated to teaching reading to adults with low literacy skills. The Laubach approach emphasizes the use of volunteer tutors on an Each One Teach One basis, using structured literacy books and easy-to-read follow-up literature.

The student groups that adhered to a traditional notion of leadership with an elected executive were the groups that were successful in formulating and meeting some of their goals. These groups also followed traditional organization forms such as decision making by majority vote.[6] Action Read unconsciously chose a grass-roots model that promoted shared leadership, agreement by consensus, and structurelessness. I use the word unconsciously because, to the best of my knowledge, the Action Read staff and students never discussed the issues of leadership and decision making, although it could be argued that a core group of interested students is necessary to begin exploring leadership. Although the Action Read student group formulated goals in the sense that they listed ideas and activities they wanted to pursue, their only success in terms of reaching their goals was the development and analysis of the Student Involvement Questionnaire.[7]

This next section examines how students who have never held leadership positions responded to their new role as leaders. The four students who were elected to president or student representative were quick to tell me that it was the "first time they had ever been involved in stuff like that" and that it "was a big experience for [them]." In the following narratives, we can see how Peggy and Paul were uncertain about their roles and how Jean and Paul were uncertain about group process. This section focuses on the students' struggles as opposed to the benefits they derived from being in a leadership position.

Learning the Ropes: The Question of Role

In 1991, Donna was elected to serve on the ALFA board as the student representative. At the beginning of this study it became apparent that Donna's role as student representative had not been communicated to the student group. During one of our interviews, Barb explained that students can "funnel their ideas [through Donna] to the board." When asked if the students were aware of this process, there was a pause in our conversation, followed by laughter. Barb then responded, "We never discussed it. But, good point.

---

[6]See Adamson, Briskin, and McPhail (1988, chap. 7) for a discussion on feminist organization and feminist process.

[7]Three of the students wanted to develop a questionnaire to find out why students were not attending meetings. The results of the Student Involvement Questionnaire indicated the majority of respondents preferred activities where they could interact with their peers. This questionnaire was mailed to 83 Action Read students and 39 (47%) responded. The results of the questionnaire indicated that 29 (74%) of the respondents wanted to be involved in student-centered activities such as student get togethers and welcoming new students into the program, whereas a smaller number of students (19) wanted to be involved in program-centered activities such as evaluating the program, choosing library books, *planning* social activities, serving on the board, and training tutors. A mere 7 (18%) of the respondents wanted to be involved in outreach activities such as public speaking, fundraising, planning conferences, and talking to the media.

It should be mentioned to them." Donna was also unaware that, as student representative, she was in the position to take the students' views and concerns to the board.

Toward the end of the study, I asked Peggy what she needed in terms of leadership training. Although Peggy had been president for a year, the following exchange reveals she was an actor in an unfamiliar terrain; she was mystified about her role in navigating others through this terrain.

> Peggy: I still have a hard time, like 'cause I don't, I don't know how to do it right.
>
> Pat: Ok.
>
> Peggy: For me to, someone to show me, or teach me how to do my job right not just to come in, like I come in without really knowing, I still don't really know for sure what to do.
>
> Pat: And sometimes when you don't know, you don't even have the words to explain what it is that you don't know. Does that make sense?
>
> Peggy: Yeah, like sometimes I, at a meeting Barb wants me to say, but I, a lot of times I can't because I don't know, I don't know how to do it, I guess.
>
> Pat: I know what you mean. But that just makes sense, cause if you hadn't had experience in it before, then you wouldn't know, so you need almost some training.
>
> Peggy: Yeah, like if someone, for a president you must have to do, you know, certain things in certain areas, which I don't even know. I wouldn't even know which areas to begin in.
>
> Pat: So, wanting to know what you should do and how to do it?
>
> Peggy: Yeah, what your part would be of what you want to be like.

Throughout our conversation, Peggy was grappling for the words to name the confusion about her role. She spoke to the need for a well-defined set of duties so that she would know what was expected of her. As well, Peggy was concerned about her performance as president. In observing Peggy at student meetings and at public events and through my conversations with Barb, the coordinator, it was clear that Peggy had acquired leadership skills, such as the ability to chair meetings, to speak publicly, and to set and reach goals. Peggy was even beginning to use the language associated with chairing meetings such as, "Is there anything else from the floor?" Despite her achievements and the support she received from staff and students, Peggy was still concerned about her ability to do it right, and unclear about her duties and responsibilities. This suggests Peggy needed constant reassurance and moral support about her performance as president.

After discussing what she needed in terms of leadership training, Peggy informed me she wanted to resign from her duties as president. She still wanted to be part of the group, but she wanted a smaller role. Immediately after our interview, Peggy informed Barb of her decision. Peggy's decision prompted Barb to realize that she "should have been telling [Peggy] what her role was and teaching [Peggy] more about her role." Peggy was a mother and was attending college full time, so it should be noted that this situation dictated the amount of time Barb could spend with Peggy.

Paul, the president of the Virden student association, was also unclear about his role. He expressed this uncertainty in a brief, but illuminating exchange:

Paul: Why they got me like is I talk quite a bit, eh, and joke around and they figure 'Well, he'll be good for a president.'

Pat: You can speak.

Paul: But after I got in there, I didn't know what to say.

Providing opportunities for students to have a voice does not necessarily mean they will know how to use their voice, simply because this is such a new experience for them.

Learning the Ropes: The Question of Process

In Virden, the student association generated a list of goals, one of which was to buy books for beginning readers. Early in the study, I asked Paul whether the student association had pursued this goal and we engaged in the following cryptic conversation:

Paul: Well, we never talked too much about it after that, like you know.

Pat: That's the thing is how to once it's ...

Paul: Yeah, I figure once it's on paper maybe it, maybe they will jump to it.

Pat: Who's they?

Paul: I don't know. I'm giving a hint here.

In this exchange, we can see how Paul attributed power to the written word and to an outside force, which he referred to as "they." Paul's comments suggested to me that within the realm of an educational institution, he was mystified about and alienated from the processes needed to convert ideas into action. According to Sarup (1982), "The working class itself has not been involved in the decision-making process [within the educational system], but has been acted upon; 'good' has been done to them" (p. 113).

Paul, a working class student, had always been a passive participant on the receiving end of educational services who followed and obeyed the decisions and rules made by others, rather than being an active participant who had a role in shaping and defining the service.

Jean, the president of the Haines Junction student association, seemed to be the clearest about her role and how to turn ideas into action. In terms of process, Jean requested staff assistance whenever there was "a situation that [the students couldn't] handle together," because she was unsure of how to resolve conflict within the group.

The Need for Leadership Training

Of the three presidents, two expressed a need for leadership training. Rather than learning through a vicarious experience such as observing presidents in action at meetings, they wanted direct training either through a one-to-one mentoring relationship or through workshops. These were their comments about training:

> Someone to show me, or teach me how to do my job right. (Peggy)

> There should really be workshops.
>   Well, the only support that the guy could get is somebody that had experience that teach us what to do. Get somebody that's been in there for three or four years, eh, that has been a president and tell us what, you know, to do, what we don't have to do, like you know, just on and on. (Paul)

Peggy was the only president who was involved in a mentoring relationship with her literacy coordinator. Peggy informed me that Barb "helps me out lots." Although Peggy was appreciative of Barb's efforts, she still doubted her own abilities. Paul, on the other hand, reported that "the only support I'm getting is from my students."

Fostering Leadership Skills

Socialist and feminist pedagogies aim to address the issue of the educator's role in fostering leadership skills (Briskin, 1990; Maguire, 1987; Reed, 1981; Schniedewind, 1983; Youngman, 1986). Youngman (1986) argued that socialist pedagogy acknowledges the expertise, authority, and leadership of the educator:

> Socialist adult educators bring to the education situation a necessary expertise and they initially assume a position of authority and leadership (a position which is itself the product of the unequal personal development that

capitalism generates). They take responsibility for making their expertise available in a way that will further the learners' interests. They participate in a collaborative process which aims to raise the level of awareness and competence of the learners and hence their position is not static. (p. 207)

According to Youngman, students initially lack, to varying degrees, the knowledge and skills needed to assume a position of expertise or leadership. Therefore, it is the educator's responsibility to share his or her expertise with the students. As the students' awareness and competence are raised and developed, the educator's role changes and he or she begins to recede into the background. In this study, it was evident that the students lacked leadership experience and wanted training and support to develop their knowledge and skills in this area.

Although Barb would not define herself as a socialist educator, she was aware of her expertise and was willing to share it with the group, and in particular with Peggy, the president, and Donna, the secretary. Barb recognized that the students had never held a leadership position and consequently needed assistance with their new roles. She described how Peggy would look to her for cues: "But, sometimes you'll notice at the meeting Peggy's looking at me [as if to say] 'What should I do now?' and that's ok to begin with." Barb realized students would initially depend on her and she hoped they would eventually become independent as they developed leadership skills and confidence in their abilities. In other words, she assumed a dynamic rather than a static position with the students.

Barb was the only literacy worker who employed direct training through a mentoring relationship. As a mentor, she provided training and moral support. For instance, she discussed and formulated the agenda with the president and secretary before the meetings. After the meetings, she assisted Donna, the secretary, with the minutes. Barb taught Donna how to use the computer and how to compose business letters. Barb informed me that she was "teaching her all the things that I think a secretary of a group should know." Barb also recognized the need to expand direct training to other students by having "leadership workshops and discussions on leadership."

Some feminists also believe that teaching leadership should be the responsibility of educators because "those who are outside the 'culture of power' learn best how to access that culture when the rules of that culture are taught explicitly" (Delpit cited in Briskin, 1990, p. 14). Those who advocate a bottom-up approach might argue that teaching leadership undermines student autonomy and is undemocratic. However, Briskin (1990) said that "acknowledging teacher expertise does not necessarily negate the authority of the students' expertise" (p. 13). In other words, is it possible for an educator to instill leadership skills while still maintaining a bottom-up approach?

The remaining literacy workers in this study did not directly teach leadership skills through a mentoring relationship. There was even a reluctance to share their facilitation skills during the group meetings. Shelley was reluctant to provide direct leadership training to the Action Read student group. The following statements indicate she did not want to use her knowledge of standard facilitation techniques unless the group requested them:

> They wanted [their ideas] on paper because they were forgetting and because it was just these ideas come and then they go. And so it came from the group that I should write it down and that was really positive because I didn't want to just start introducing the writing down stuff.
>
> Even though I wanted very much to draw up an agenda and attack the items in order, I realized the ideas and pace must come from the group. (Shelley—journal entry)

Shelley's comment suggested she believed introducing facilitation skills would not be consistent with the bottom-up approach. Maguire (1987), a feminist educator who conducted participatory research with a group of women who had been abused, also discussed her "reluctance to utilize [her] full range of training skills and techniques with the group" (p. 162). Maguire thought these skills might intimidate the women. Upon reflection, Maguire realized her reluctance was a mistake and she had "lost many opportunities to introduce structures and activities that would have made equal and meaningful participation more possible" (p. 163). Demetrion (1993), a manager of a literacy program who was involved in promoting student support groups, also discussed his "hands-off approach" with the group. He was "apprehensive that [his] pragmatic drive to make things work may have overriden the emerging efforts of the learners" (p. 43). Toward the end of the study, Shelley expressed a preference for promoting vicarious experiences, rather than direct training, in her comment that students could learn all kinds of skills by attending meetings and being exposed to "things, like how to run a meeting, how to organize to get things done, how to delegate authority, how to follow up, how to arrange a speaker [and] how to arrange a function."

It is interesting that at the end of the study, Jody, Shelley's supervisor, had recognized a need for direct training. Jody reported, "I think we need to provide just a bit more structure for them and help them along a bit more ... by giv[ing] them the benefit of [our] knowledge and [our] expertise." Jody's perception of the role staff need to adopt parallels the role of the animateur, a role in which the educator nurtures leadership ability and acts as a catalyst and resource person in a democratic process (Brookfield, 1983; Kidd, 1971; Titmus, 1981).

Initially, Liz believed in the virtues of vicarious training. In monthly professional development days, she set up situations in which the students could learn through modeling. Later, when I shared Paul's need for assistance, she became more open to developing a mentoring relationship with the students.

CONCLUSION

Participatory literacy practices created possibilities for literacy workers to question their pedagogical approach with students—an approach that rested on social relations more than methodology. Shelley, for example, soon realized that the bottom-up approach was unfeasible because most students were used to being passive recipients of a program's services as well as being users rather than doers in the wider socioeconomic context; they were used to having people tell them what to do. Therefore, by introducing a bottom-up approach, one is introducing a sudden change in social relations between the educator and the student.

In this study, the literacy workers spoke of their fear of and reluctance toward listening to the students' personal stories within the student groups and associations. As well, there was a belief that listening to personal narratives was a form of therapy and this was not part of adult basic education. As educators, we need to acknowledge the importance of personal narratives and facilitate a process where students can see that personal troubles are often social issues (Kirby & McKenna, 1989; Mills, 1959). In turn, this means literacy workers need to develop a stronger knowledge base in critical theory and pedagogy. I fear that a move in this direction could result in nothing more than a 2-day course on popular education. What I visualize though, is more of a process where literacy workers can begin to examine their positions about literacy education and the assumptions that underscore these positions. Certainly, literacy workers would benefit from professional development in how to work with groups in ways that allow them to examine critically their issues and experiences. As well, literacy workers would benefit from professional development in how to deal with differences among individuals in group settings.

The findings indicated that the students, particularly those who held leadership positions, were confused about their roles and concerned about their performance. Therefore, educators need to work closely with students, particularly the group leaders, in student groups and associations. Rather than adopting a bottom-up, hands-off approach, literacy workers need to move between top-down and bottom-up approaches, and develop a mentoring relationship with the students. As educators, we need to view our facilitation skills and techniques as socially constructed attributes that have been developed through years of education and experience. Our skills did not come naturally; rather, they are part and parcel of social location and privilege. People with low literacy skills are often outside the circles of opportunities where one can develop these attributes; therefore, as educators it is our responsibility to teach, share, and perhaps demystify facilitation skills and techniques.

Finally, the findings indicated that literacy workers viewed participatory literacy practices as an action- and production-oriented mode of activity; they placed importance on doing. The students, on the other hand, wanted to be engaged in a dialectical process of being and doing; they appreciated the chance to simply "be" with other students, to discuss and share ideas. Within the realm of functional literacy, there is a focus on product, on skills, and on doing. Therefore, it was not surprising that the literacy workers spoke of a need to do in the student group versus a need to be. As educators, we cannot underestimate the importance and the benefits of spending time discussing ideas; the concept of dialogue needs to be supported. Therefore, we need to challenge and contest the production-oriented discourse that shapes our practice. Rather than viewing participatory literacy practices as activities and events such as serving on the board, forming a student group, and speaking in public, we need to view participatory literacy practices as a process that evolves over time. This, in turn, may alleviate the frustration and disappointment the literacy workers felt when students did not turn up for events. Perhaps literacy workers need to understand that participatory literacy practices do not originate with the formation of a student group or having a student serve on the board; rather, they originate from a way of thinking about egalitarian social relations.

REFERENCES

Adamson, N., Briskin, L., & McPhail, M. (1988). *Feminists organizing for change.* Toronto, Canada: Oxford.

Briskin, L. (1990). *Feminist pedagogy: Teaching and learning liberation.* Ottawa, Canada: Canadian Research Institute for the Advancement of Women.

Brookfield, S. D. (1983). *Adult learners, adult education and the community.* Milton Keynes, England: Open University Press.

Demetrion, G. (1993). Participatory literacy education: A complex phenomenon. *Adult Basic Education, 3*(1), 27–50.

Freire, P., & Macedo, D. (1987). *Literacy: Reading the word and the world.* New York: Bergin and Garvey.

Giroux, H. A. (1983). *Theory and resistance in education: A pedagogy for the opposition.* South Hadley, MA: Bergin and Garvey.

Giroux, H. A., & Simon, R. I. (1988). Schooling, popular culture, and a pedagogy of possibility. *Journal of Education, 170*(1), 9–26.

hooks, B. (1988). *Talking back: Thinking feminist, thinking black.* Toronto, Canada: Between the Lines.

Horsman, J. (1988). The social dimension of literacy. *Canadian Women Studies, 9*(3&4), 78–81.

Horsman, J. (1990). *Something in my mind besides the everyday: Women and literacy.* Toronto: Women's Press.

Horsman, J. (Keynote Speaker). (1993). Alberta Association for Adult Literacy: Voices and Visions Conference. (Cassette Recording). Edmonton, Canada: Kennedy Recordings.

Kidd, J. R. (1971). Adult education, the community, and the animateur. In J. A. Draper (Ed.), *Citizen participation: Canada* (pp. 137–158). Toronto: New Press.

Kirby, S., & McKenna, K. (1989). *Experience, research, social change: Methods from the margins.* Toronto: Garamond Press.

Lincoln, Y. S., & Guba, E. G. (1985). *Naturalistic inquiry.* Newbury Park, CA: Sage.

Maguire, P. (1987). *Doing participatory research: A feminist approach.* MA: The Center for International Education.

Miles, A. (1990). Women's challenge to adult education. In F. Forman (Ed.), *Feminism and education: A Canadian challenge* (pp. 247–271). Toronto, Canada: OISE Press.

Mills, C. W. (1959). *The sociological imagination.* London: Oxford University Press.

Reed, D. (1981). *Education for building a people's movement.* Boston: South End Press.

Rockhill, K. (1991). *Dis/connecting literacy and sexuality: Speaking the unspeakable in the classroom.* Unpublished manuscript.

Sarup, M. (1982). *Education, state and crisis: A Marxist perspective.* London: Routledge and Kegan Paul.

Sauvé, V. L. (1987). *From one educator to another: A window on participatory research.* Edmonton, Canada: Grant MacEwan Community College.

Schniedewind, N. (1983). Feminist values: Guidelines for teaching methodology in women's studies. In C. Bunch & S. Pollack (Eds.), *Learning our way: Essays in feminist education* (pp. 261–271). New York: Crossing Press Feminist Series.

Shor, I. (1980). *Critical teaching and everyday life.* Chicago: The University of Chicago Press.

Stanley, L., & Wise, S. (1993). *Breaking out again.* London: Routledge.

Titmus, C. (1981). *Strategies for adult education: Practices in Western Europe.* Chicago: Follett.

Wang, C., & Burris, M. A. (1994). Empowerment through photo novella: Portraits of participation. *Health Education Quarterly, 21*(2), 171–186.

Youngman, F. (1986). *Adult education and socialist pedagogy.* Dover, NH: Croom Helm.

4

"Why Would They Listen to Me?" Reflections on Learner Leadership Activities

Jenny Horsman
Spiral Community Resource Group

When I began researching the impacts of trauma on women's literacy learning, and reexamining approaches to literacy programming in the light of these impacts, my suspicion was that the aftermath of violence might affect all aspects of literacy involvement, including learner leadership. At that time I wrote that where impacts of violence are not adequately addressed in literacy programs there is a cost for learners, because they face barriers to successful learning; a cost to literacy workers, because they are frustrated by lack of knowledge about how best to support survivors in overcoming barriers to learning; and a cost to programs as a whole, because learners struggle to participate effectively as leaders sharing in running their programs. This research into trauma and learning revealed a wide range of impacts and suggested many possible shifts to literacy work.

This chapter explores insights the research offers for rethinking the problems of learner leadership and the complex conflicts that arise during attempts, in the literacy movement in Canada, to support learners taking substantial power and control. Silences in the literacy movement, and in society broadly, about violence generally and connections between violence and learning in particular may lead to the belief that learner leadership and trauma issues are separate. Yet research on the impacts of trauma suggests not only profound implications of trauma for all learning, but also that central areas in learner leadership are particularly fraught and complex terrain for trauma survivors. Learner leadership activities usually fail to fulfill the promise of power sharing they offer, if we are to develop possibilities for meaningful change in the literacy movement. New angles from which to examine this practice are urgently needed.

Considering impacts of trauma on learning is key for adult literacy work. First, we must recognize that though there is not one agreed-upon statistic assessing the numbers of adults, both men and women, who have experienced sexual, physical, or emotional abuse in childhood or as adults, there is increasing acceptance that the problem is widespread. Second, I believe anecdotal evidence from large numbers of literacy workers and learners suggests the incidence of survivors of trauma may be even higher in adult literacy programs than in the general population. Frequently, literacy workers speak of working with groups in which every member has experienced major trauma. Experiencing trauma as a child may well have contributed to difficulties with learning to read in the first place. Experiences of violence and being controlled as an adult may contribute to the urgency of desire to improve literacy skills to enhance the possibility of making further changes in their lives. ESL literacy learners may well have left situations of war, oppression, imprisonment, and torture. Third, few adults who have limited literacy skills will not have experienced the violence of oppression, of marginalization around issues of poverty, class, race, ability, and language. Most will have experienced daily put-downs and erasures that oppress and contribute to a well of anger and frustration. Looking at the impacts of trauma on learning in general, and on learning to take leadership, may be crucial for all learners.

I write as an insider who has been involved, usually as the facilitator, in many of the initiatives in Ontario and in the national movement, to increase learner leadership. I draw particularly on two projects in Ontario that I planned and facilitated with coworkers.[1] I am not offering an analysis of all learner leadership activities, but rather a personal musing and rethinking of some examples. This rethinking is informed throughout by research I recently completed on trauma and learning (Horsman, 1999/2000). A focus on the impact of violence on learning potential offers new insight into why attempts to increase learner leadership so rarely lead to the hoped-for shifts in power and control in literacy programs.

Though I have facilitated many learner leadership events, I am also in some ways an outsider. I am not now a literacy worker—in the sense of working on a day-to-day basis in a program—nor am I a literacy learner, so I hold neither key position in the dance around learner leadership. As a person with those "big papers" learners often speak about, it is clear to learn-

---

[1]In 1992, I codesigned and cofacilitated the Ontario Literacy Coalition Learner Training Institute with Maggie Killoran. Throughout the Metro Toronto Movement for Literacy's Learners' Leadership Project in 1996, I worked with Donna Jeffery.

ers that, though many may see me as an ally, I am one of "them," one of the privileged who are not to be trusted to truly share power. I can still see the image learners role-played, during some long ago workshop, where they showed workers handing them the rope of "control" and then yanking it back again, as a way to illustrate their experience of learner leadership.

Though learner leadership is a frequently used concept in the adult literacy field, it is open to wide interpretations of meaning. It has become a central tenet of much literacy work, especially community-based literacy programming. In community-based programs, the term is often used to refer to learners taking "leadership" in their programs, through sitting on the board of directors, the usual organizational form of governance. Other forms of taking control or sharing power in such programs may include participating in committees, including hiring committees, or participating in a learner-directed group. Learners often participate in the creation of collections of their writing or newsletters. Occasionally, the focus of leadership activities has been toward encouraging learners to take more control in other areas of their lives, rather than only within their literacy learning and the organization of the program itself. In school board or community college programs with more structured hierarchies, the potential for shared power may seem more limited, but some classes and centers do create student committees to influence direction and decision making within the program.

Part of the commitment and focus of community-based programs has been a desire to create an equitable organization, and through that to contribute to the creation of a more equitable society. At this period in Ontario the contrasts between community programs and more institutional structures may be challenged by the introduction of a myriad of policy changes and regulatory practices, while the basic principle of support for increased learner leadership has been entrenched as a requirement of "quality standards" for literacy programs. This period, with workers feeling increasingly anxious and disempowered by shifts in policy, is a challenging one in which to consider the possibilities for increasing learner leadership in ways that make real changes in the balance of power and control in programs.

In this chapter I focus on learner leadership to participate in decision making and to share power in literacy programs. It is here that major tensions frequently surface and where, in spite of the enormous amount of staff energy frequently expended to try to make it "work," few learners seem to feel a greater sense of power. Even though I think participating on boards is a problematic area, it is a central place in most programs where decision making occurs and where the power appears to reside. However, I want to acknowledge that the form of the board, a format required by charitable organizations, may in itself create problems for power sharing. Tensions often arise between staff and board. The structure can leave people of all education levels, not only literacy learners, feeling mystified, silenced, and stupid. A useful direction in community-based programs might be to re-assess whether there is any space within the regulations, or to make changes in the regulations, to permit differences in the organizational structure. Different models, such as a worker-user cooperative, could offer different possibilities for power sharing.

WE'RE ALL IN THIS TOGETHER

We're All in this Together is the title of a book about *Leadership and Community* at a literacy program in Brooklyn. But from what I have observed, much of the experience of learner leadership might be more aptly titled "Us and Them." More often learner leadership activity seems to lead, not to good feelings of being "in this together," but to endless frustration. Learners often talk about feeling they are not listened to or that they are set up to fail. One learner, describing a leadership project, said, "I don't think they expected that we'd be able to do it."[2] Workers and volunteers often fear that learners won't be able to work effectively on boards or committees or feel frustrated by the form participation takes and "the students' reluctance to speak their minds and state their opinions" (Campbell, 1996, p. 131).

Recently Sheila Stewart, a literacy worker in Toronto, told me she feels sad and full of questions sitting on a board with a learner and realizing the talk provides few "points of entry" for the learner. She spoke of her sense of the anxiety of workers as they struggle to keep up with all the work involved themselves. Learners are often either very appreciative of whatever workers do for them, or extremely angry. Learners argue that "they"—the workers—don't really want to hand over power to learners because their main interest is their jobs. As one learner said, "They do as much as they can with the money they're given as long as it doesn't threaten their livelihood. . . . They wouldn't have the job unless we had gone to school and not learned to read and write, if there wasn't us that don't fit then you wouldn't have all these social agencies getting money from the government and not quite meeting the need." Though that learner says there are "a few of you who are real" she is angry at most workers, who she feels say they are giving control to learners but do not really want to give up power. That analysis echoes in my ears. I seem to have heard it over and over again over the

---

[2]I want to thank three participants in the MTML Learners' Leadership Project for spending the time to reflect on the project and discuss learner leadership with me. Donna Lovell and Susan Macdonald of Frontier College spent a precious morning (assisted by Donna's wonderful baking) thinking through these issues. A learner from another Toronto-based program, who chose to remain anonymous, told me about her experience on boards and challenged my thinking. All unsourced quotes draw from these discussions. Quotes from Donna Lovell's words, or descriptions of her ideas, are included on pages 5, 21, 23, 25, 34, and 36.

years from learners who have been active in the literacy movement. And from workers I often hear a sense of not feeling very powerful themselves, of questioning what approach might make a change to the patterns.

The analysis that those who enjoy the privilege of inequality may not always support sweeping change that will undermine their own privilege is a widely held view, not only among literacy learners but more broadly. The "privileged usually are not inclined to protect or advance the interests of the oppressed, partly because their social position prevents them from understanding those interests, and partly because to some degree their privilege depends on the continued oppression of others" (Young cited in Campbell, 1996, p. 130). Learners often speak angrily of how little workers understand their experience:

> I know everyone means well and they all care about the cause, but do they really know what it's like to be poor, illiterate and without hope? . . . I don't think they can even imagine one ten thousandth of the fear and pain I feel when they talk about cutbacks in social programs. (Lovell in Metro Toronto Movement for Literacy, 1996, p. 57)

Campbell (1996) also explored some of the ways in which workers' perspectives from their experience can shape their judgment of issues that may feed into a deficit perception that it is learners' "lack" that inhibits them taking power:

> Shelley is frustrated by the students' reluctance to speak their minds and state their opinions; she attributes their reluctance to speak to a lack of confidence and ability to articulate, lack of interest, lack of commitment and lack of social skills. The meanings which Shelley ascribed to the behavior, actions, and words of students appear to be colored by her social identity as a white, middle-class, educated woman; her subjectivity affected her interpretation of the world. Shelley perceived the students' behavior was in sharp contrast to the behavior of people (friends, family, colleagues) that she usually associated with in her daily interactions, yet she did not question why the student's behavior was different. Consequently, Shelley was locked into a deficit perspective of the students which painted them as lacking confidence, social skills, commitment, interest, and ability to articulate, rather than looking at how the intersection of class, race and gender played a significant role in their participation and willingness to speak their mind. (pp. 131–132)

This description sounds familiar to me. I have heard myself and others struggle with why learners often sit silent during a meeting and then complain afterwards: that nobody wanted to know what they thought, or when they have spoken, if their ideas are not followed, that no one ever listens, and so on. Questioning whether I am caught in a deficit discourse, when I frame these questions, might help to reframe the question. Shifting from deficit discourses, where I see the problem in the learners' lack or deficit, might allow for a different sort of attention to *what* silences learners. Moving to examining "What is happening here?" rather than "What is wrong with them? Why don't they . . ." may offer new possibilities. But sometimes, even the exploration of what is going on is limited by the silence we might want to explore.

When I think of meetings I have run, I am aware of (and have been reminded by learners) the times I have moved onto a new topic without hearing from all the learners, because accomplishing the task before the end of the meeting seems more important than getting everyone involved. As I reflect now, I may question whether that was always "necessary" or whether I assumed I wasn't losing any crucial opinion when I left some learners behind. But, I am cautious about descriptions that can seem simply to blame workers for operating from the perspective of their own location and "subjectivity" and struggling with pressures and demands from all sides. I wonder, how can we create more spaces for critical reflection so that both workers and learners can question the gaps between our intentions and our actions and learn more about what the world looks like from both sides of the learner–worker divide?

Campbell (1996) also explored how complicated it can be when a literacy worker's discourses of "collaboration, democracy, equality, participation" meet a hierarchical institutional discourse of control, discipline, and authority, and she drew attention to the conflicting discourses within which literacy workers frequently work. In particular, the contradictory demands from government that learners be involved in running programs and the pressures of time tied to increased demands for "efficiency," "accountability," and the expectations of rapid learner "progress" are not often discussed. Workers and learners are caught in a series of contradictory demands. Workers may become "shock absorbers" in the system, stretched and pushed from all sides.

When I think about the "us-and-them" framework that learners have for learner leadership, I am discontented with this simple divide and the way it can cause differences *among learners* and *among literacy workers* to disappear from view. I worry that I can only reject this division between learners and the rest of "us" because I am *not* a learner, so the division does not look so central to me. But I want to question the validity of that simple divide between learners and others. I believe it is created through the discourses that "other" literacy learners and, like the wheelchair that is viewed as the defining feature of a person with a mobility disability, view lack of literacy skill as the central identifying feature for a literacy learner. This focus draws attention away from all the other identities that may be significant. However, this divide clearly speaks to the sense that learners often have of being "different." It perhaps leads to the conviction that some learners hold that learners *ought* to be able to find common cause:

> We have let the big THEY have the right to direct us because we haven't
> worked together to learn and change the old ways of dependency. . . . As long
> as we continue in this divided, dependent and self destructive way the estab-
> lished literacy community will continue to use the "we know what's best for
> you" attitude and our voices will never be heard. A united voice will be heard.
> I would like to see a solely run coalition of students with a united voice
> funded by the government and employing consumers only. (Lovell in Metro
> Toronto Movement for Literacy, 1996, p. 79).

Perhaps the belief that learners must share common cause against the
"rest" leaves learners few options for an explanation of the divisions between them, except self-blame and criticism of learners' failure to work together.

Learners sometimes argue that workers are naive when they deny there
is a crucial divide between learners and workers. Some learners suggest the
approaches workers use contribute to the divisions within the community
of learners. They also sometimes suggest workers put one or two learners
on a pedestal, contributing to jealousy and division. These learners' observations prompt questions for me about how to support communities of
learners' taking more power and avoid isolating one or two learners as representatives on boards and committees. I was interested in a Brooklyn example I read where a group of students made decisions about hiring new
staff in the program, with only one or two staff members participating in the
process. It sounded different from the examples I heard about locally,
where the one learner on a hiring committee often complains about not being heard. One Brooklyn staff person wrote:

> Whenever we have to hire a new teacher, we form a committee of students and
> staff to interview candidates and decide who to hire. Usually I'm on the com-
> mittee with maybe one other staff member and six or seven students. Most of
> the students are usually from the class that needs a teacher, but we try to have
> some students from other classes as well. It helps to have people who can look
> at the needs of the whole school.
>   I see my role as trying to help people figure out what the strengths and weak-
> nesses are and what the person has to offer the school. I don't offer any opin-
> ions of my own until there has been a lot of discussion and even then I don't say
> whether I think we should hire the person. I try to help the students come to
> some consensus. They generally make the decision. (The Open Book, n.d., p.
> 46)

Of course this example is written, so we don't hear about the tensions
and problems. For example, what happens when the students don't come to
consensus or what would lead them not to be the decision makers? I wonder when staff feel they have to intervene. Most of all, I think about how
time consuming the process sounds. They wrote about continuing to inter-

view, sometimes six or seven people, before someone was hired. But I remember how time consuming the tensions are when the one learner on the committee continues to be angry for a long time because she or he doesn't feel heard. One challenge seems to be to explore ways of supporting the building of community among learners and looking for models of power sharing that move away from seeming to set individual learners on a pedestal.

As I think about the conflicts among learners, I realize I have heard learners, while arguing for the value of a united front, criticizing the current learner in power and angry at what they see as the self-importance of the current "star" learner. The focus on limited literacy skills as the defining feature about learners can shift attention away from the inevitable divisions by gender, race, intellectual "ability," and physical disabilities. Hierarchies among learners often replicate mainstream society. Language, especially, creates divisions. Learners who have difficulties with speech, who communicate using technological devices or Bliss symbolics, can as easily be left out by other learners as by workers, and learners who use long words can silence and exclude others.

Many years ago, I worked with a national committee of learners who were preparing a presentation to convince the board of the Movement for Canadian Literacy (MCL) that they should support a motion to create a board comprised 50% by learners. One of the group often seemed to be off-track, not grasping the question and telling stories that didn't seem relevant. I could feel the tension among the other learners, who seemed anxious she would show learners in a bad light. I thought they didn't want to be associated with her, because she might fit the popular stereotype of the learner and they wanted to distance themselves from that inferior status. Fortunately, in that instance, we had the time to work together. The group had already met many times, much trust had built up, and we were still planning and talking when she suggested a brilliant piece that she could say as part of the presentation. There was palpable surprise and relief in the room that she had "got" it and perhaps a new clarity about the problems of judging anyone's worth through the standard hierarchical conceptions. Reflecting now, I realize that our focus on the task meant we didn't take the opportunity to speak about and explore the meaning of the tensions and judgments that could have divided the group.

As I remember the presentation to the MCL board, where the motion to have 50% learners on the board was accepted, I remember the learners' jubilation that a new era had begun. I was not involved in the process after that point and I cannot reflect here on what made up all the complex elements that caused later discontent and disappointment and a move to a different model. The experiment of 50% learners on the board seems to have been part of a hope that has been lost, something that was tried, but failed.

My desire through this writing is not to judge, but to renew discussion about current possibilities for meaningful change.

The impetus for the process of increasing the numbers of learners on the board was put into writing in 1991 by the Learner Action Group of Canada, as part of its mission statement. It hoped to "lay the foundation of strengthening the adult student/learner voice" by suggesting:

a) That the 50/50 partnership for adult student/learner involvement existing in 1 to 1 tutoring be extended by 1995 to all levels of literacy organizations, including programs, boards and networks, to ensure that we get the most out of what is available to help the largest number of people. This is to include representation on executive, personnel and finance committees, etc.

b) That programs build financial and moral support to adult student/learners who want to be involved.

This statement heralded a period when many organizations increased the number of learners on their boards, some actually moving to 50% learners. Now many have moved away from that commitment into experimentation with other models. I think there is a widespread sense in the movement that the experiment didn't work. Many literacy workers argue that the earlier attempts to increase the number of learners on boards created a group of discontented "professional learners" and that new models of advisory committees and representatives on boards allow learners to be heard. Many of those discontented learners argue that workers did not want to hear what they had to say or deal with their anger and so a new "token learner"—as one learner put it, a new "golden child"—is selected to replace the "troublemakers."

TEACHING "SKILLS" OF LEARNER LEADERSHIP

Reflecting on past experiences in the light of trauma research may begin the process of revealing alternatives. In 1992, when increasing the capacity for learners to participate in boards was seen as key, the Ontario Literacy Coalition created a residential week-long Learners' Leadership Institute in Paris, Ontario. The focus of the Paris institute was the idea that what learners needed to be able to take leadership roles in their programs was a set of skills that they were lacking. Learners were asking for this course, and there was some tension about whether they should be solely responsible for planning and facilitating it. As I write, I can see that to some extent we were all operating from a deficit approach that said learners lack something and if we just give "it" to them—skills for facilitation and planning and knowledge and understanding about how boards work, about the structures of the network organizations, and about the bigger picture of learner involvement in the province—they will be able to take on leadership roles successfully. I argued then that it was important to "teach" learners and not simply set them up to fail by expecting them to take on roles for which others would receive training. Much of the content of the course was generated by asking learners what they wanted to learn. Learners had the opportunity to learn about facilitation and try it out, rather than just diving in and facilitating the whole thing, a direction I had resisted, fearing that some learners would take power and others be silenced.

Now I question the framework. I think we looked mainly to concrete "skills" and knowledge they needed to acquire. During the residential week, learners led sessions and taught each other about fundraising, public speaking, participating in board meetings, and running learners' groups. It was a training week; the one unusual addition was a session exploring anger and how people dealt with their anger. This was not a skill session—not about anger "management"—but rather exploration and shared reflection about feelings. It was a surprising, but popular and moving piece.

At the end of the course I talked about it laughingly, saying that I could give two accounts of the week. One was a story of resounding success, the other of chaos and disaster, and both were true. During the week learners were excited about what they were learning. They worked long and hard and took time for everyone to understand the structure of programs and networks. Learners had been involved with the Ontario Literacy Coalition or their local network, but were often confused about what each organization was. I felt that I had been right. There was a lot of value in getting the bigger picture. Learners formed into groups to run the morning session each day and designed sessions that gave others the experience of being at a board meeting or a learners' committee. This process, where learners conceptualized and ran a mock version of a meeting to illustrate how it worked, rather than providing abstract description, was innovative and effective.

There were many other elements that seemed useful. We all returned at the end of the week proud of what we had accomplished. But there was another side to the picture—a series of crises: students who harassed others, students who consequently did not feel safe, students who found the institutional setting or the mixed group triggered flashbacks of trauma, and students who became extremely sick. Tensions and anger simmered and erupted in the group as different needs—to go slowly enough to fully understand, to go fast enough not to get bored—conflicted. Looking back, the details have faded but the sense of enormous needs that we as facilitators tried to balance—needs that pulled us in all directions, stretched us beyond our limits—stays with me. We sought desperately to address these needs, which we saw as our responsibility. One learner who participated surprised me when she said recently that by feeling so responsible, we kept control over how to address the tensions and kept issues to ourselves and prevented them from becoming collective problems.

At the time I felt strongly that the skills focus of the course was useful. I believed learners needed an opportunity to learn skills and to learn about the larger picture, or they were being set up to fail. The emotional upheaval and the incredible breadth of demands on us as facilitators I simply saw as part of work in the literacy movement, a challenge but irrelevant to the main matter of learners' learning to take more power in their programs, a distraction from the main business at hand. Now, with hindsight, and the experience of the research on impacts of violence on learning, I see emotional issues and questions as central. I wonder now how the picture might have been changed had we taken all that emotion and tension and put it in the foreground, as the matter to be explored together.

Another possible "story" about the success or limitations of the course was revealed when the group got back together later for a follow-up session. At this meeting, many learners talked about how they had gone back to their programs keen to take on more but soon felt frustrated. They felt they had changed, but the program was still relating to them as before. They reported that their attempts to take on more leadership in their programs were not welcomed and supported, but more often were blocked and sabotaged. It seemed that if learners were to take on the battle to be heard in their programs there was more they would need to learn. I also began to think it wasn't only learners who needed to learn skills. Program staff, too, needed to learn new skills to support learners who wanted to take more leadership in their programs, and perhaps new approaches and processes to facilitate change and new attitudes of openness to change the ways things have always been done, to embrace different styles, and to let go of some control.

I don't want to simplify the picture of the approach we took and offer a revisionist history to illustrate my point for new approaches. The course was not a simple deficit approach; the approach was respectful to learners' existing knowledge and skills and sought to build new knowledge onto existing knowledge, creating processes to support learners trying out ideas, playing with those ideas, seeing if they worked for them, and reshaping them if they didn't work.

This workshop was the first time I made plasticine available and discovered the impact for many participants of having something creative to do with their hands while they thought and listened. I have used it ever since with a wide variety of participants, learning that for some it is a crucial aid to the process of reflection. We also tried to respond to the mood of the group. A moment stands out in my memory, when most of the group came back substantially late after lunch. Our reaction was to check in with the group and ask them what it meant. We problem solved together. They were tired and restless. It was a beautiful sunny afternoon. We had work we thought they would want to cover. We quickly agreed to take the afternoon off and instead do the planned work in the evening. They were amazed that rather than being mad at them and telling them off for being late, we wanted to work with their feelings, not push them down and get on with the work. We also sought to create a safe learning environment, but only realized in retrospect how much more we could have done to explore, at the outset, how to create a safe space for everyone, recognizing diverse needs and concerns.

Looking back, I see the complexity of the picture, and though I do not now want to ignore the value of teaching skills nor forget the value of concrete accomplishments, with the insights drawn from understanding impacts of trauma, I would in the future want to shift the emphasis away from skills. I would want to include a focus on feelings and allow more space for reflection and work directed toward building connection and exploring divides between learners and workers. I would now question how we might have shifted "ownership" of the problems rather than feeling we were solely responsible and explore issues of control. I would spend much more time on creating a safe environment, building trust, and creating strategies together for what to do when working in a group became difficult for whatever reason. I would create a holistic approach recognizing the whole person in a myriad of ways. I wonder now what new possibilities for change might have been opened up had we offered learners more experiences of holistic learning, not only words, words, words!

CARRYING OUT A LEARNER LEADERSHIP ACTIVITY TOGETHER

Remembering the problems of that course, when I next had a chance to shape a learner leadership activity, I thought it would be valuable to include a group from each program rather than a lone learner. I thought that if a learner worked with some allies from his or her program, it would support increased learner control in the program. In proposing this grouping I knew I was going against the desire several learners had expressed for a course for learners only. Although I could see many reasons why learners might prefer a group for learners only, I thought that strategically a mixed grouping, including volunteer or paid staff from programs, might increase the possibilities for change in programs. I always value opportunities to illustrate the common ground and similarities between literacy learners and workers. From the location of learners, in spite of similarities with workers, the key difference is frequently seen as exclusion and difference. This makes it harder for learners to see any value in working alongside those who are on the other side of the divide—included and "normal"—who participate in excluding and marking learners as different. I wonder now about the different learning that could have happened in a learner-only group, with teams of learners from each program. I would love to imagine, what seems an impossible dream in the current climate, the possibility of a parallel course for workers and volunteers only, where we could critically examine our own practices, and the opportunity for the two parallel streams to come together and do further work on how to engage in the process of change together. Conceiving of this project, I had a notion of scheduling time when the two groupings of learners and workers would work separately and come back together. Limits on time, space, and energy meant that I found only minimal ways to put that vision into practice.

Although I wondered about workers' resistance to change and questioned what training opportunities might be necessary to allow workers to learn how to support learners in taking control, I now see that when I began to conceptualize this second project I was still operating within a deficit mode. I thought that it was a different set of "skills" that learners lacked. I thought of this lack as "persistence." I wanted learners to learn how to push, to reframe their goal if necessary when they met resistance, and to find new ways to persist such as restating their point so they would be heard and get what they wanted. I wanted to encourage them to be open to challenge, to rethinking, and to listening to what others wanted them to hear. I wanted them to take the initiative to demand to be heard, rather than to wait to be asked. I hoped that meeting as a whole group we could reflect on what they were accomplishing, or what changes they needed to make, to accomplish more and support each other to think through new options.

The framework was that teams from seven or eight programs would each choose an activity to carry out in their program that they felt would increase learner leadership in their program. We suggested various types of activity, such as learning something and teaching others, running a new learner orientation, or running a learners' committee. They would have an opportunity to attend workshops to learn skills to help them do their activity in their program and they would meet regularly with the rest of the group to talk and write about how their activity was going, so the whole group could provide support to each other. At the end of the process, they would teach others in the literacy community about what they had done in their program and what they had learned from the process, so others could benefit from the experience. They would also help put together a book from the project so those who couldn't attend the workshop could still learn something to help them try a leadership activity in their program.

It was an ambitious project. We only had 6 months and the demand for a "good product" created anxiety to move forward long before everyone had even decided whether they wanted to be part of the group, before some had fully understood what was meant by an "activity," and before the group had cemented into working supportively together. The framework was still one that included learning skills, but that wasn't the sole focus. The chance to carry out an activity and create a group of supporters for this process to help learners, volunteers, and staff to reflect, to rethink, and to teach others was also part of the project. As I reflect now, I realize that to some extent the pressure to have a good product was a demand of the funder and the organization, but also I wonder how much I fell into that need to create a good product myself. Perhaps I could have argued for something more moderate as the goal and allowed more time to develop the process together. I would not want to lose focus on the accomplishment of a task, but I would like to see more time for focus on process and reflection. Often I think the demands to see results or outcomes from a project lead to more emphasis on product than process.

Again, it is easy for me to simplify and suggest the project was totally product oriented. I was surprised when I suggested to a learner and literacy worker team that I should have stopped to address the process issues, because they both insisted that we *had* stopped to look at what was going on! The writing of one volunteer who participated in the project also suggested a sense of balance:

> as each week went on, my trust of the facilitators, learners and tutors grew from my being able to be a participant in a group where questioning of the methods was encouraged and where we stopped when someone got stuck, abandoning the agenda to prioritize healing . . . that's what has always messed me up in school—when it gets tense, or someone becomes lost and the teacher keeps on going because it is easier than sticking around to clean it up . . . once I realized how safe our group was I put away all my defences because I knew if something awkward or annoying arose I would be protected by our honest and sensible approach to conflict . . . I didn't spend all of my energy putting on layer after layer of armour just to walk in the door . . . this may sound exaggerated or dramatic but this is the first time I have participated in a group where things moved, where we had time to focus on ourselves because we weren't plowing ahead towards some ridiculous or unrealistic goal . . . the learning occurred in showing up and trusting ourselves to share information and finish tasks. (Hillhouse in Metro Toronto Movement for Literacy, 1996, pp. 81–82)

I suspect many of the learners would not have shared that tutor's sense that there was the right balance during the project, which reminds me of the impossibility of finding a balance that seems right for all.

During the project we took time regularly to reflect as a group. One useful process we included was a round during which participants brought their problems to the table and other participants helped them problem solve. I wrote about another important moment of reflection during our regular writing time:

> One favourite moment in the project was when Rachel [our workshop facilitator] acted out different responses [to a situation] and we could all hear the difference. The next session, people talked about the ways they had tried to respond differently, or noticed other people's responses, over the last weeks. So many people had noticed something and seen more options for themselves. That for me was a central skill for leadership. (Horsman in Metro Toronto Movement for Literacy, 1996, p. 77)

We included a workshop to help everyone prepare for giving presentations, which explored assessing risk and examining our defensive behavior. On reflection, I would have explored such ideas much earlier in the process. One of the learners reminded me that by bringing a disparate group together we were setting up a terrifying situation where most would feel extremely threatened, creating the perfect situation for everyone to escape into their familiar patterns of defensive behavior. Her assessment fits well with my knowledge of trauma impacts, which suggests that any challenging situation may bring back memories of trauma and earlier methods of coping with terror.

Although there was an enormous sense of accomplishment for most of us at the end of the project, when I recently talked to some of the learners involved in the project I was aware of how much that glow has faded, leaving them still angry and frustrated and feeling powerless. However well intentioned many of us in literacy may be, however strong our commitment to equity, the many blocks to the process of making "real" changes in the balance of power seem to be enormously complex. Even when learners have taken their places on boards, as Malicky et al. (1997) suggested, it is "unlikely, however, that this type of involvement significantly increased either their sense of power or their actual power" (p. 99). Later Malicky et al. mentioned that when they were checking with one of the interviewees whether she had an "increased sense of power . . . she responded, 'I don't have power on anything'" (p. 99). I sometimes wonder whether participation on boards and committees increases learners' sense of powerlessness, further silencing them and contributing to their anger at themselves for being "stupid" and at others for not valuing or listening to them. These comments draw my attention to a need for much more in-depth exploration about what power sharing might look like. What would real power for learners mean? I think workers too often feel as if we don't have any power, yet from learners' perspectives, the power we hold may be more visible, leading to the judgment that we are trying to hang on to it all and are not prepared to let go. The opportuntity for more in-depth reflection is crucial if the literacy movement is to move out of frustrating patterns of "failed" or limited learner leadership.

RESEARCH ON TRAUMA AND LEARNING

With these two experiences of learner leadership projects in mind, I am prompted by learning from research around literacy and violence to question the value of skills-building training to increase leadership and to see a little more of the complex picture around making change. I don't want to dismiss "skills" and new knowledge. I do want to explore the effect attitudes and old "knowledge," which haunts learner leadership attempts, have on explosions of anger and ongoing frustration for learners and workers alike.

When I talked to one learner about why she found it hard to speak out on the board she is on, she first said, "Why would they listen to me?" This old "knowledge" she operates from will not easily be shifted by learning new skills. Yet, when I had conceptualized skills learning that I needed to introduce in the second project described earlier I thought in terms of persistence rather than exploring *why* learners often don't persist, *why* they often give up when not listened to, and *why* they are often not "present" when they sit in a meeting. I thought in terms of learning speaking and listening skills. I had not thought much about that complex combination of learners sometimes feeling "Why would anyone listen to me" and not speaking out in consequence, and workers sometimes not listening, perhaps thinking a learner has nothing worthwhile to say, or just too hurried and anxious to move forward to notice that a learner hasn't spoken or doesn't really seem to agree. Teaching learners skills to help them to make others listen would not unearth information about that feeling of not being worthy of being listened to, nor reveal how such attitudes of both learners and workers might shape the interactions. The learner's belief that she has nothing worth saying, combined with her fury when anyone else suggests, through their words or behavior, that they might share her belief, points to the complexity of the interaction. The extent to which workers are embedded in hierarchical discourses that value those with more education as "smarter" and the conflict between such discourses and those around equity and social justice might reveal further layers of the complexity of the picture.

As part of a possible rethinking of leadership activities, I want to recognize that many workers and learners have experienced trauma and see whether, rather than only teaching knowledge or skill, a different sort of exploration might lead to new insights about interactions between workers and learners. Many of the key areas of tension in learner leadership are reflected in the situations that trauma survivors face. I am not suggesting that issues of violence should be taken up directly during leadership activities or that workers should be figuring out who are survivors and who not. One learner told me that if we had addressed issues of violence directly in the recent learner leadership activity "you wouldn't have seen me for dust" and suggested that another learner "would have died right on the spot." However, we both thought indirect exploration might be useful in activities designed to increase learner leadership in programs.

What follows picks up some themes from the first discussion paper (Horsman, 1997) I wrote from the research into trauma impacts that seem relevant to the learner leadership process.[3] I talked about these themes with some participants in the later learner leadership activity and together we reflected on what we now saw differently in the light of these insights and what we might do differently in a future activity. Although my research focused on the experiences of women, I think the issues that were raised are relevant to all learners. I introduce each one with an extract from the paper and discuss how it might influence future leadership work.

Control, Connection, and Meaning

In the discussion paper I called the first grouping of themes "Looking at Learning in the Face of Trauma" and introduced the section with a discussion of Herman's (1992) definition of trauma as caused by events that "overwhelm the ordinary systems of care that give people a sense of control, connection and meaning" (p. 33). Many writers suggested that therapy for trauma victims should be directed at helping the survivor to regain a sense of control, meaning, and connection in her life. This helps us see an overlap between literacy and therapy, even if programs are not aware that learners have experienced trauma or that the literacy involvement can be therapeutic. Issues of control, connection, and meaning are central to literacy learning (Horsman, 1997, p. 10).

Control, in particular, seems to be central to the concept of learner leadership and the question of shifting locations of power and feeling powerful because trauma entails being controlled by others and being out of control. One effect of trauma is that control becomes a complex and difficult terrain. Seeing learners continue to struggle with control—feeling that they can't have it, trying to hold on to it, not wanting to be responsible—may be crucial to understanding some interactions in a literacy program. When literacy programs seek to be learner centered, to encourage learners to set

[3]*But I'm Not a Therapist": Furthering Discussion about Literacy Work with Survivors of Trauma* is available to download on the Internet at www.jennyhorsman.com. *Too Scared to Learn: Women, Violence & Education* presents the findings in depth.

goals, and to take a role in running programs by sitting on committees and boards of directors, they can take learners into that same fraught terrain of control. At best, only limited support is provided for learners to learn to navigate their own processes of being effectively in control. Asking learners to "take control," while failing to help them to explore safely what that means or support them in learning about control, sets learners up for failure. Yet what adequate support looks like has yet to be explored (Horsman, 1997, p. 10).

Thinking about how to support "learners to learn to navigate their own processes of being effectively in control" is a central question for learner leadership. I have described control as being like walking in a minefield while assuming you are walking in a field without danger in sight. A key insight might be just to know it is a minefield, to tread warily and at the ready, and perhaps not to retreat rapidly. The need may be to stand still and do lots of exploration of what is happening and proceed with care and consciousness. Of course, it is important to recognize it may not be a minefield only for learners. Workers, too, may struggle with issues of control. Learners, volunteers, and paid staff who are attracted to take part in leadership activities may be those for whom exploring the potential to be in control is particularly important and difficult work. The minefield analogy can perhaps be taken one step further. Like actual minefields, it is not enough just to negotiate the mines hoping not to get hurt. A ban on mines is also needed. Similarly, a focus only on picking up the pieces of the impact of trauma is insufficient. Increased awareness of the dimensions of violence and the extent of the damage is also crucial.

When I discussed this with a learner who had participated in the earlier project she thought that control was a crucial issue. She thought a lot of time and energy was spent by learners testing "are we really in control, even if you don't like what we do." She argued she often feels learners are being offered a false promise in literacy. She feels the implication is that everyone will have control, but that is only a game and control will get taken back as soon as something goes wrong, with the judgment "they just weren't capable." In our discussion, we struggled to understand each other. I felt that rather than thinking the learners are not capable, I was liable to hang on to a certain amount of control, feeling I am paid to take responsibility for accomplishing the agreed-upon task. If I snatch back control as things begin to get messy, I am likely to do so thinking *not* that "they" can't do it, but that *I* got it wrong and I may fail. We laughed over our different analyses and the realization that we both had control issues and both were convinced we would be judged to be at fault! The richness of the conversation made me think it would be interesting to open up discussion about such issues early in a project process. We agreed that not everyone would find it easy to engage in such discussion, but thought there could be ways to make the discussion straightforward. Introducing ideas such as what would count as success and failure in a project, talking about places in our lives where we feel we have some control and what we do when we feel out of control, and talking about blaming others and taking responsibility could all be ways to negotiate such talk.

In our conversation, we also recognized that not everyone wants control and that some of us do at some times and not at others. Avoiding responsibility and blaming others was a pattern we both knew well. We thought it was crucial to make as much of this visible as possible; otherwise, learners may judge that any example of workers taking back some control is not because the person leading became scared, but because "they didn't really think I could do it," or they just pretended to give control. Then, the sense of the workers' dishonesty, the distrust, and the layers of anger can build up each time something goes wrong and may become an insurmountable barrier.

Learner leadership activities might be a place for exploration of control and a practice ground where learners can explore taking control without being judged. Several learners talked about how hard it is to risk saying no or disagreeing. One learner said that "you think they're going to give up on you" if you disagree. The opportunity to build trust and to reflect might offer important possibilities. If I were running a leadership project again, I would try to be much clearer about the control I intended to keep. Naming my role, my sense of my responsibility, and the aspects of the project that were agreed in the funding proposal or in my contract clearly at the outset might avoid the appearance that I am trying to hang onto control. I would want to make as much of that visible as possible, so the group could explore together what was open to negotiation by the group. Then, too, we would want to make visible as much as possible the complexity of group decisions to explore whether some members are listened to more than others. Continually opening up questions about who feels in control here—is there an OK balance between participants and facilitators?—and generally opening up a project to more exploration with less pressure to accomplish might be valuable.

Much of Herman's (1992) book, *Trauma and Recovery*, explored in depth how control, connection, and meaning are areas of difficulty for survivors of trauma. I am beginning to think through what these issues might mean in literacy. Reporting on my research I wrote that connection requires trust, and that speaking and listening and reading and writing are about connection to others and trust that it is possible to communicate something. During my research several learners talked about the "smiling face" as a way of hiding the pain that they were experiencing (Horsman, 1997, p. 11). It also became clear how many of the connections around the shared experience of violence cannot easily be drawn on because of the profound silences around violence. In the learner leadership group I led I would guess that many learners, volunteers, and paid workers had experienced trauma, but rather than leading to connection and solidarity, it seemed to lead to competing needs. One learner said that she thought many learners "have never had enough attention" so they are always trying to gain the attention of the facilitators. Learning to listen to each other and support each other is a challenge that takes time and practice.

The language that all learners are in it together assumes there will be connection. Experience shows me this is not necessarily so and may be a dangerous assumption that fuels future disappointment and blame. This awareness would lead me in the future to design a wide range of activities to build connections between learners, including exploring their commonalities and differences and examining what creates divisions and competition among learners. Taking on a common task together built a sense of shared purpose by the end of our working together. Several connections have been developed subsequently, but more often along the way it seemed that the tensions and animosities within the group were increasing rather than decreasing. In the future, I would stop and spend time along the way to explore this perception carefully.

I would want to explore questions about meaning in a similar manner, because Herman referred to a loss of meaning. In literacy that may also lead learners to have difficulty dreaming of possibilities or imagining goals. Learners often have difficulty trusting their own knowledge. Many learners have enormous difficulty finding meaning in a text, even when they are able to decipher the words. Much of this difficulty may be about limited vocabulary and lack of experience with a wide variety of words, but the concept of loss of meaning suggests new questions (Horsman, 1997, p.12). In the future in a learner leadership project I would want to build some sense of shared meaning on various levels early in working together. I would want to look at the meaning of "learner leadership," of learners' past experiences in their programs, and of the project in progress.

When I think of the importance of time to process questions of control, connection, and meaning, I can imagine the value of a regular meeting for learners who sit on the boards of programs and networks to explore these issues among themselves. Caucuses are increasingly used as a tool for people with shared experiences of oppression to define their own problems, explore common experiences and shared meanings, and develop collective strategies to support their participation in coalitions. Opportunities to explore the value of such caucusing in literacy might be useful.

Impacts of Violence

Another theme that emerged from my research that I think is relevant to learner leadership work is what I called "Responding to Impacts of Violence in Literacy." Through this theme I explored issues not usually visible, which take energy away from the literacy learning process for many students who are survivors of trauma. Much current talk in literacy is focused on outcomes. This talk needs to include the complexity of what many learners are dealing with. Much of the learning that has to take place, and that takes the energy of the learner, is not visible even to learners or workers, let alone planners and funders (Horsman, 1997, p. 17). In learner leadership activities, perhaps our focus is too much on the product—for example, getting learners to sit on boards—and we have too little awareness of what is going on for many learners as they try to take on this challenge while living with the impacts of trauma.

The concept of presence, which emerged strongly in the research into trauma impacts, is central to the leadership project. Rather than use a framework in which it is "normal" to be present, and "abnormal" to be dissociated, I used the word *presence* to focus on the nuances of presence and to create a positive way of speaking about the challenge for learners to explore what hinders and supports their presence. I suggested that programs recognize that many learners have difficulty staying present for various reasons and talk about this with learners. The concept could be normalized and space created for learners to notice when they are less present and what is contributing to it. Do they have crises happening in their life? Are they having nightmares and trouble sleeping? What do they think or feel about the topic of the class? Are they anxious and panicked? If spacing out is named as something many learners struggle with, and the program or class is a place that is accepting and supportive of the challenges learners are facing, learners can be encouraged to strengthen their awareness of their degree of presence, to build knowledge about what they need to stay present and what they learn from leaving, and to learn to ask for what they need to support their learning processes (Horsman, 1997, pp. 18–19).

I was aware during the learner leadership project of the varying degrees of presence for different participants on different days. I was fascinated and frustrated by the ways in which those who seemed most absent drew my attention. I felt less and less able to reach those who were present, as I watched those who stared out of the window, who seemed disengaged from the process, who regularly arrived late and frequently missed sessions, or who often stood near the door or distant from the group. That observation remained my private struggle to pay better attention myself and not to be distracted by the various distancing activities that participants were using. Now that I review the activity from the perspective of impacts of trauma, I can see the value of taking time to talk about it. In a class I am teaching currently, I have begun to ask about what is helping or hindering their presence in class that day. Though they are not literacy learners, the lesson I have learned from this process is that sharing the types of issues and problems that are distracting and exhausting the learners seemed to help them to set those things aside and focus. Though they didn't speak about issues of violence, an awareness about presence in general made visible to all of us our collective challenges and built connection.

Another pattern I have become more aware of through the trauma impact research is one of "all or nothing" and crises. In conversation, therapists talked about trauma survivors as frequently showing opposing patterns at the same time, about moving between taking complete control and abdicating control, complete trust and no trust at all, a defended self and no boundaries or self-protection at all. They spoke of switching between extremes and having enormous difficulty with ambiguity. They suggested it would be healing to learn to find middle ground. One therapist stressed that if one pattern is present you could expect to see the opposite also there. Some people spoke of another dimension, of the all-or-nothing concept of "totalizing," which explained a tendency to move instantly from experiencing one example to concluding "it is always this way." For example, one mistake means "I always make mistakes; I am stupid and nothing will change it." Or, "You let me down once I can never rely on you; you always let me down, I will never trust you again over anything." Small failures are complete failures (Horsman, 1997, pp. 20–21).

Now that I am aware of this pattern, I am more able to observe it and less likely to get offended, for example, when learners who at the end of the learner leadership project were describing it as "wonderful," are later telling me that it was "completely useless." I can see the comments as part of the pattern of all or nothing. I noticed, too, that in my own reports of a project I would want to decide whether it was good or bad, leaving little space for an assessment that includes both the strengths and weaknesses. Working on making the middle ground visible, exploring what makes an activity a little better or a little worse, might help to make visible the pattern of all or nothing and create more choices.

Being aware of patterns of crises and explosions might also help a facilitator move away from self-blame and get less defensive, freeing up everyone to explore the pattern. All-or-nothing ways of relating to the world can mean that trauma survivors live with regular crises. In my research, instructors talked a lot about the crises in learners' lives and the energy they consume. One literacy worker I spoke to said, "They are too busy being upset to learn." Therapists and the therapeutic literature talk about how scary it can be for someone who is used to living in a state of crisis to live without crises. The tension of waiting for the next crisis creates a state of continual expectation, so that for some women it may be easier to provoke the crisis than wait for it. A group of workers described crises as a way of "putting off success and change." One learner said that after living with crisis all her life she had no sense of who she would be if she were not in crisis (Horsman, 1997, pp. 21–22). I have noticed that learners' descriptions of involvement on boards and hiring committees are often descriptions of a series of crises. I wonder how much these crises are also a way of controlling the situation and avoiding the possibility of rejection by others. Exploring the meaning of crises and looking at new ways to make meaning of the experiences could perhaps begin the process of creating new patterns.

Moving away from all-or-nothing concepts in terms of power, and in terms of options for learner leadership, might offer new understandings. Perhaps we are operating within too small a range of choices in which either learners have power and are on boards and committees, or they have none. Could we look more creatively to come up with more options, more increments to acquire more power? Can learners assess what power looks like for themselves and use tools of evaluation for experiences and degrees of power? For example, a leadership activity in which students (and others perhaps) tried out roles and observed possibilities, such as sitting in on the board *and* exploring multiple meanings of what is happening, working as a group to analyze the board process and become clearer about possibilities to intervene, and even role playing, might free learners from some of the defensive behaviors that come into play when they are anxious and create new possibilities for taking power in a situation. Such options might shift away from the simple either-or choice of becoming a board member or not taking part in that process of program governance at all. Examining what power looks like and feels like and what its effects are might be a valuable process for many learners and workers to see nuances. Where divisions of all or nothing shape the perception, both learners and workers are likely to feel they have no power. Exploring the nuances might make more possibilities visible.

When I discussed the leadership project with a learner who participated, one of the first things she said was, "It was difficult for me because I have trust issues." As we talked further, we soon saw the ways in which testing and checking out the possibilities to trust was a central theme. Reporting on the trauma impact research, I identified trust, or the attention required to assess whether it is safe to trust, as another issue that workers and counselors spoke about as taking up energy and impeding the learners' presence in the program. In that research, one worker suggested that the energy expended to check out whether a person was trustworthy added time to the learning process. A survivor described the problem as more profound: "The first thing I learned, in a long list of strategies to survive my childhood, was not to trust anybody. The second thing I learned was not to trust myself" (Danica, 1996, p. 17).

If you cannot trust yourself, you cannot figure out whether to trust others. Your gut or instinct is not to be relied on and you cannot know who to trust and who not to trust. You can also have problems with knowing whether to trust your own sense of danger. Therapists used the term *hypervigilance* to refer to the level of alertness that survivors may use to observe the tensions in a room. I think this research should alert literacy workers to continually question whether we are being trustworthy and whether our behavior in any way replicates abuse because we have authority (Horsman, 1997, pp. 22–23).

As a facilitator, had I realized that many of the conflicts and clashes were about testing my trustworthiness, I suspect that I would have found it easier to weather the process. As it was, I would go away from a session where explosions had occurred desperately trying to figure out how to do it "right" next time. After talking to learners, I wondered what difference it would have made to me, if, instead of seeing myself as getting it "wrong" I had seen myself as being tested. I think it might have helped me to continue to stay present without getting angry or defensive, or becoming exhausted by my sense of failure. I might have been at least less likely to blame myself.

Questioning what it means to be trustworthy may also be crucial. When workers assure a learner that it is great to have them on the board but struggle with the tension of slowing the board process down to work for the learner, does the learner read that they are a burden and should not trust the worker's assurances? One learner said of the learners in the leadership project that "we are a bunch of watchers" with incredible skills at watching people and sensing danger. Exploring what is observed in that watching process might reveal information useful to all participants in an interaction. Processes to build trust in any group—committee, board, or leadership project—would be crucial.

Building trust is also part of creating a safe environment where it is possible to take risks. When a group is brought together they may feel threatened and retreat into earlier patterns of defensive behavior. A learner who participated in the leadership project commented, "If you bring a bunch of learners together who all have trust issues, they will feel threatened and if you say 'work it through' well it's going to explode on you." If we talk about what our defensive behaviors are when we feel threatened and explore the different baggage we all bring to working in a group, it might be possible to create an environment where it feels safe to practice taking control and building connection. This learner stressed that it is not fair to learners to bring a group together, put them under pressure to produce, and blame them when conflicts blow up. She said that it is important to have plenty of time to work through the tensions, to address the baggage that everyone brings to the learning situation, and to build trust and connection before trying to accomplish a task.

Recognizing the impact of trauma on all aspects of the person has also led me to see great potential in fully holistic approaches to learning that recognize the body, mind, emotion, and spirit. Thinking about these four aspects of the person challenged me to think about how the "damage" to each area I have heard about in my trauma impact interviews could also lead to new possibilities for literacy work. A focus on body, mind, emotions, and spirit could be far more than just addressing damage. It could lead to a process where each aspect of the person was fully engaged in a creative learning process. A more holistic literacy might support healing, integration, and lead to a highly successful educational process (Horsman, 1997, pp. 34–35). Thinking creatively about how to involve all aspects of the person in learner leadership activities might help us to nurture "damaged souls" and move from places where we are stuck in frustration and tension.

CONCLUSION

Learners and literacy workers are involved together in a dance of interactions to increase learner leadership in literacy programs and networks. I have argued that we need to step out of that dance and engage in critical reflection about these interactions. Questioning the current possibilities for learner leadership in literacy programs and envisaging new structures for power sharing for all involved in literacy programs might contribute to shifting the dynamics around learner leadership. New structures instead of traditional boards of governance might offer new possibilities. Further reflection on power issues, unpacking assumptions about "them and us," could lead to the creation of activities to explore the connections and separations between learners and staff and among learners, and lead to more complex understandings of power and powerlessness.

Recognizing the impact of trauma may help us to step back from deficit models of teaching skills for learner leadership and support new possibilities that pay more attention to identifying control, developing connection, and exploring meaning. Noticing the tensions around presence, trust, "all or nothing," and crises can open up new approaches to explore possibilities for increasing learner leadership in programs. Stopping the dance, not only to reflect and question what is happening for all the players, but also to create more holistic ways of working, may lead away from frustration and toward new possibilities for learner leadership.

REFERENCES

Campbell, P. (1996). Participatory literacy practices: Exploring social identity and relations. *Adult Basic Education, 6*(3), 127–142.

Danica, E. (1996). *Beyond don't: Dreaming past the dark.* Charlottetown, Canada: Gynergy Books.

Herman, J. (1992). *Trauma and recovery.* New York: Basic Books.

Horsman, J. (1997). *"But I'm not a therapist:" Furthering discussion about literacy work with survivors of trauma.* Toronto, Canada: CCLOW. (www.jennyhorsman.com)

Horsman, J. (1999/2000). *Too scared to learn: Women, violence and education.* Toronto, Canada: McGilligan Books and Mahwah, NJ: Lawrence Erlbaum Associates.

Malicky, G. V., Katz, C. H., Norton, M., & Norman, C. A. (1997). Literacy learning in a community-based program. *Adult Basic Education, 7*(2), 84–103.

Metro Toronto Movement for Literacy. (1996). *MTML's Learners' Leadership Project.* Toronto, Canada: MTML.

The Open Book. (no date). *We're all in this together: Leadership and community at the Open Book.* Brooklyn, NY: The Open Book.

5

Getting Our Own Education: Peer Tutoring and Participatory Education in an Adult Literacy Centre

Mary Norton
The Learning Centre Association

The Learning Centre is a community-based adult literacy and education center, located on the north edge of downtown Edmonton. From 1994 to 1997, a number of women and men who come to the center were engaged in a peer tutoring project: adult students tutoring other students.[1]

The peer tutoring project started serendipitously one spring day in 1993. At the time, the Learning Centre was housed in a small room in the basement of a former city courthouse. The windows were open to warm breezes and the room was bursting with people and their learning. Being short of volunteer tutors, I asked Mary, a student, to give Barb a hand with her reading. Mary and Barb were content with their lesson, and Mary was eager to tutor again, although concerned that she "do it right."

Mary's interest and questions led me to apply to the National Literacy Secretariat for a grant to undertake the peer tutoring project. Having found few resources about peer tutoring in adult literacy work, I proposed to develop a peer tutoring program, to produce a handbook and video, and to research some outcomes of peer tutoring. I posed questions about how peer tutoring would affect students' learning and literacy development, their participation in the program, and relationships among students, peer tutors, and other volunteers.

---

[1]Adults at the Learning Centre use the term student, rather than learner, to name their main role at the Learning Centre.

The day I asked Mary to tutor Barb, I acted out of expediency; I had no idea where the request would lead. Although I have had a long-standing interest in participatory education, I never imagined how the peer tutoring project would be a catalyst for participatory approaches to take hold at the Learning Centre. This chapter is about the peer tutoring project, some outcomes, and how it contributed to participatory education at the Learning Centre. It is addressed to literacy educators and others interested in the adult literacy field.

THE LEARNING CENTRE: CONTEXT FOR THE PROJECT

The Learning Centre started when Sister Beryl Stone began tutoring literacy at an inner-city women's program in the early 1980s. Sister Beryl and some coworkers created a quiet Learning Room near the kitchen where neighborhood women gathered for lunch. Some of the women started going to the Learning Room to write and read their stories with Sister Beryl and other volunteers who joined her. An advisory committee formed and they obtained a grant to hire a coordinator for the emerging program.

The Learning Room grew into the Learning Centre and moved to a new space, first onto the stage of an old theatre located in the same building as the women's program, and then to the previously mentioned basement room.[2] Here, women and men came to work on their own or one to one with volunteer tutors. The center became known as a place of welcome, warmth, and acceptance.

In 1991, the advisory committee incorporated The Learning Centre Literacy Association. Association members elected a board of directors that included students, tutors, and other volunteers. I was hired as coordinator in 1992, following the retirement of the first coordinator. During the next year, I explored ways to invite students into collaborative work. Some became involved in organizing the annual Christmas party and year-end picnic. Some worked on a photo-story together and recognized potential benefits of learning in a group. Three women read a story written by a women's group in Toronto and suggested we start a women's group at the Learning Centre.

In 1993, the Association undertook a visioning process and the board responded to students' expressed interest in expanding the program. We obtained grants to contract instructors to work with groups, and other grants enabled us to move into a larger room. More students could come, more of-

---

[2]This room was made available to the Learning Centre by the Boyle Street Co-op, a community services and resource agency. The Learning Centre continues to be housed and closely affiliated with the Co-op.

ten. There were areas where people could work together and spaces to work alone or with a tutor. This was the context in which the peer tutor project started.

THE PEER TUTORING PROJECT

In January 1994, three men and three women attended an inaugural meeting about peer tutoring. I had informed all Learning Centre students about the meeting, but had also spoken directly with these six for various reasons: One had already indicated a desire to tutor, two served on the board and were active in organizing and supporting program events, two had moved from individual to group work and seemed ready for a new challenge, and one had been nominated by other students because she was viewed as a good reader.

The six who attended the meeting decided to participate in the project. They were soon joined by another woman whose husband, a student at the center, had encouraged her to volunteer as a tutor. She was uncertain about tutoring and she identified socially with the students at the center. With the encouragement of some peer tutors, she joined the project.

Approaches to training and supporting peer tutors evolved with the project. Generally, I met weekly or biweekly with peer tutors to hear about their tutoring and to introduce tutoring strategies. We were sometimes joined by other students and community tutors. For a time during 1995–1996, support for peer tutors was minimal because my attention was directed to relocating our program. (After a prolonged search, two temporary moves, and living with renovations, we resettled in June 1996.)

From the start of the project until 1997, 25 students were involved as peer tutors, in some cases briefly, but more often for extended periods. They tutored with at least an equal number of students, for a short period or almost daily for several months. Four of the first seven peer tutors continued to tutor in 1997, and some of the students they first tutored had taken on tutoring roles.

Initially, peer tutors worked one to one with other students. Some tutored steadily with the same student for a while; others worked with more than one over time. During the last year of the peer tutoring project, the Learning Centre program was reorganized to include learning circles that met three mornings a week. Each circle involved 10 to 15 students and a facilitator. Peer tutors, as well as community tutors,[3] assisted in two of the circles. Peer tutors also tutored one to one at other times and some worked

---

[3]Community tutors are tutors who are not also students at the center. We use this term rather than volunteer tutors because peer tutors are also volunteers.

with small groups, such as a Readers' Theatre group. One peer tutor tutored youth in a neighboring school.

In 1997, around 10 students identified themselves as peer tutors. They had tutoring assignments and attended biweekly tutor meetings. However, many other students were now involved in helping each other learn. It was not uncommon to see two or three students reading together, puzzling out words and ideas, and asking a peer or community tutor for help as they needed it. Peer tutoring—and peer learning—was now a fundamental and vital dimension of the Learning Centre program.

UNDERTAKING RESEARCH ABOUT PEER TUTORING

In writing the project proposal in 1993, I did a literature review and concluded that peer tutoring among adult literacy students had not been widely developed, documented, or researched. Suggesting a need to develop and document peer tutoring practices, I posed the following questions:

- Does peer tutoring affect the participation of peer tutors and other students in the Learning Centre program, and if so, how?
- Does tutoring affect students and peer tutors' literacy development and related abilities, and if so, how?
- Does peer tutoring affect the relationships among peer tutors, other volunteer tutors, and staff, and if so, how?

I engaged Herb Katz as a researcher for the peer tutoring project. Herb became familiar to all of us at the center as he tutored, participated in peer tutor meetings, facilitated some groups, and conducted other research. For the peer tutor research, Herb interviewed project participants and observed peer tutor meetings, tutorials, and other interactions. I also made notes about meetings and observations and did some interviews. Because Herb could not continue as researcher after the first year and a half of the project, I completed the research analysis and the write-up that follows.

Because peer tutoring occurred in a complex, changing context, Herb and I realized the research would be "messy." We would not be able to attribute changes in people's literacy, participation, and relationships solely to peer tutoring. For one thing, students and peer tutors did not learn only with each other; they were also involved in other learning activities and contexts that would have influenced developments. Peer tutors and students participated in the project for different lengths of time. We were also aware that the many changes that occurred at the Learning Centre could influence developments.[4]

The research questions were broad, particularly given the context and resources available. However, they provided starting points for sifting through the interviews, notes, and other information collected during the project. They also provided categories for reflecting on what I found: participation, literacy development, and relationships.

PARTICIPATION

Participation has many meanings in adult literacy education. In one common use, the term refers to enrollment and attendance in programs. However, as Jurmo (1989) described, attendance is the most basic form of student participation. More active participation means students having "higher degrees of control, responsibility and reward vis-à-vis program activities" (p. 17).

While writing about participation, I realized that peer tutoring is about students having responsibility for a fundamental activity in literacy programs: learning to read and write. Through peer tutoring, adults who are developing literacy themselves help others learn. As one peer tutor remarked, "We are getting our own education." At the Learning Centre, peer tutoring was both an exploration of participatory education and a model for applying participatory approaches throughout the program.

In reviewing the literature about participatory education, I found much in common between what I observed as outcomes of peer tutoring and what others, such as Jurmo (1989), described as benefits of participatory approaches: enhanced learning, enhanced personal development, and enhanced ability to transform the larger social contexts.

For some educators, the last possibility—realizing and enhancing capacity to act for social change—is what ultimately distinguishes participatory education from other collaborative educational approaches. Educational efforts concerned with social change recognize connections between low literacy and the conditions with which people with low literacy often live. Further, these conditions are understood as a reflection of inequitable distribution of power in society.

In some cases, participatory education is a process through which participants work together for change in their communities.[5] This process of-

---

[4]Others (Goodlad & Hirst, 1989; Melarango, 1976) noted the challenges of researching peer tutoring among school-age children because of the complexity of the endeavours and the number of variables that can affect outcomes.

[5]When operating from a social change perspective, participatory education has much in common with popular education. For an engaging and thoughtful discussion about participatory education and related movements see Sauvé's (1987) *From One Educator to Another*. For a discussion of popular education, see Beder (1996).

ten engages participants in analyzing the roots and causes of a common issue, identifying and researching potential solutions, and taking action to
implement the solutions (Beder, 1996). In literacy programs, participatory
education may be seen as providing opportunities for people to experience
more equitable power relationships—at least within the program—and to develop skills and confidence to speak up about issues that matter to them
(Campbell, 1994; Jurmo, 1989). Speaking up in programs may be a rehearsal
for speaking out in other contexts.

At the Learning Centre, peer tutoring enhanced learning, nurtured
growth in confidence and self-esteem, and enabled the development of personal relationships among students. Peer tutoring also invited a shift in social and power relations among students, tutors, and staff and provided
new opportunities for students to make their voices heard. These ideas are
developed throughout the remainder of this chapter.

LITERACY DEVELOPMENT

When I wrote the project proposal, the available research on peer tutoring
among adults in literacy programs focused on personal or affective outcomes, such as growth in self-esteem (Goldgrab, 1992; Jurmo, 1987). I found
no reports about the effect of peer tutoring on adults' reading or writing.
For this reason, an objective for the peer tutoring project was to research
whether and how peer tutoring affected participants' literacy development.
By this I meant: Would peer tutors and the students they tutored improve
their reading and writing skills?

Research about peer tutoring with children indicates that both the tutor
and the "tutee" can make gains in literacy. The peer tutoring project seems
to have had similar benefits. In reporting on gains made by students, peer
tutors offered comments such as the following:

> One book he picked out, he read the whole thing. You go back a couple of
> months and you can see the difference. Its unreal how much he has learned
> You can see the confidence in him too. He understands what he reads. (Ben)

> When I used to read with her she couldn't really read too good. . . . Before she
> could hardly read, now she's improving. (Mary)

> Writing with L. . . . A lot of times before she would say she can't do this or she
> didn't know how to put it. Now you make a couple of suggestions and she'll go
> right through and whiz through it. (Ross)

For reasons noted earlier, most examples of improved reading or writing
cannot be attributed to peer tutoring alone. However, in one instance, a tutor and student read together almost daily for 6 months. By the end of the

match the student was reading more difficult books, and she reported that she had "caught up" with the tutor. (An informal reading inventory, administered for another purpose, indicated an increase in the student's reading level.) Because the student read more with the tutor than in other contexts, her increased reading ability might be attributed to peer tutoring.

A more direct relationship between peer tutoring and literacy development was observed for some peer tutors. Learning by teaching was a recurring theme.

> It's practice for what we've learned too. If you've learned something and then you help someone else with it, you're teaching them but you're also refreshing yourself. So you're still learning. (Ross)

As an example, Mary was a peer tutor who had some difficulty composing her ideas in writing. In a videotape of Mary helping another student with a language experience activity, it was evident that Mary was assisting ably with organizing ideas as well as with scribing. It seemed that as a scribe, she was freed from having to generate and remember ideas as well as write them down. Intrigued by her ability to scribe for someone else, Mary anticipated that tutoring would help her with her own writing. She also mentioned that she had always been interested in being a secretary and that this was a way for her to apply that interest.

Mary also commented a number of times during the project that she had greater comprehension of materials since she had started tutoring: "When I'm reading with [student] it helps me learn my reading too. . . . When I listen to her reading, it helps me understand." Another student, Ross, had been assisting a woman with writing. He described how he had honed his own writing skills: "It helps me look at it and put it into paragraphs so everyone can read and get the point and not just rattle on."

These examples suggest that peer tutoring helped both peer tutors and the students they tutored to develop their reading and writing. An exploration of the participatory nature of peer tutoring provides some insights about how it helped.

PARTICIPATORY LEARNING

> *Many scholars have begun to appreciate the impact that the development of community and connection can have on learners. Scholarship . . . has emphasized the power and importance of the social role of connection in educational settings. . . . Programs must be more supportive of learners' need to communicate and connect with each other.*
>
> —Sissel (1996, pp. 98–99)

Cognitive Development

Among other benefits, participatory learning enables students to share ideas and construct meaning together, to engage in critical and creative thinking, and to model cognitive strategies for each other (Jennings & Xu, 1996). Participatory learning occurred at two levels in the peer tutoring project: among the peer tutors in their weekly meetings, and between peer tutors and students. An event during one of the peer tutor meetings provides an example of participatory learning among peer tutors.

In working with peer tutors I initially focused on the cognitive and metacognitive aspects of reading and writing, and a part of most peer tutor meetings were devoted to presentation and discussion about reading and writing strategies. One time, in an attempt to model a one-to-one writing *conference*, I had drafted a letter with the intention of reading it to the peer tutor group and requesting feedback. I would then use their feedback to revise the letter. The letter was addressed to the premier of our province and expressed my fatigue and sadness in the face of recent cuts to welfare benefits. My efforts to model a writing conference fell flat as participants responded to the content of my letter and launched into their own discussion of current events, experiences, and feelings.

Through their discussion about welfare cutbacks, peer tutors concluded there was limited government support for literacy programs because politicians did not know about the people who attended them. They decided to organize visits to the Learning Centre by Members of the Legislative Assembly, with a view to raising awareness among the politicians about people's lives and hopes for learning. In this event, peer tutors engaged with each other as well as with my letter. They constructed meaning and engaged in critical and creative thinking as they analyzed reasons for limited program support and identified ways to address this issue. As the facilitator, I modeled strategies such as summarizing ideas and inviting participants to respond to ideas.

Reflection about the writing conference event helped me recognize that I was attempting to introduce strategies, such as a writing conference, that were new to peer tutors. They had not had opportunities to learn or practice these strategies themselves. How could they be expected to model them for others? When I started to facilitate a weekly writing workshop, in which most peer tutors participated, I found that peer tutors began to apply strategies from the workshop to their own tutoring. Similarly, I found that as students learned strategies in their learning circles they began to coach other students in using them. This has implications for training and support for peer tutors.[6]

---

[6]Training and support for tutors is discussed in the second part of the publication in which this chapter was originally published.

Peer tutoring also contributed to cognitive development between peer tutors and students, but not in the ways I had anticipated. During much of the project, I had been concerned that peer tutors and students were mostly "just" reading together. For the most part, a student would read aloud and the tutor would help with unknown words. As one student reported: "We read together first and after that I try to read it myself and if I get stuck they help me." I felt that tutors should be doing more direct instruction of reading strategies. I have since realized the value of reading together as a way for people to engage with each other as well as with what they are reading. I also recognized that although not teaching strategies directly, peer tutors were modeling, and practicing, strategies as they read and wrote with other students.

As one example, after writing about the rural one-room school of her childhood, a student decided to research and write about "school in the old days." The tutor helped her read the books she had borrowed from the library and found himself getting caught up in "learning the history of the old schools, going through it with her and reading the books myself finding the way things were."

This tutor had also been assisting the woman with writing, as noted earlier. He modeled how to generate ideas through prewriting discussion. At the same time, he picked up ideas that he could write about: "I started helping her put sentences in order and then getting [her] ideas ... down on paper. It was also giving me ideas, so I came up with ideas for myself."

When a group of peer tutors and other students started meeting weekly to practice reading, they alternated between oral reading of a shared text and lively sharing of experiences related to the content. They also reported the following cooperative learning and reading strategies on flip-chart paper:

- We read aloud. We read a paragraph each.
- If someone doesn't understand a word or idea, we talk about what we think it means.
- If someone doesn't know a word, someone else reads it for them.
- We stop every so often to see if everyone understands what is happening. We talk about the story.

During a break, I overheard one woman comment to another that they hadn't finished reading yet, as they still had to *talk* about the story. Clearly, some of the women in the group were conscious of and modeled strategies to support reading development.

While demonstrating some outcomes of participatory learning, these examples also illustrate the social nature of literacy and literacy development that contrasts with some notions about literacy and schooling. For example, when asked what people need to do to improve their reading, some peer tutors responded they need to *go to school* or otherwise find someone who can *teach* them.

Several people who come to the center refer to it as "the school" and refer to themselves as "students." Calling the center a school may be a way for some people to complete unfinished business. Or it may indicate that people haven't been presented with alternate models. Perhaps peer tutoring offers another way to view literacy development. It may also suggest ways to support literacy development in informal settings where adults gather around texts.

Affective Development

> It helped me with my self-esteem, built my confidence back up again. Got my level up there where I could start learning again. (Gordon)

> It was good to prove that we could actually do something and become something. (Joyce)

Affective development emerged strongly as one of the benefits of peer tutoring at the Learning Centre.[7] Peer tutors indicated they had increased in *confidence*, *self-esteem*, and *self-respect*. Though these terms are sometimes used interchangeably, subtle distinctions seem important.

For some peer tutors, their participation in the project provided an opportunity to transform how they valued themselves. Literacy development can be a vehicle to change self-esteem in any case; as people tell and write their stories, they reflect on their past and start to write new futures. For those engaged in such personal change work, the peer tutor meetings seemed to add another avenue for learning about oneself, reflecting on that learning, and coming to see oneself in a new light. The early meetings, with their focus on learning and how to facilitate it, may have promoted such reflection. For some participants, the meetings were a first opportunity to gather with peers and talk about themselves, their experiences, and their ways of relating with others.

For most peer tutors, the project led to increased confidence in their abilities to help others. Some noted they had been nervous or scared at the start of the project, or had felt they didn't know enough to tutor. Peer tutors gained confidence as they tutored, developed skills, and received helpful feedback. They transferred this confidence as they took on other roles in the Learning Centre, such as receptionist or board member. From an indi-

---

[7]Jurmo (1989) suggested that personal development such as growth in self-esteem results from participatory approaches. Other reports about peer tutoring with children and adults also suggested that tutors experience an increase in self-esteem or self-confidence (Dooley, 1984; Goldgrab, 1992; McLachlan, 1990).

vidual-oriented, psychological perspective, changes in both self-esteem and self-confidence may be related to personal relationships that developed through peer tutoring. From a community-oriented, sociological perspective, these changes could be related to concepts of social relations.

RELATIONSHIPS

In posing the question about relationships, I wondered how peer tutoring would affect relationships among peer tutors, other students, other tutors, and staff. Although not stated as such, I was thinking primarily about the power associated with the various roles and whether that would shift. As I worked with the project, perspectives and insights about personal relationships emerged as well.

Personal Relationships

Peer tutoring provided opportunities for students to relate one to one with other students. These relationships benefited peer tutors and students because the relationships were person centered and were "helping."

Person-Centered Relationships

When me and Mary work together . . . sometimes we laugh, right. If I can't say the words we just started laughing and we'd try again. (Alice)

It wasn't just about reading and writing . . . understanding people before you could tutor. (Gordon)

In reviewing interviews and notes, it seemed that some peer tutors were practicing what Rogers (1980) described as person-centered relationships. Rogers named three essential elements of person centered relationship: genuiness or being oneself in a relationship; nonjudgmental acceptance of a person; and empathetic understanding—accurately sensing a person's feelings and personal meanings. Rogers advocated that when these elements are applied in a relationship, such as a tutoring relationship, students start to accept themselves, listen to themselves, and become more genuine themselves, and thus enable themselves to develop.

They helped me a lot. They're the reason why I can read now, and to realize who I am. (Alice)

Empathetic understanding was a recurrent focus for peer tutors. One of the women often described her empathy for the students she tutored. "It hurts when you're in that situation. I feel for what people are going through." She noted that she felt it helped students to know that she had been through the same thing. One of the students she tutored reflected this perspective: "When I have a problem I talk to them and it seems like they listen and they understand."[8]

Development of personal relationships may have strengthened the community in the Learning Centre.

> It brought us all together. (Mary)

> I feel comfortable. When I go home I miss this place. (Alice)

> For some reason this place is just a great place to come. Everybody works together. (Mardge)

In turn, the strengthened community supported learning and encouraged participation, both in attendance and in more active ways.

Helping Relationships

> What I learned I can hand off to somebody else. It makes me feel good . . . that I can pass it on to someone else. (Helen)

> I'm getting a lot out of it so what I want is to put something back in. (Ben)

Helping others and giving back to the program were key among the reasons participants gave for becoming peer tutors. Other studies of peer tutoring point to the value of tutors becoming ones who *help*, a change from the traditional student role of being *helped*. Studies of peer tutoring by university students suggest that being in a helping role has positive psychological effects for tutors. Other studies with children point to the way students, when placed in the responsible role of a tutor, tend to grow to meet the expectations. Being in helping relationships can lead to increased sense of personal adequacy (Goodlad & Hlrst, 1989). As Learning Centre students moved into roles as helpers—roles traditionally played by staff and students—possibilities for shifting social relations also emerged.

SOCIAL RELATIONS

As used here, the concept of social relations has to do with how people, particularly groups of people, are positioned in relation to each other. Social relations are based on distribution of power and are thus influenced by

---

[8]As with any helping relationship, peer tutoring also offers invitations to advise people or take some action to "fix things." Further, there can be a fine line between empathetic understanding and overidentifying with a person. Hearing others' stories can recall painful stories for the peer tutor-listener. Discussion about tutors' roles and boundaries in such situations became an important part of peer tutor meetings.

factors such as social class, income, race, sexual orientation, gender, and culture. Social identity is a dimension of social relations; consciously or unconsciously, people identify themselves and others in terms of their social positions. Social identity can influence how people relate to others.

In literacy and other education programs, the most obvious relations have to do with teacher or tutor and student roles. As well as traditionally having different power positions, these two groups usually have different identities related, at the least, to education and income. The peer tutoring project provided insights into identity, social relations, and power at the Learning Centre.

Identity

> All of us were in the same boat before. We can tell them we were in that situation. (Mary)

> The Learning Centre is not just for people who can afford it. It's for everyone who did not have a chance when they were young. (Bill)

When peer tutors talked about advantages of involving students as tutors, they emphasized the experiences they had in common with other students and how this experience helped them relate to each other. Common experiences referred to shared histories of not learning to read and write, but also to shared life and work experiences, like getting *the boot* (from a job). Although expressing appreciation for the skills and efforts of community tutors, some peer tutors indicated a belief that given their different experiences, community tutors could not relate to or empathize with students in the same way as peer tutors.

> If you talk to someone who had a perfect time in school . . . I figure its just not me. If they haven't been through it, they can't understand. (Ross)

In naming differences between themselves and community tutors, peer tutors were recognizing identity and social relations among students and community tutors. Although not stated as such, there was an awareness of "us" and "them."

I never explored the concept of identity with students during the project. For instance, I didn't encourage peer tutors to examine assumptions that might underlie the belief that we are all in the same boat. Although almost all of the students at the Learning Centre are living with incomes below the poverty line, they are otherwise a heterogeneous group. Nor did we explore the different experiences and skills that peer and community tutors have to offer.

In retrospect, peer tutoring also introduced opportunities to explore identity issues with community tutors, although they were not pursued. For example, during the first year of the project, students, peer tutors, and community tutors were interviewed about their perceptions of peer tutoring. One community tutor questioned the idea of having workshops with peer tutors, indicating that some things might be difficult to discuss. Notes from this interview do not indicate whether the tutor was referring to the nature of the topics, such as particular students' needs, or to the complexity of topics and to differences in community and peer tutors' language and knowledge. At the Learning Centre, involvement of community volunteers is valued, among other ways, as a means to promote exchange and understanding between people of different classes, cultures, and abilities. Campbell (1994) suggested that an intentional exploration of identity can provide a foundation for changing power relations.

Discovering New Voices

> I like the meetings because they were with people I already knew that helped me to speak out and even though a lot of times I feel stupid, its never stupid in the group. It helped me learn new ways to deal with people. (Dawn)

Having a voice refers to people's capacity to "express ideas and opinions with the confidence that they will be heard and taken into account" (Stein, 1997, p. 7). Peer tutors talked about how the project had helped them with this. When asked about accepting a position as secretary of the Learning Centre board, a peer tutor commented:

> I think [peer tutoring] gave me the confidence to take the position, because I never felt that I could do it. . . . If I had been asked last year I would have said no, because I didn't feel I had the confidence because I had a hard time talking with people. Tutoring has really helped me because you have to forget your shyness and just do it. (Mardge)

Campbell (1994) discussed the concept of shyness as socially constructed, rooted in one's identity and social relationships. Shyness may reflect experiences of not being heard in a milieu where dominant voices are different from one's own. A peer tutor noted how hearing familiar voices helped him overcome his shyness about reading in public:

> Talking to people I don't have a problem but to read, even at home I won't read out loud in front of a bunch of people. The reason I can do it now is . . . with peer tutoring and listening to other people read has given me the confidence to read, and a lot of people here I know and we've all been in the same

boat, it just makes it a lot easier to be able to read in front of people that you know or people that have been going through the same thing. (Ross)

Campbell (1994) and Jurmo (1989) suggested that literacy programs can offer safe places for students to practice using their voices. The peer tutoring project provided such places through the peer tutor meetings and other activities.[9] The project also led to shifts in the kinds of power relations that may have contributed to people's "shyness" in the first place.

EXPANDING ROLES AND SHIFTING RELATIONS

The way power is distributed is an essential issue in participatory education, particularly how power is shared between students and tutors or students and staff. Community tutors at the Learning Centre had always been encouraged to develop person-centered partnerships with students; at the same time, as tutors they had distinct roles that traditionally carry more power than students.

As the peer tutoring project got underway, peer tutors began to expand their roles to include tutor as well as student. Through weekly meetings, they also started to relate to each other as a social group. Some peer tutors seemed aware of how their expanded roles could affect their relations with other students and with community tutors. Early in the project, peer tutors expressed concern that they not be seen as "better than" the rest of the students in the program. We spent some meeting time planning how to publicize the project and ensure that everyone felt welcome to participate.

Some peer tutors also expressed concern that the community tutors not feel as though they were being "pushed out" by the peer tutors. This led to a workshop attended by both community and peer tutors. Participants talked about their involvement in the Learning Centre and worked together to practice some tutoring strategies. Community tutors responded positively, with a number commenting about seeing students in terms of their capacities rather than just in terms of needs.

These examples suggest that peer tutors were aware of the power related to their tutor roles. They recognized how this power could distance them from their peers and be construed as a move to take over from the community tutors. They actively chose to share their power and, in doing

---

[9]During the project, peer tutors and other students spoke with Members of the Legislative Assembly; they spoke up in workshops with community tutors; they met and spoke with literacy program coordinators and graduate university students in professional development events. During the last election, students hosted and spoke publicly to the Prime Minister Jean Chretien during his visit to the Learning Centre.

so, opened a door to shifting the established, though unacknowledged, social relations.

LEARNING ABOUT SHARING POWER

Sissel (1996) suggested that social relations between educators and students are related to issues of power, privilege, and personal politics. As facilitator for the peer tutoring project and a coordinator at the Learning Centre, I was aware of the power that accompanied my position. I approached the project with the intention of learning about how to share that power. I was soon faced with contradictions between my beliefs and my practices.

For example, at the start of the project I spoke with participants about the power that a facilitator could assume in a group and expressed an openness to sharing power. I was very excited when a peer tutor initiated and facilitated an ad hoc committee of students to deal with a task that emerged. Yet I felt anxious when some peer tutors suggested they take on a role that I felt was my territory. While talking about how tutors might share the work of supporting new students, one suggested that peer tutors could interview new students and do some informal assessment of their reading. I was amazed afterward at how threatened I felt by this suggestion. After all, I had invested years in becoming a "reading specialist." As I unpacked the feelings related to this event, I realized I was both reluctant to give up my authority and reluctant to suggest that students might not have the skills needed to do interviews and assessments, at least as I defined them.

During peer tutor meetings, I was aware of my reluctance to let go of topics that I wanted to address. I was also aware of my need to control the agenda when peer tutors went "off topic." Yet the meetings where I followed topics that emerged were among the most energized. The previous discussion about welfare cuts stands out as one example.

Later in the project, I was delighted to observe students' active participation in a Reader's Theatre group that was facilitated by a peer tutor. Yet when a group of women approached me about practicing reading together, my first response was to think of which community tutor might help. I soon realized the women had arranged to help each other and were asking only if they could use a particular room to meet. I had been advocating student participation but failed to recognize it in action!

CONCLUSION

Peer tutoring is not a new concept. Historical accounts identify its use in addressing teacher shortages in the 1700s (Goodlad & Hirst, 1989). More recently, many teachers working in one-room schools applied the concept, if not the term. Peer tutoring may be introduced to meet instructional needs in large or multilevel classrooms or, as at the Learning Centre, where there is a shortage of volunteer tutors. It offers other possibilities as well. Through peer tutoring, students and tutors develop literacy skills and self-confidence. Relationships among students may develop or strengthen, and a sense of community can be fostered. But above all, peer tutoring can prompt a shift in power relations as students take more active roles in teaching, learning, and other aspects of their programs.

In conversations with students, tutors, and staff from other literacy programs, I have found an interest in encouraging active student participation. Peer tutoring could be a starting point for students to become more involved in volunteer tutor programs. It could also be a way to introduce or extend participatory learning in classroom-based settings.

ACKNOWLEDGMENTS

Getting our own education was written as part of a project funded by the National Literacy Secretariat, Human Resources Development Canada. Alberta Learning is a partner in the cost-shared national literacy program. This chapter was first published by the Learning Centre Literacy Association as part of *With a Common Thread*, a resource kit about peer tutoring. As noted in the original publication, writing this chapter would not have been possible without project participants' generously sharing their words, ideas, and actions. I thank them and I hope I have used their contributions respectfully. I also thank the colleagues who kindly read and responded to drafts.

REFERENCES

Beder, H. (1996). Popular education: An appropriate educational strategy for community-based organizations. *New Directions for Adult and Continuing Education, (70)*, 73–83.

Campbell, P. (1994). *Particpatory literacy practices: Having a voice, having a vote*. Unpublished doctoral dissertation, University of Toronto.

Campbell, P. (1996). Participatory literacy practices: Exploring social identity and relations. *Adult Basic Education, 6*(3), 127–142.

Dooley, M. (1984). Peer teaching in an ABE special education setting. *Lifelong Learning, 7*(8), 20–30.

Goldgrab, S. (1992). Activating student participation. In J. A. Draper & M. Taylor (Eds.), *Voices from the literacy field* (pp. 231–242). Toronto, Canada: Culture Concepts.

Goodlad, S., & Hirst, B. (1989). *Peer tutoring: A guide to learning by teaching*. London: Kogan Page.

Jennings, C. M., & Xu, D. (1996). Collaborative learning and thinking: The Vygotskian approach. In L. Dixon-Krauss (Ed.), *Vygotsky in the classroom. Mediated literacy instruction and assessment* (pp. 77–92). White Plains, NY: Longman.

Jurmo, P. (1987). *Learner participation practices in adult literacy efforts in the United States*. Unpublished doctoral dissertation, University of Michigan, Ann Arbor.

Jurmo, P. (1989). History in the making: The case for participatory literacy education. In A. Finguret & P. Jurmo (Eds.), *Participatory literacy education* (pp. 17–28). San Francisco: Jossey-Bass.

McLachlan, C. (1990). Supporting and developing adult learning. Peer tutoring: An approach to learning for adult literacy students. *Adults Learning* (England), *2*(4), 110–112.

Melarango, R. (1976). The tutorial community. In V. L. Allen (Ed.), *Children as teachers: Theory and research on tutoring* (pp. 189–197). New York: Academic Press.

Rogers, C. (1980). *A way of being.* Boston: Houghton Mifflin.

Sauvé, V. (1987). *From one educator to another: A window on participatory education.* Edmonton, Canada: Grant MacEwan Community College.

Sissel, P. A. (1996). Reflection as vision: Prospects for future literacy programming. *New Directions for Adult and Continuing Education, 70*, 97–103.

Stein, S. G. (1997). *Equipped for the future: A reform agenda for adult literacy and lifelong learning.* Washington, DC: National Institute for Literacy.

COMMUNITY

6

Power and Program Planning in a Community-Based Context

Sue M. Scott
Margo Schmitt-Boshnick
University of Alberta

Community-based program planning attempts to address the needs of both individuals and the community at large and can be undertaken in various forms ranging from determination by "experts," with little community involvement in the process, to determination by communities themselves. Unfortunately, much of the program planning that occurs within community-based situations relies on "expert" advice and is required to follow prescriptive models. This denies the community opportunities to grow and develop. Models that emphasize step-by-step procedures in program planning focus on the outcomes or content of program planning. This approach produces programming but often fails to promote community. Recent theorizing in program planning, however, stems from the critical perspective that attempts to build community through democratic processes while examining contextual factors and power relationships.

This chapter seeks to demonstrate the effectiveness of participatory program planning as a means of allowing individual and societal needs to be acknowledged and met. Significant education occurs in the process of planning and implementing programs, particularly through dialogue and community building that is inherent in community-based organizations. In turn, the degree of learning is affected by both the interests that each participant brings to the situation and the power relationships that exist in the situation itself. How these two contextual factors, interests and power relationships, are negotiated is key to the realization of community programs.

The move in recent years toward standardization and efficiency in programming reveals societal trends that are more concerned with the bottom line than with learner development. This occurs throughout the educational process, as students have less control over their education. Appropriate process is sacrificed for product. The planning of educational programs is affected in that programs are prescribed, determined by someone other than the learner. The concern is primarily outcome based focusing on specific skill development. It is difficult for students to own the process of education when it is irrelevant and insensitive to the needs of the learner. Fortunately, there are still pockets where a more holistic notion of education is practiced. The case study presented here examines the program planning process in an organization, Canora, that serves women who have been marginalized for various reasons. The planning process provides the women with a means of becoming empowered within their own lives as well as within their communities. The question that guided us as we entered Candora was to what extent do power relationships affect the program planning process in a fundamentally democratically conceived community-based organization?

Sork and Caffarella (1989) analyzed program planning theories and models from the last 40 years and determined six elements were common to all of them: (a) scan the environment, (b) run a needs assessment, (c) develop an administrative plan, (d) develop an instructional plan, (e) implement the program, and (f) evaluate the program. They also admitted, however, that little is known about how planners deal with contextual factors. Cervero and Wilson (1994) investigated the "political richness, ethical dilemmas, and practical judgments of planning practice" (p. 6) in institutional settings. They concluded that each planning situation is affected by the *interests* that each party brings to the exercise, the *power relationships* that exist within it, and how the program planner *negotiates* these interests and power relationships in developing the program. They suggested the planner should be promoting a democratic ethos in the planning situation. Drawing upon Forester (1989), they developed four strategies that planners could use depending on the boundaries or limits that exist for various situations. They referred to their model as bounded rationality in program planning.

The case study that follows uses this theoretical framework, but it extends Cervero and Wilson's (1994) work into a community-based context. In such settings, community programmers usually use a community development planning model; however, that model does not explain how negotiation occurs in collectivity, nor does it highlight the dilemmas the planners encounter when attempting to practice democracy in community. The research reported here addresses these problems. Specifically, it seeks to illuminate processes that are important in overcoming the fragmentation of contemporary society: relationship building, critiquing power structures, and acting in concert on shared goals.

The community-based organization selected for this case study is different from other groups with similar purposes in its orientation to planning and in the functioning of the organization. As a women's collective, Candora serves low-income women who come together to overcome problems of poverty, family violence, child care, unemployment, language barriers, and settlement issues. They operate on a consensual basis, and programs are developed based on the needs and interests of these women.

The following involves both descriptive and theoretical analyses drawn from the data and the literature. A discussion then illustrates the ways they fit with the bounded rationality model of Cervero and Wilson (1994) and ties the findings back to critical social theory.

CANDORA

Candora is a nonprofit organization that was originally established as part of the consumer education project of Grant MacEwan Community College in Edmonton, Alberta. It grew out of the Abbotsfield Women's Project, which came into being through a participatory education approach (Sauvé, 1987). This approach was new to the consumer education project because it had previously followed an "expert" approach to program planning. Candora continues to operate on a participatory model in which community members determine their own future.

The mission statement of Candora involves a series of principles as follows:

> We, of the CANDORA Society of Edmonton, are people working together to effect change in our lives and our community.
>
> 1) We honor the strengths and capabilities that we have;
>
> 2) We are the experts on our life experiences;
>
> 3) We have the potential for change and growth;
>
> 4) We maintain the control of our lives;
>
> 5) We participate in education for personal and social change;
>
> 6) We employ skilled people;
>
> 7) We strive to create a cohesive and mutually supportive atmosphere for all who live our neighborhood.

The residents of Abbotsfield and Rundle areas determine the programs that are offered; a coordinator is hired by the board. Many residents are hired to work as community facilitators. The participatory approach is helped along through the interests of the first coordinator, as well as women in the community who have had experience in this type of grassroots community development in their native Latin American countries.

Candora stands for Can Do in Rundle and Abbotsfield, which are areas of the city of Edmonton located in the northeast quadrant. These two areas were built in the 1970s during the boom years in Alberta and were intended for low income housing. Although the city originally provided funding for the housing complexes, this eventually ceased with dwindling municipal budgets. Eventually, the decreased value of the declining housing made them affordable to those on social assistance and to the working poor.

Single-parent families, primarily headed by women, make up a large portion of the population of the communities. Many of the women who live in the area are isolated, without family or friends, and operate in the private sphere rather than in the public sphere. Candora provides a space for these people to come together, to meet people, and to identify and to take action on some of the problems they are experiencing, such as unemployment, poverty, family violence, parenting, and child-care concerns. The community is also home to a diverse group of immigrants, and Candora provides them with a place to address their language and settlement concerns in a collective manner. Other programs in Candora include native crafts, sewing, cooking, parenting, a Spanish support group, and collective kitchens.

The organization is based in the local Abbotsfield Mall and is open 4 days per week. The programs and staff are funded through Alberta Social Services, City of Edmonton Community Support Services, and various private foundations. The staff consists of a coordinator, the Building A Business Towards Self-Employment program coordinator, three outreach workers, an administrative/financial coordinator, and a child-care worker. Programs include the Personal and Community Enrichment Program (PACE), which provides most of the base funding, and are designed to give those who have been out of the workforce for a long time a preliminary introduction to the workplace. Residents participate in a Tuesday morning weekly "life choices" program (part of the PACE program) and are paid 5 hours per week for work in Candora. It is in this group where programs are planned, where women give voice to issues, and where a constant renaming of who they are takes place. Programs are initiated and implemented in the life choices group; it is here that the knowledge the women possess is exercised, taken seriously, brought to fruition, and realized. Women who participate in this program learn they have potential and a contribution to make to society. They learn to cope with their difficulties, and they learn to be confident so they can step out of poverty and take an active role in society. In affirming the success of the project, one official in social services said, "Candora is *where* we all need to be."

THE VOICES AT CANDORA

To determine how program planning occurs in Candora, both a group interview and individual interviews were held in the summer of 1994. The group interview, comprising about 20 people, was conducted during the Tuesday morning life choices program. At a later date three staff members and one resident were interviewed.

The information that came out of the interviews was analyzed according to: (a) the various stakeholder interests (the women, the staff, the funders), (b) the power relationships within and outside of Candora that affect the way programs are planned, and (c) how these interests and power relationships are negotiated in the program-planning process. We present the themes unique to Candora within the framework of their interests, power relationships, and negotiations and highlight the ways Candora women practice program planning. We have called these last themes fundamental elements in the participatory, democratic, community-based communities and present them toward the end of this chapter.

INTERESTS

Cervero and Wilson (1994) quoted Morgan (1986) in defining interests as "predispositions embracing goals, values, desires, expectations and other orientations and inclinations that lead a person to act in one direction or another" (p. 29). Each stakeholder brings his or her own interests to the program-planning situation. With Candora, these are the women, staff, and external groups whose interests must be given consideration.

Women of Candora

The women who participate in Candora have interests ranging from personal self-interests to public self-interests (Scott, 1991). Specifically, the personal self-interests include the need to connect with others to talk about personal crises or to overcome loneliness. The need to connect with others is an undertone in the following statement by a resident: "I didn't know what to do or where to go, and I was really new to this community. I found people were hard to get to know and it was very difficult. So I finally got up enough nerve to come to Candora." In time though:

> When Candora began I came here, and after some months I know the necessity to help in this neighborhood because people live in poverty and I was aware of the [need in] the Spanish community. . . . I began to visit house by house to convince them to come here to the centre to do sewing and crafts because I understand they need to do something that they like, like sewing, crocheting, and cooking too. In this way I am here six years.

Many of the women depend on the Candora group for support and therapy when there's trouble at home. "Family violence is an issue in the Spanish community. The Centre addresses this issue." They "depend on these people [who] help many people." As another women described Candora: "This place is for everybody. It is important for me and everybody. It a place for coming and for stay three or four hours. After you go here, you go clean."

What does it mean to leave someplace "clean?" Somehow the social interaction of the group becomes a catharsis—a place to get rid of the dirt. Sorting through the feelings, assumptions, and beliefs that confuse their lives in a supportive nonjudgmental group allows the women to go away clean, feeling better about themselves and knowing that others felt the same way or have moved away from immobilizing thoughts and emotions. This kind of group interaction is life giving. It affirms the self as basically good at a time when partners and society continually call them bad. As one woman put it, "Candora is my umbligo." *Umbligo* in Spanish means umbilical cord, a cord that connects a new unborn baby to a nurturing mother. Thus, metaphorically, the Candora women are being birthed and nurtured through a cord of life found in the group. Through this cord, personal interests, in time, shift from a concern for only themselves as individuals to a concern for all the women in like circumstances. They learn to address larger issues such as family violence and poverty.

The personal interests articulated in the group dialogue can be considered an emancipatory process because each woman recognized she had an interest and a need to become connected to other women. As the women congregated with others with similar problems, they gradually moved to the question, "What are *we* going to do about our situations?" Instrumental interests emerged that revolved around skills for employment. For example, one woman stated, "I got involved because I was willing to share the skills I have with the sewing department, knitting and crocheting." The women understood that their strength was in "the traditional kinds of things like cooking, cleaning and sewing. In order to be able to compete for other jobs, you need to look at a whole other area, and it seems to me that we are always doing catch up." But some are making money using their traditional skills.

> I came to Candora in 1992. I was here for six months, but then was . . . sick [and] did not come for one year. I went to school too. I came back in March 1994 and am volunteering again, and have another mission. I am now seeking to have a catering group, and about one month ago we took the first job, catering for about 40 people and for this Thursday, they are going to do a lunch for about 60 people for Candora's annual general meeting.
>
> We are trying to do something like that. I was in the employment program and in the tailoring shop. I was learning to do jackets and alterations. (As translated from Spanish to English by one of the staff members during the interview.)

Although economic interests are paramount to their livelihood, the women understand they need to work through their psychosocial needs as well. In time, the opportunity to share and see the larger picture in a safe and comfortable environment moved some of the women to action projects outside their own homes and outside Candora itself.

Staff at Candora

The full-time staff also express interests that are philosophically and altruistically based. They adhere to a community development model that asserts the ability of the women to define their needs and to solve their problems and issues. One of the staff's interests includes "a different way of working and a different philosophy that [attempts] to be worked out in practice. We talk a lot about honoring people and looking at strengthening capacity or working a different way but we [hardly] ever do it." In Candora, however, there is an attempt to walk the talk, to act on principles they believe in. Candora provides an opportunity to work in an egalitarian structure that honors relationships, caring, and compassion rather than hierarchies and linear thinking.

The women actively critique why they are kept poor by society in a dynamic dialogical process of naming the situation "as it is." There is an interest in working in a place that promotes "social justice and change," in a place that is congruent with personally held beliefs that social change is good and necessary for advancement of human development and quality of life:

> So my interests were to work in a different kind of structure. I had done some workshops in popular theatre and education, some on community development; I was in the one in 1988 with John McKnight. I had harboured these thoughts that I would like to be part of this.

The staff hoped community members would take ownership of the project. They saw their staff position as temporary and in the background, rather than in the foreground of planning or doing. The staff understood that "you plan *with* the community rather than *for* them because [planning for them] never works; nobody will ever show up. I mean that's the nature of it." Members of the community need to articulate their needs and wants from their own experiences and be able to fulfill those needs if they are to grow and develop.

The staff see a "poverty of hope ... amongst the women in this community." The women of the community often don't believe there's anything of value in a ghetto or run-down area. It takes a process of "naming the strengths of this community. There are a lot of wonderful things here and [recognizing] that makes people reconsider the value of this community, to stay and make those connections."

The staff view their mission as drawing from "something within us that would give possibility for change." A facility is not enough; it takes personal integrity in the staff to work themselves out of a job as the community becomes more involved and committed. It's "an intent that the community finds its own potential and dynamic and they can work that through rather than my need to be there all the time. And that is really what we hope will happen."

These interests require a deep commitment on the part of staff because they believe their work is more than a "job"; it is a vocation. They have a vision with a philosophy, one that means committing to the daily life in community on a long-term basis. This prevents them from being prescriptive, rigid, or formulaic about community development, a factor that is highly important in participatory program planning. The program unfolds and becomes relational and interconnected, and the planning process itself is facilitated *with*, not "dictated" *by* the staff.

External Groups

Interests are not only generated from within Candora, but also outside of it. Funders, in particular, have interests that affect the programs that occur at Candora. In many cases, the programs that funders, particularly large bureaucracies, are willing to fund must be within their prescriptive and rigid guidelines, and they will not tolerate deviation. It is in their interest to maintain the efficiency and accountability of the programs they fund. Recent policy changes that focus on the number of people that can be "put through" programs in the least amount of feasible time fits with the conservative philosophy and interest of the present government. Because the funders' interests do not always match Candora's interests, conflicts and tensions about programming develop.

> The one thing that is becoming increasingly apparent to me is that the way we operate already has come in conflict with the expectations of funders because we try to be responsive, fluid, flexible, yet we are hearing strategic planning, long term goals, accountability and those things may or may not be compatible. It puts us in some kind of jeopardy because how can we honour the strengths here and be responsive to the women and children and what is important in the area if we are being dictated to by people who say that you will use your money in a certain way.

Other external groups often request input by Candora on proposed programs. In many instances these organizations or individuals have not really talked to the residents of the community to any large extent, and their programs or suggestions are prescriptive. The women of Candora articulate their opinions and thoughts on these issues or programs, and in general these outside interests do not seem to have much influence on the programs that are developed at Candora. It is apparent that the programs that are successful in the Candora area are conceived, initiated, and implemented by the Candora women themselves.

POWER RELATIONSHIPS

Cervero and Wilson (1994) suggested that power relationships exist in all human interactions and it is a vital part of the relationship among people in the program planning process. They quote Isaac (1987) in defining power as "the capacity to act, distributed to people by virtue of the enduring social relationships in which they participate" (p. 29). Essentially, power relationships define what people are able to do and say.

Power relationships occur both from outside of the group, as well as within. The major external power relationships occur with the funders. Because of Candora's philosophy of "people before programs," the organization has a bottom line that they are not willing to step over in compromising their principles for the sake of funding. The most classic example that jeopardized Candora's future is a funding proposal for a long term existing program. The guidelines for this program had changed, and the funding agency required that the same program be completed in a much shorter period of time. The funder was a government agency and the approach was consistent with policy from a new government pushing for standardization and efficiency. The staff at Candora knew that they needed a longer period of time to accomplish what was best for the participants. They stood firm, presented their arguments, were not willing to become an extension of the state, but ultimately the funding for the program was revoked. This base funding has not been fully replaced, and as time goes on the ability to continue to fund programs and staff becomes increasingly difficult for the organization. The power of the dominant system continues to threaten Candora's survival.

Although power relationships are easier to identify outside an organization, internal organizational power relationships exist. Candora considers itself a flat organization structurally; however, the existence of a paid professional who acts as coordinator implies some hierarchy. She described her position:

> The staff attempts to ground me, but I am in a different position, and even though we work in an organization where everyone's input is important and so on, there is still some leveling that is bound to be the case because you are the boss so you have to take that role on at certain times more than others.

Staff members have certain authority over their respective areas, but they make every attempt to ensure equality within the group. In terms of program planning, although staff may introduce an idea for a program that they feel is appropriate, the decision is still up to the women, who may or may not go along with these ideas. Still, the staff have power in that they decide on what type of funding to apply for or what issues to bring to the group. Certainly, there is leadership here and staff must be aware of their motives.

Power relationships that emerge and cause conflicts within the group are handled through dialogue with the group as a whole. Power relationships within the organization can be fragmenting, and the group attempts to prevent this from occurring through a culture of respect and tolerance for everyone.

NEGOTIATION

Cervero and Wilson (1994) suggested that negotiation is the main activity planners undertake in developing programs. It allows them to connect and balance the interests and power relationships that exist in the planning situation. Planners negotiate their interests *with* others, as well as negotiate *between* other interests and power relationships. As this occurs, they negotiate *about* the interests and power relationships that structure the situation. Planners then can act *within* the social context and act *upon* it through the planning process. Cervero and Wilson's research comes from institutionalized situations where the planner is charged with more direct responsibility in program planning. In participatory education, the planner becomes more of a facilitator, but ultimately must be the one to ensure that planning occurs and is implemented.

With various interests and power relationships occurring within Candora at any given time, the task of negotiating these is primarily up to the coordinator, who serves as the facilitator of program planning. Because philosophies differ, negotiations between Candora and the funders can create situations where Candora is either successful in putting their ideas across, or unsuccessful. Both situations have occurred and continue to occur:

> I don't know that I can verbalize that, I just do it, and I don't know if I do it real well but I just do it the way it seems to work for me. I guess that if I don't like what happens at a government level and a funder level I give voice to it and try to negotiate with them so they can relax their hard line approach. And certainly [I say] written or verbally, "I don't think that you are looking at this the right way." In the end I might still have to do it and that was really true of evaluation. We gave voice really strongly and we submitted what we thought evaluation should look like and in the end it wasn't honored and we were told

"you get the funding and do it this way," and we had to live with it. I still hold the philosophy that the community needs to define for itself what has to happen.

Negotiating between interests of participants is another part of the process. For the most part, all interests and needs are respected, although the needs of the majority are given the priority. Individual voices are provided for to the best of the collective's ability, which may mean individuals are referred to other programs or agencies that are better able to address specific needs more fully. Because of the collective nature of the group, there is a sense of equality that becomes apparent in the negotiation process:

Negotiations are on-going and there is freedom to express negative feedback without fear of reprisal of some sort. . . . And there is the freedom, there isn't the fear of losing a job or that you are going to be alienated.

People's needs are taken into account when negotiation happens. This fits with Candora's philosophy that the people in the programs are more important than the nature of the programs themselves. This creates a different emphasis on the context and on the programs that are eventually decided on. They are not prescriptive, but rather interactive to allow for the growth and development of each individual.

THE FUNDAMENTAL ELEMENTS
IN COMMUNITY-BASED ORGANIZATIONS

Although democratic program planning is woven throughout the descriptive analysis of interests, power relationships, and negotiation outlined here, it is a secondary descriptive analysis that continues to show the uniqueness of this community-based study. Three themes were identified that have significant effects on the program-planning process in Candora. These are fundamental characteristics, we think, of community-based programming. The dominant theme is equalizing power, and the other two themes are empowerment for self-sufficiency and self-confidence, and advocating for the interests of women. They are all interconnected, but it is useful to pull them apart to illustrate the effects they have on program planning.

Equalizing Power

The main theme, equalizing power, suggests power is consciously acknowledged by the staff of Candora, who attempt to level the playing field in all contexts. Thus, the staff of Candora generally see the structure of the organization as being circular or flat. This creates an ambiguous or messy situation for the coordinator who often struggles to define her role:

> I struggled with, and I still do, what is the role of the coordinator in a circular or flat structure. . . . To me it's like we are sitting in a circle and the board of directors are part of it, as am I, as are community residents, as are the children involved in our project, the Neighbor Next Door. But inherent in that means that I have responsibilities as project coordinator to funders, and I need to make sure that those responsibilities are carried out.

Equalizing power relationships to create this circular structure involves negotiating with the power relationships both inside and outside of Candora. In terms of funders, Candora's principles are made clear in all proposals, and although some funders are responsive, others are not willing to allow for any deviation from the prescriptive nature of their programs. The collective is willing to garner support from their board members, as well as local and provincial politicians, should this become necessary in ensuring their existence and in dealing with difficult funding agencies.

Equalizing power is probably more evident within the collective and its day-to-day operations than in the conflicts with outside agencies. In an effort to promote egalitarian relations and to equalize power, the coordinator told a story that illustrated what happens when visitors to Candora are not given preferential treatment.

> The other thing that we used to do when we used to meet a bit more formally, like around our employment programs, we always had people coming and going. When we did introductions, . . . they think that they are going to sit at the front of the room when they are going to make a presentation, and you say, "Well, just take a chair," and it is funny to watch some people. They are not sure what to do. They don't know where to sit, or should they be moving towards the front of the room. Men in particular are bad for that if they come to visit. Really they are. And when we go around the room, all of us introduce ourselves, so there really isn't anything special done. And then we might say, "and today [we have so-and-so with us] and this person is here to talk about whatever." But there is not this whole lauding given to that person that makes some sort of "stand up here above everyone else." It's trying to equalize again and give women the opportunity to feel that they have as much dignity and as much right to be sitting around that table as the big shot.

This method provides for an atmosphere where the women can sit at the same table with authority figures and feel they are on equal footing and are not "lesser people." Even among themselves there is an acknowledgment that they are all equal. Equal time is also given to the women themselves who tell their stories in the group as funders and guests listen, often hearing for the first time their clients' voices. Despite differences in language, education, and so on, no one individual stands out above the rest. The women have come to expect that their opinions and voices will be heard, and they will call the staff on it if they feel that this is not happening. Ultimately, this feeling of collectivity provides them with a sense of power that builds their individual confidences in equalizing power in their own lives.

Empowerment for Self-Sufficiency and Self-Confidence

Through the experience of being involved in a group that promotes a culture of equalizing power when necessary, women are given the skills and confidence to undertake this kind of activity for themselves. The fact that their voices are respected within the group can be a new experience for many of them and give them the personal power to overcome some of the obstacles that have kept them in a dependent state:

> You can put something on the table and say, "What do people think?" And some reaction can occur as opposed to saying, "Well, here it is." There is a danger for people in being honest in those kinds of cases. They probably haven't got a lot of reinforcing about that in the past. If they haven't agreed with people in positions of authority, doctors, teachers, in their past, why would they risk it? But here is hopefully a place that they can do that with us being there to say, "Feel free to disagree," and they have been.

Respect and dignity are the key components of Candora, where people come together to help people help themselves. The notion of empowerment is inherent in everything they do. As people find power within the collective, they can overcome the lack of self-confidence that may have been holding them back from confronting the difficulties that they face. By giving voice to their opinions and being able to guide the direction of programs, their self-confidence and growing skills build their abilities to escape the cycle of dependency and to become self-sufficient. This type of empowerment, though, is not promoted from a standpoint of individualism, because it has its roots in community. Instead, it is a notion of independence through interdependence.

Advocating for the Interests of Women

During the program-planning phase, particularly with outside agencies, the staff must continually ensure that the interests and needs of the women of Candora are communicated. Problems that these women, most of whom are single mothers living on social assistance, encounter are created by the patriarchal society in which they live. The issues they confront on a day-to-day basis, such as poverty and violence, are systemic; they are not an individual's problem but rather society's problem. There is an effort to assist the women in understanding they are not to blame for these problems, and various tools for doing this, such as popular theater, are used. Candora's continual voice assists in getting these issues onto the agendas for change. The education of government and agency representatives as to an alternative method of doing things, another way of looking at their "clients," promotes further understanding of what is occurring. It promotes an awareness of a reality or world view that many bureaucrats may not be willing to understand or adopt. However, advocating these interests, refusing to take a client submissive orientation, is no guarantee of change:

> But the people in power have never been . . . the people that share the kind of vision that John McKnight had. It is almost anti-power, so of course, the politicians and especially the civil servants are an entrenched group of people making good salaries that have no desire to see the status quo change.

By reinforcing the needs of these women with external forces on a continual basis, Candora has been able to remain true to its mission and principles.

Putting the Three Themes Together

All three of these themes are interrelated and affect the program-planning process. The type of process, as well as the type of program that eventually comes out of it, is imbued with the philosophy of the staff, particularly of the coordinator, who is the one to pull all these threads together in providing for opportunities for the women of Candora. The program planner needs to be democratic in orientation and to become aware of his or her sense of agency to deal with the structures that affect the program plan. From the research completed in this case study, it is evident that the program planner is much more openly democratic than those in the examples Cervero and Wilson (1994) provided, which were all institutionally based. It appears the grassroots nature of Candora and its noninstitutionalized orientation contributes to the ability of the program planner to undertake a democratic role in negotiation because of the lack of direct constraining elements on the organization. These elements appear to be more autonomous and directed from the ground up rather than top down. There is less concern about the political positioning of the coordinator, although the attempts to stand up to power brokers could have more of an overall effect on the organization than they did on the individual program planners in Cervero and Wilson's examples. For instance, in the Cervero and Wilson cases, if one of the program planners chose to advocate for a dramatic change to the status quo, he or she could be moved out of the job quickly. In the case of Candora, a coordinator who advocates for too dramatic a change is likely to cause funders to stop supporting the program, thus affecting himself or herself as well as the rest of the organization. Despite this, there appears to be more room for the democratically oriented program planner to work within a community-based organization as the power comes from the grassroots.

BOUNDED RATIONALITY

Cervero and Wilson (1994) offered a schematic for understanding the strategies that program planners use in negotiating interests and power relationships. They provided a four-quadrant model (see Fig. 6.1) that "offers a conceptual scheme that delineates four different ways that relationships of power and associated interests can structure the situations in which program planners must carry out their work" (pp. 127–128). The model displays the political boundedness of nurturing a substantively democratic planning process. Essentially it draws upon the rationality of the program

Source of the Power Relations

Relations Among Legitimate Interests	Socially Ad Hoc	Socially Systematic
Consensual	Bounded Rationality I Individual Limits ********* Strategy: **Satisfice**	Bounded Rationality II Social Differentiation ********* Strategy **Network**
Conflictual	Bounded Rationality III Pluralist Conflict ********* Strategy: **Bargain**	Bounded Rationality IV Structural Legitimation ********* Strategy: **Counteract** (Equalizing Power)

FIG. 6.1. Bounded rationality for program planning. From *Planning Responsibly for Adult Education: A Guide to Negotiating Power and Interests*, p. 128, by R. Cervero and A. Wilson, 1994, San Francisco: Jossey-Bass. Copyright 1994 by Jossey-Bass. Reprinted with permission.

planners based on the constraining features of the program-planning situation. The horizontal axis of this model consists of the source of the power relations, which could be either socially ad hoc or socially systematic. The first of these means the program-planning situation is conducted on an ad hoc basis, where stakeholders come together for one specific program-planning exercise. Socially systematic situations imply the planning process is ongoing and occurs within an institutionalized atmosphere. The horizontal axis consists of the relations among the legitimate interests, and these can be either consensual or conflictual. For each quadrant, the program planner must use a specific strategy based on a rational decision that will be appropriate for the particular constraints within each situation. According to Cervero and Wilson (1994):

> If planners are to nurture a substantially democratic planning process in situations marked by conflicting interests and asymmetrical relationships of power, they need to use strategies that will give all legitimate actors an equivalent voice in constructing the program. (p. 129)

For the first quadrant, in which the source of the power relations is socially ad hoc and the relations among the legitimate interests is consensual, the program planner would be constrained by individual limits and the strategy to be used would be that of satisfice. This means relations would be consensual, and all parties would agree to head in the same direction. The only limiting factors would be the amount of time that the program planner can reasonably spend on the process, the amount of funding, and so on. This means the optimal or ideal project or process could not be undertaken, but it would be satisfactory.

The second quadrant is again consensual in nature, but it is institutionalized, so these power relations occur on a continual basis. In this instance, individuals or organizations would be working together on a long-term basis such as with a consortium of various agencies. Here, the limits are the social differentiation (differences) of the stakeholders, and the strategy is to network, to ensure effective communication among them.

The third quadrant is socially ad hoc, but it is conflictual in nature. In this situation the parties come together in the short term and those involved have opposing interests in the process. An example of this is a comming together of a skill-based learning institution such as a community or technical college and a community-based organization to address the needs of the community on a one-time basis. In many instances these groups hold different, opposing interests and ideologies. The program planner is then given to bargaining as the appropriate strategy.

The fourth quadrant is conflictual as well, but it occurs within an institutionalized ethos of power relations. Here the constraints are those that perpetuate the existing structural relations of power. An example here is a community-based agency that must relate to funders and policyholders who continually require strict instrumental adherence to their planning frameworks. It is likely the planner will have little room to move and thus must mobilize others to counteract these structural inequalities that keep the agency from realizing its goals. Cervero and Wilson (1994) drew upon Forester (1989) who suggested that the strategies needed here are derivatives of practices of political or community organizing practices. Cervero and Wilson (1994) state:

> Fundamentally, these strategies involve mobilizing groups of people to counter the effects of established interests. This may take a variety of forms, from providing information to potentially affected groups to active interventions to bring all affected groups into the process. (p. 135)

Although all strategies are used in Candora, because of the nature of the philosophy of the organization—that of people before programs—they appear to be involved in Quadrant 4 and use the strategy of counteracting power to a much greater extent. Quadrant 3, bargaining in the face of pluralist conflict, is also used, but to a lesser extent because the organization is not willing "to prostitute themselves for the sake of funding." This is illustrated by one of the staff:

> So I think we are facing, that's part of the reason that we are meeting this afternoon, we are facing a time of conflict between what we are, what we hope to continue to be and what we might need to conform to at least on a short term basis in order to remain alive. It becomes a very difficult position that we are put in, but I'm hoping that all of us can come to some kind of resolution about that such that we can go with a united front to the funders and say, "This is what we are willing and able to do within the constraints that you give us, but you have got to give us some room to move too, because the way that we plan programs, and the way that we do things here is this way. If we don't do it this way, then we are not Candora." So which way does it go?

SUMMARY AND IMPLICATIONS

The Candora case study attempts to examine community-based program planning through a grassroots participatory democratic model of planning. In explicating the critical perspective, this research uses models such as bounded rationality to further demonstrate the democratic nature of the community-based situation. Through identification of interests, power relationships, and negotiation strategies, program planning in grassroots organizations becomes fundamentally an educative process, particularly when all are involved in this identification. When program planning operates from the ground up as opposed to a top-down approach, it is possible to create a situation where women have more say in the programs than in other situations. The prescriptive nature of much program planning is resisted to the best of the organization's ability, often leaving it susceptible to the withdrawal of funds by governments and foundations. The program planner plays a key role in that he or she must ensure there is continual communication among all parties to develop an understanding of Candora's goals and directions. The approach can be considered "critical" in that it questions the prescriptive and authoritarian nature of certain funding agencies, and it is prepared to take some action against them to equalize the power should this become necessary. It is also critical in that it assists women to come to an understanding of their own situations and the societal structures that create a cycle of dependency and poverty. These elements are all present in program planning that occurs within a community-based organization.

Are there implications from a situation like this for more institutionally based organizations? Candora is able to provide more freedom to its members in program planning because of the absence of an organizational culture that demands conformity. As well, there is a commitment to work with people at their level rather from where they "should be." This is a messy process and Candora was not always successful because problematizing power relations can be a tense and difficult exercise. It requires engagement by all the parties involved in the organization. Institutionalized organizations that have a profit orientation, or large bureaucracies that are committed to the needs of efficiency and accountability over the needs of people, may find it difficult to use this approach. However, examples like these demonstrate the nature of true democratic program planning and can offer direction and guidance to organizations about the way things can be carried out.

Collectives have some characteristics that need to be taken into account in drawing implications for program planning in other settings. First, conflict may arise as various interests surface. Conflict is not seen as a negative, but rather as an inevitable factor in the planning process. It draws out the real interests and needs of those involved in the process, and stakeholders must learn to deal with these to have a truly effective program-planning process.

Second, equal status among all members of the group is important to sustain a democratic process. This involves equal pay and similar job responsibilities, which promote a sense of equality in the group. In an institutional setting, this means certain departments or groups could operate as a collective, as long as their responsibilities and status are relatively equal. It would be difficult to operate this way where there are large discrepancies in pay or status, such as with a mixed group of professionals and laborers. It is difficult to overcome these established parts of the culture of the organization.

Third, leadership must be more facilitative than authoritarian. To achieve equality, the leader needs to be aware of the needs and interests of the group members as well as his or her own motives, as the group furthers the goals of the organization.

REFERENCES

Cervero, R. M., & Wilson, A. L. (1994). *Planning responsibly for adult education: A guide to negotiating power and interests.* San Francisco: Jossey-Bass.

Forester, J. (1989). *Planning in the face of power.* Berkeley, CA: University of California Press.

Isaac, J. C. (1987). *Power and Marxist theory: A realist view.* Ithaca, NY: Cornell University Press.

Morgan, G. (1986). *Images of organization.* Newbury Park, CA: Sage.

Sauvé, V. (1987). *From one educator to another: A window on participatory education.* Edmonton, Canada: Grant MacEwan Community College.

Scott, S. M. (1991). *Personal transformation through participation in social action: A case study of the leaders in the Lincoln Alliance.* Unpublished doctoral dissertation, University of Nebraska, Lincoln.

Sork, T., & Caffarella, R. (1989). Planning programs for adults. In S. B. Merriam & P. M. Cunningham. *Handbook of adult and continuing education* (pp. 233–245). San Francisco: Jossey-Bass.

7

Strategic Planning in Rural Town Meetings: Issues Related to Citizen Participation and Democratic Decision Making

Jeff Zacharakis-Jutz
Iowa State University Extension

The political economy of power in North America is concentrated in hierarchical status structures that include location, family, education, gender, race, income, and culture. Invariably, small rural communities located outside the commuter's reach of urban and suburban corporate engines fall near the bottom of these hierarchies. Yet many of these often forgotten communities are vibrant places where people pride themselves on knowing each other; where local government is accessible and responsive; and where churches, schools, and neighborhoods are important social political networks of support (Ryan, Terry, & Woebke, 1995). Although being careful not to romanticize rural living, these communities are rich in social capital yet have limited financial, physical, and human capital (Ryan, Terry, & Besser, 1995). Their social capital, characterized by the democratic decision-making processes in local organizations, requires maximum participation by every citizen. This chapter takes a phenomenological look at one of these democratic processes: town meetings in rural communities.

Iowa State University Extension to Communities' mission is to assist communities and nonprofit groups in using public processes to analyze their situation and gather relevant information and data to make informed decisions and develop action plans. Our mission captures the spirit of adult education's traditions in popular education and participatory research that emphasize democratic processes and the ability of everyday people to make informed decisions on complex and difficult issues.

The decline of North America's rural communities is a trend that has accelerated since World War II, resulting in access to fewer resources. Census records show that in Iowa 38 of her 99 counties had their greatest population before 1910, and most of her recent economic resurgence has occurred in only 12 counties. These types of statistics are not unusual for rural areas in North America. State and federal governments are investing fewer and fewer dollars to these rural communities, while corporate America looks upon them as a source of cheap labor. Often rural residents are place bound, having deep ties to family, farm, and community, making it difficult if not impossible to move. What these communities do have is a strong communitarian culture where everyone is valued for their potential contribution. The town meeting may be the one institution that best captures this democratic spirit.

THE SETTING

For large public gatherings, people in rural communities historically have met in school gymnasiums, cafeterias, or local church basements. With large-scale school consolidation, many communities have lost their local school, and with this loss, their largest public gathering place. As a multipurpose room that serves as auditorium, gymnasium, and cafeteria, bleachers can be folded against the walls, basketball hoops folded against the ceiling, and folding chairs and tables arranged throughout the room for even the largest community function. With the hard echo against the cinderblock walls, wood floor, and rafted ceiling, it is hard to hear the soft-spoken person while those with loud voices sound particularly sharp. Each table can comfortably seat eight people, an ideal number for small group discussions.

For most rural towns, the local school historically has been the strongest symbol of community unity. In a photo history of Dakota's small towns (Strand, 1992), a slide presentation depicted the present condition of over a hundred small town main streets located on the semiarid high prairies. Each slide was shown for a mere 5 seconds. As these images flashed by and one town became blurred with the next, the audience was left with the impression that each community was unique yet the same. It seemed as though each town had its school located at the top of a gentle hill at the end of main street. All of these schools were the most massive structure in town, two-story symmetry with the entrance at the center, constructed of brick intended to last many lifetimes. As an enduring symbol of each community's vitality, all but a few of these schools were abandoned or in need of serious repair. The vision of the many people who settled these small towns a hundred years ago was embodied in these now antiquated schools, only to fade into distant memories.

Those towns that were fortunate enough to win the lottery of school consolidation and keep their schools have rebuilt them into modern ranch-style buildings with one floor, few stairs, and large parking lots. Most new schools are built on the edge of town on relatively inexpensive farm fields. These new schools no longer represent the binding glue that historically held the community together. Now on the edge, almost hidden from public view, without sidewalks connecting the town and school, kids are bused to school. This new physical, postmodern reality has seriously hurt the fragile downtowns and retail businesses whose early vitality depended on residents walking by rather than driving by. Once in their cars, after picking up their kids at school, parents find it just as easy to drive to the next larger community to buy groceries or a new pair of shoes than to go home and walk uptown.

As the largest public meeting place in town, the history of small towns has been negotiated and renegotiated in their school auditoriums. If their walls could speak they would tell more than about past sporting events and school concerts; they would trace the many decisions and deals—both formal and informal—made during town meetings and other social gatherings.

THE CRISIS

The crisis in rural America is not new. It is a perpetual theme, with reoccurring events, sometimes highlighted by Willie Nelson and Neil Young's Farm Aid Concerts, but most of the time buried under news headlines that center on national, foreign, or urban themes. The trend toward larger farms, fewer farmers, and cheaper commodities (when inflation is factored in) is closely related to the industrial revolution that has consumed other artisan economies over the last hundred years. One result of this concentration of capital among fewer people in rural communities and the out-migration of capital to urban centers is the inevitable slow death of main street. Not only have people and capital fled these rural communities, the quality and character of industrial and physical investment that remains has changed. In Gaventa's land use studies of the coal mining regions of Appalachia (Gaveta, 1980) and his industrial migration studies of Mexico's Maquilladoras (Gaventa, Smith, & Willingham, 1990), the structure of power and its relationship to rural communities and their people are clearly mapped. Although there is uneasiness, there is also quiescence among people who feel helpless to stand up and proactively address the issues that face them. People are not nearly as mobile as is capital and technology. Hence, multinational corporations can easily move capital and technology to locations that have an economic advantage of cheap labor. Although rural people tend to be tied to their community and land through family and history, migrating to an urban setting for a better paying job may provide short-term economic relief for some families, but it does not address the larger systemic issues related to community survival.

State and federal governments are often not a source of solutions for these "at-risk" communities. For the federal government or most states, it may not be financially feasible to invest limited resources in rural communities, unless they are the county seat or are located at the intersection of two major highways. As economies have evolved from agrarian to industrial to postindustrial to service, the economic purpose of communities have changed, unfortunately rendering some communities obsolete from an economic perspective. Yet, there is an inextricable relation between the economic and the spiritual components of any community. Farmer-poet Wendell Berry throughout his writings identified the rural crises in the faces and personalities of the most oppressed. In Berry's (1987) essay, *Does Community Have Value*, he argued that value must be measured in economic terms as well as emotional or spiritual. When a community has a tangible economic value it will thrive. Using the life history of Loyce and Owen Flood, Berry traced their survival in rural Appalachia over the last 50 years relative to the strength of their community. With improved roads, telecommunications, and jobs to which neighbors must commute, these communities have lost much of their economic value. The economic forces that brought people together to form communities in the 19th century have been weakened since World War II, resulting in archaic reasoning for many communities to exist. How often do we become involved in our neighbor's lives? If we want to speak to a friend or family member we pick up the telephone, hop in our car and drive, or send e-mail. If we want a better job, we move family and household. More perverse is the growing trend to find friendship among the faceless community of cyberspace.

One of the most effective lobbies for family farms in the United States is the Center for Rural Affairs (1998). In its annual report (1998) the center argued that "we must employ new strategies that build on our unique and enviable strengths, while reaffirming the values that have stood the test of time—that community matters; that hard work deserves a fair reward, even among the least powerful elements of society; that wealth and power should be widely distributed; that ownership and control should be vested in those who work the land and operate businesses; that we are all responsible to our neighbors and future generations to be careful stewards of the environment and that society is governed best by participatory democracy" (p. 5). This populist sentiment is strong throughout rural America.

We are told that farms need to grow, that schools need to be consolidated, and that people want to live in communities that are large enough to offer the services and amenities that Americans have come to expect. It is essential to understand the political economy of community if we are to develop sustainable rural communities.

PARTICIPATION

This crisis is compounded when rural people become unable to see beyond the immediate issues and personalities of their city. When this occurs, it becomes difficult to craft developmental strategies without an outside perspective. Iowa State University (ISU) Extension to Communities has a long track record of helping communities develop strategies that assist their residents in making decisions, including town meetings, focus groups, surveys, and organizational development. As an Extension Community Development Specialist, I am frequently called on to assist in planning and facilitating town meetings. When I get these calls, my first question is who will be sponsoring the town meeting? Is it the city council, the chamber of commerce, the ministerial association, the county board of supervisors? My second question is who will be on the steering committee to organize the town meeting? Will there be any young parents, single parents, teenagers, senior citizens, women as well as men? I often use a matrix developed by the National Civic League in Denver for organizing committees that asks about gender, ethnicity, length of residency, language, income, age, physically challenged, education, marital status, and sexual orientation. In every community, there are some questions that are just not asked. Yet this single sheet of paper gets people thinking about the different interests in their community without personalizing the problem. One question that must always be asked in the democratic decision-making process is who are the people in our communities who never attend or participate, and, more pointedly, who are the people we never invite?

Part of the crisis in rural communities can be attributed to who participates and who does not. Participation creates that tangible sense of place, where people feel they have more ownership in community activities and therefore greater responsibility to each other. Although it may be difficult to address geopolitical questions that affect these communities, it is imperative that we do not overlook local factors that can be changed, all of which center on broad participation in local decision making. Although there are many key elements to a successful town meeting, getting a true cross-section of the community to participate is essential to both the success of the meeting and implementation of any agreed-upon recommendations.

THE POWER OF ONE

There are many clichés that hold true in community development and popular education. One I have found to be true is that it takes an entire community (or group depending on the setting) to develop and implement an activity, but it takes only one person to sabotage or stop a project (Bleiker &

Bleiker, 1981). During the spring of 1993 I received a phone call from a mother concerned about the "new" sex education curriculum the local school district was about to implement. She asked me to help her develop a plan so she could influence the school board and school superintendent. During our 20-minute phone call we discussed half a dozen ideas. One was to seek out other parents who shared the same concern and form a committee that would have greater political clout. This suggestion was never pursued. Two weeks later I received a call from the school superintendent's office asking how they might deal with "one parent's opposition" to implementing the new sex education curriculum (I believe the school got my name from the women whom I had spoken to several weeks earlier). We discussed several approaches to working with opposition groups and several strategies to neutralize opposition groups. Over the next few months, I received several more phone calls from both parties, both looking for ISU Extension to serve as an intermediary that would not take sides. Ultimately, I was asked to facilitate a public meeting on the issue, an invitation I declined because I was too close to the issue and the contesting parties. A colleague who was not connected to the problem did facilitate the public meeting. The final outcome of this situation was that the school district decided the timing was not right for this new curriculum. Only after their decision had been made did I learn that this mother who worked so hard to stop the school district only had preschool-age children. It takes only one person to stop a project. The school district might have been able to proceed in spite of this women's opposition, but by the time a decision had to be made the school board believed it did not have the political capital to overcome the opposition.

One rule of thumb that I use when planning town meetings is that everyone in town is invited three times to participate. Because many rural communities do not have a town newspaper, other methods to invite people are required. Posting flyers in the post office and local stores, sending invitations on postcards in their utility bill, making announcements at local churches, and placing public announcements in the nearest newspaper such as the county weekly are just a few opportunities to invite people. Mailing out invitations using first-class mail is sometimes an option if it does not present too much of a financial burden. Regardless, the most effective way to neutralize opposition is to make sure everyone gets an invitation to participate. A common response from people who want to see a community activity stopped is to claim that "I was not involved in the planning; if I was invited I would not have protested." If someone is against a community program, their best strategy is to stay out of the public planning process. This strategy is nullified if the invitation process is public and widespread.

ACCORDING TO SEASONS

In agrarian cultures, town meetings are held according to the seasons to maximize participation. In Iowa, such meetings are not held in July or August because of field work and vacations, nor late September through October because of harvest, nor late March through May because of planting. Ideally, we try to schedule town meetings for November, January, February, or early March. For many rural communities that operate in sync with the seasons, reflecting their agricultural traditions, this is the time of year when people can gather, reflect, and make decisions that will affect the community the rest of the year.

Iowa's winters are usually cold with brisk winds resulting in a thin veneer of ice covering cement walks and steps. Although the school is probably less than a half of a mile from the homes of most town residents, the weather challenges them to stay home, warm and safe. Iowa has the highest per capita population of people 85 years or older in the United States, and third highest of people 65 or older. This segment of the population is the backbone of most rural communities in terms of leadership and financial strength. During the farm crises of the early 1980s, many communities survived because these same people did not abandon their community for more prosperous regions. They had accumulated personal financial resources that enabled them to weather falling land prices. Today, in the late 1990s, these communities are not only aging, their traditional leadership is slowly dying. At most town meetings, I always see an older cohort of participants who have been active in the community for 30, 40, or more years. A key factor to the outcome of any town meeting is the weather.

Although the brisk wind and the freezing temperature do keep some people at home, many people arrive in groups of two, three, or four. Very few people come by themselves. There is a social aspect to this gathering that complements the business at hand. A strong inherent sense of responsibility draws people from their homes to this gathering. Everyone understands why they are here; everyone is welcome regardless of their social standing. This is a town meeting, and they are the town.

A SOCIAL EVENT

Putnam (1995), noted for his research on social capital, pointed out that television has become our most popular source of entertainment. No longer do we gather for card games, or quilting, or barn raising. Rather, we focus all our energy on building an isolated world around us full of creature comforts and technological toys intended to make our lives easier. According to

Putnam, bowling in America is at an all-time high; more people are bowling than ever before. Yet, participation on bowling teams and leagues is declining. Individual accomplishments do not contribute much to a community when they are done in isolation of the community. Bellah, Madsen, Sullivan, Swindler, and Tipton (1995) saw not only the decline in community, but also less willingness to make sacrifices for the "common good." Yet, they argued that "only greater citizen participation in the large structures of the economy and the state will enable us to surmount the deepening problem of contemporary social life" (p. 6). Lasch (1979) identified this malaise as symbolic of a narcissistic culture based on escalating consumerism and self-indulgence. Both argued that individual achievement cannot solve our social problems.

When working with rural businesses, we discuss the shopping experience as a form of entertainment. To "feel good," people will drive an hour or more to the closest urban mall, passing through not only their own languishing downtown, but also through several more small town main streets to what is often referred to social activity of a shopping experience in an urban center. Automobiles, good highways, and an inner need for excitement—a commercial metaphor created by popular advertising—all lead to the demise of rural social capital and economic obsolescence of rural main street.

As people arrive for the town meeting, they mill around the sign-in table, visiting, updating each other on the harvest, who is sick, where their kids are living and working in Chicago or Des Moines. A large coffeepot is on a corner table next to a plate of cookies and bars—sweets are an essential ingredient to a successful town meeting. Everyone writes their first name on the name tag and sticks it to their shirts or sweaters, even though almost everyone knows each other. There are a few new faces, possibly a new schoolteacher, pastor, or a new in-law to a "born and bred" family. Most people in the audience have lived here for more than 20 years, raised their kids, and formed many linkages in the community creating an extended family. These linkages are the foundation of their community's social capital.

Yet, there are cliques, husbands and wives, brothers and cousins, those connected with the volunteer fire department, and other smaller spheres of influence. These micro polities affect every community initiative, from planning to implementation. These spheres can and will shape the outcome of any town meeting, regardless of the community's size. Mills (1963) in a speech to the Center for Liberal Adult Education in 1959 described power as a universe with competing polities within a sociopolitical setting. The size of each sphere is weighted, reflecting its political strength. For example, within Mills' scheme, state government or General Motors would occupy large spheres, whereas rural communities would reside in small spheres, and individuals would be isolated dots. In every community there is a complex set of competing polities, where the city council, the volunteer fire department, or the local bank and trust occupy large spheres, and family businesses and the grain elevator might occupy smaller spheres representing their limited political capital. Although these relations are important and will affect any community initiative, activity, or decision, they have little influence on events outside of their community. For most small rural communities it is essential to negotiate between all competing polities to develop an agreed-upon agenda, a set of common values and goals most residents can live with. A universal polity within a community will result in greater potential to influence county, state, and federal policies. Although the community as a cohesive polity remains weak and fragile relative to the corporate state, it is critical that the competing polities within a community not only work together but also with other rural communities with similar interests. Politically, a large and well-organized polity must evolve to advocate for the common interests of rural communities. The evolution of this political economy begins with the formation of social capital during the local democratic process such as a town meeting. Successful socializing is the first step to a successful town meeting.

CREATING A NEW POLITY

With this theoretical perspective in mind, as the outside facilitator, I find it essential to break apart the small internal polities and the potential cliques they represent—thereby minimizing their influence—when they enter the door of the auditorium. For community brainstorming, the dynamics are enhanced when people who normally do not interact on a day-to-day basis sit side-by-side. The possibilities for new understandings and friendships are enhanced during the evening. Moreover, individuals within a small polity or clique often never have their perspectives on community issues challenged because they never seek competing views. Within these town meetings consensus can only be achieved when competing perspectives are articulated and subjected to negotiations.

I often use a simple technique to disperse a community's subgroups during a town meeting. In preparation for the meeting, a small, almost inconspicuous number that correlates to a specific table in the room is written on each name tag. People who arrive together will end up with different numbers on their name tag, resulting in mixed groups sitting together at the tables and preventing, for example, husbands sitting with their wives. As the facilitator, I can manipulate the location of where people are seated and the dynamics of the meeting.

Once people have signed in and had a cup of coffee, they are asked to sit at their tables. The evening begins with a short introduction followed by a short description of what we hope to achieve by the end of the evening. The goals need to be established before the meeting by the organizing or steering committee. Occasionally, these goals can be negotiated during the first part of the town meeting. Regardless, there needs to be a set of established goals so the meeting will have direction in case group interaction becomes heated or if outcomes are contested. These goals must be clear to everyone. I usually have them written on a flip chart for everyone to read. If for some reason the goals or meeting objectives change during the town meeting, opportunities to challenge the outcomes will arise, even after the meeting has adjourned.

Bleiker and Bleiker (1981) argued that people will accept decisions they may not fully agree with, or decisions that may cost them monetarily and only if they perceive the process is fair. Although fairness is an objectification, it has to be the foundation of any town meeting where decisions will be made. On the flip side, people will not accept decisions, even if they personally benefit from them, if they perceive the process to be unfair. Recognizing there is an inherent power advantage to the outside facilitator in any town meeting, this power relationship can be easily challenged if the process is perceived not to be balanced and fair. More than once I have witnessed public meetings where the outside facilitator, in a moment of desperation, exerted too much control and was subsequently accused of taking sides on a controversial issue such as siting landfills locations or industrial hog farms. There is a fine line between "too" much control and democratic balance. This line is usually determined by how clearly objectives and goals are established at the beginning of the meeting.

THE GUIDING QUESTION

The guiding question is the catalyst that pulls a diverse community together to form a more effective polity. An effective town meeting begins with one or two open-ended questions, that is, questions with more than one correct answer. For example: What would you like your community to look like in five years? How should we dispose of our solid waste? What do you think are the three most critical issues facing your community? The clarity and quality of this "guiding" question will significantly affect the success of the town meeting. During the planning phase, before the meeting, the nature of the question can solidify the steering or organizing committee by giving purpose to the meeting. If the issue is not critically important to the community, people will not attend. A concrete question without abstraction is a question that can be solved leaving people with the feeling they can make a difference. The keenest questions address local issues. Whereas rural people might feel powerless to address systemic issues of racism or youth violence, they will come together to address similar issues or problems if they focus on local racism or youth violence.

The same holds true when developing a time frame. Based on my experience, 3 to 5 years seems to be as far as most people can develop strategies for local issues, even if these issues demand longer term strategies. A shorter time span, say 6 to 12 months, is more attractive. If a long-term strategy is required, it should be divided into short increments where long-term progress can be benchmarked.

This guiding question needs to be developed by the organizing committee, not the outside facilitator. This facilitator as an adult educator can assist this group in framing the question, possibly bring in examples from what other communities have accomplished, and facilitate the development of the question. But this outside person cannot decide what the question is for the community. Agreeing on a guiding question is a negotiated process. Sometimes the steering committee crafts a question that misses the crucial issue the community may be facing. Subconsciously seeking to avoid conflict, the steering committee will agree on a question that is far too safe to evoke critical reflection during the town meeting. At this point in the planning, the outside facilitator can challenge some of the committee's assumptions and criteria for the question.

PRIOR KNOWLEDGE

Prior knowledge of community issues and personalities can give the facilitator some insight into knowing when or when not to challenge committee assumptions. Prior knowledge can also be a two-edged sword for a community developer. When you know more about a community, you inadvertently become more biased, thereby affecting your judgment. Yet, if you come to a community oblivious to the political landscape you may not be able to challenge the participants to think beyond the obvious. In discussions with my peers, some strive to achieve total neutrality, allowing the nominal group process to correct for poorly designed guiding questions. Others prefer to have some knowledge of the community so they might be able to interject timely suggestions or criticism.

I fall into this second category. I feel more comfortable knowing the political landscape and key issues, especially some history about how the community has worked together on past initiatives. Several times I have facilitated town meetings without understanding important issues. One time I was unwittingly manipulated by the county board of supervisors to facilitate a public visioning process for the future of unincorporated areas. The result was lending democratic credibility to a political referendum on landfill problems supported by the supervisors. I think I would have been more effective and the results would have had greater validity if I had known their agenda before the town meetings. On other occasions I have recognized that my personal biases might interfere with the democratic process. On those occasions I shared my concerns with the steering committee and let them determine whether they wanted to work with me.

SMALL GROUPS

After introductions and presentation of the guiding question, each small group of five to eight persons appoints a recorder and a small group facilitator. The facilitator's role is to keep the conversation moving ahead while making room for everyone to contribute to the dialogue. Usually the small group facilitator is a member of the community and has not had special training in small group processes. The outside facilitator as the lead facilitator can usually provide brief and simple instructions that enable the small group facilitators to accomplish their tasks. For example, make sure everyone has a chance to make comments. Politely temper the enthusiasm of the extroverted individual who may not realize he or she is taking time from others, and watch for body language of an individual who wants to make a comment but can't seem to get the words out. If the small group facilitators are having problems, they should ask the lead facilitator for assistance. The recorder's role is to write everyone's comments verbatim on a flip chart. If someone's response is not clear, the recorder may ask him or her to repeat the response so it is accurately recorded.

Within any group, rural or urban, small or large, among friends or strangers, there are always one or two persons who dominate the conversation. Stanton's (1989) study of Newcastle-upon-Tyne Family Service Unit mapped how rules of deference affect a group by decreasing democratic participation. Each of us behaves according to the setting and how we perceive ourselves in relation to others. In the company of close friends I behave in one manner; in the company of colleagues at work I behave in a different manner. I behave, consciously or subconsciously, accordingly toward people whom I perceive are from a different class or culture from my own. I look some people in the eye during a conversation; I avoid eye contact with others. The purpose of a town meeting is to create a "safe" environment for everyone to make a contribution. The small group component of the town meeting and the nominal group process is the primary arena for everyone's participation, and where rules of deference must be minimized.

To maximize this contribution and minimize chances for any one person to dominant the dialogue, a *round robin* technique is used. This process works as follows:

Step 1. Everyone writes his or her responses to the guiding question on a sheet of paper without conversing with anyone else. Within all group interaction there is a risk of what I call the "sheep" factor. That is, when the dominant person's perspective is put forth before everyone else's, there is a tendency to follow the leader. This dominant person may be a city council person, a banker, or a local pastor. He or she is usually someone with commonly recognized status. By having people write their responses privately, we attempt to minimize this sheep factor and counteract rules of difference.

Step 2. The small group's facilitator asks each person to report only one of his or her responses while the recorder writes it word for word on the flip chart. After going around the table the first time, the round robin process repeats itself until everyone has read off the second response, then third, and so on until all items on their lists have been stated. The small group has then developed a master list of responses.

Step 3. Before prioritizing, the small group members look over the list and attempt to combine responses that have similar meanings. Each refinement must be negotiated, and all are given time to advocate for their perspectives. During the lobbying, the small group facilitator is responsible for maintaining a balanced discussion, allowing space for each person to argue for particular responses, especially the "quiet" participant. During this stage, individuals are searching for common ground in their negotiated responses.

Step 4. After the master list is negotiated, group members then prioritize it by vote. There are many methods or techniques for voting. Each person gets 3 to 5 votes. To reduce the sheep factor, voting should not be done by voice or by raising hands. One solution to this problem is to give everyone adhesive paper dots (easily bought at any office supply store) and ask everyone to vote for the 3 or 5 items they see as most important. The dots are then counted and the top three to five responses are reported back to the larger group.

THE LARGE GROUP

Each small group reports back to the large group, reading off their group's top five elected responses to the guiding question. If time permits, they may want to offer a brief explanation of why theses ideas were selected. A master list of the top responses from all the small groups is developed on flip charts at the front of the auditorium. Typically, with 8 to 10 small groups there is the potential to have more than 50 responses. As in the small groups, the next step for the large group is to see if any of the responses can be consolidated by agreeing on those that are similar enough to be grouped together. For example, there may be 5 responses on how to improve recreational activities for young teenagers; when grouped together they create a supergroup that has broader support from the community. Once this refinement is completed, a final master list of the responses is printed on flip chart paper and taped to a wall for everyone to view. This list may have only 15 to 20 responses. These responses, though, should be distinct and without ambiguity so that everyone in the audience fully understands their wording and importance.

Then, everyone is asked to vote a final time for their top three or five choices, again using the adhesive colored dots or some other method where people have to get out of their chairs and walk up to the flip charts. The voting process offers another opportunity for everyone to socialize as they slowly work their way up to the wall with their dots and contemplate how they will vote. Some people vote quickly, sure of their decisions; others sit back and watch how the votes are cast. This group may strategically modify their decisions and place their precious dots next to the responses they see as having enough public support to win. As the voting comes to a conclusion, some people will step up to the flip charts and move their dot from one response to another, a decision I encourage so people have every opportunity to make the decision with which they are most comfortable. Another voting strategy used in almost every nominal group exercise is where one or two individuals place all their votes on the same response. Strategic voting like this can sway the outcomes if the voting is close and several people decide to vote as a block in support of their special interests. More than once individuals have requested another dot, which I usually provide. Is it fair to give people an extra vote? The number of votes each person makes is not as crucial to the democratic process as is the feeling that their participation counts. I have never seen an extra vote change an outcome. What is critically important is that people feel they have had ample opportunity to express themselves.

ANALYSIS, SYNTHESIS, AND ACTION

Once the votes are tabulated and the top three to five responses identified, the facilitator raises the challenge. "All right, you've done the easy part. Now it's time to begin developing an action plan based on your decisions. The only way this is going to be accomplished is for each of you to take some leadership toward achieving the vision you've crafted tonight." As people begin to look at their shoes with side glances at established community leaders who in the past have always assumed this responsibility, the facilitator needs to reach out to everyone and invite them to make a contribution to the next step in community action.

The notion of reflection, study, and action is inherent in participatory research as well as most forms of popular education (*Participatory Research*, 1982; Tandon, 1988). Within this framework, the nominal group process is merely a form of collective reflection. The challenge following the town meeting for the community is to move toward more study, then action. Without the next two steps, reflection achieved during the town meeting would have no value or purpose. At a minimum, before the meeting is adjourned and people leave for home, each of the top responses needs to be crafted into a project and a subcommittee recruited to bring the project into fruition. This must be done quickly. People have been working for close to 90 minutes to identify and prioritize issues. They are beginning to tire, willing to accept their progress as enough for one night's work. Typically, when we reach this point in the nominal group process we have no more than 15 to 20 minutes before the community will be physically exhausted.

Starting with the issue that received the most votes, the facilitator challenges the audience to develop a strategy for implementation, an action plan. To do this, a committee must be recruited and dates set so committee members can begin to study the issue in greater detail and present a set of proposals to the community via the city council, the chamber of commerce, the local media, and other key polities. They must also agree on a time frame in which to accomplish this, preferably within 6 months.

For example, the group decides that more recreational activities are needed for preteenagers. People are asked to join a special committee that will address the problem of youth recreation. If people will not volunteer to be part of this committee, it is dropped from the high-priority list identified during the night. If a committee is formed, they are given a time frame to further analyze the problem and develop proposals to the community. Once accomplished, the next priority is addressed. This one might be, as another example, to develop a solid waste disposal plan. Again, people are asked to volunteer for a solid waste committee. If there are no volunteers, there can be no committee and hence no solution to the problem. If volunteers come forth and a committee is formed, they are given a concrete time line to develop a better understanding of the problem and an action plan. This process is quickly completed for each of the responses on the high-priority list.

The selection of committees is always interesting to observe. Because I hesitate to put anyone on more than one committee, with a limited pool of established leaders the formation of multiple committees requires that fresh bodies step forward. Part of this challenge is to have both established and emerging leaders represented on each committee. Everyone who participated during the evening has to be considered to have some level of leadership ability, regardless of their past experience. If a rural community with limited resources is to survive it must continually invest in leadership development, which in turn is an investment in the community's social capital. If committees are formed to address the top three to five responses, I feel like the evening was a success. Before closing the meeting, I encourage everyone to call me if they have any questions as they move forward in their committee activities. I also remind them that by volunteering to be part of a committee they are therefore accountable to the community to complete the task of analyzing the issue and developing a proposal or recommendation.

The formation of these committees is the essence of any action plan and the ultimate goal for the evening. If people don't make a commitment to participate, the entire town meeting is usually a wasted exercise. Although this sounds logical, I have facilitated and participated in town meetings where, once the most important issues and problems have been identified and prioritized, only a few people are willing to make a commitment to serve on a subcommittee. Such a calamity can be minimized by making it clear to the steering committee (while planning the town meeting) and the participants (throughout the evening) that the ultimate goal is to mobilize the community to actively pursue strategies that address key issues identified during the town meeting. When a community invites me to help them organize a town meeting they often have not thought about what the goal of the evening is. Sometimes they say the information will be used by the city council to better understand what the community wants. Or that the city council will use the evening to gain support for one of "their" initiatives. If this is the case, the town meeting process is more window dressing than substance. Throughout the entire process, beginning with the steering committee and throughout the town meeting beginning with my introductory comments, the importance of establishing committees around the identified issues and problems cannot be understated. As an educator it is appropriate to have expectations of the group with which you are working, just as it is for a teacher to have of a student.

LITTLE DEMOCRACY

In rural Iowa, the democratic process in state and local politics is alive and well. Although this may hold true for most of rural North America, the same may not hold true with national politics. (Fortunately, having the first presidential caucus in Iowa raises the level of interest in national politics.) With voting participation at all-time lows and with the need to reform modern political campaign finance, it is all to easy for critics to argue it is the elite who benefit most from our present political system. Cohen and Arato (1992) pointed out that this argument has been fodder for public discussion for more than 50 years. The elite model of democracy is based on a pragmatic principle where "democracy is defined not as a kind of society or as a set of moral ends or even as a principle of legitimacy but rather as a method for choosing political leaders and organizing governments" (p. 4). This type of government prides itself on efficiency and efficacy. Democracy is maintained in principle merely by giving people an opportunity to vote even though access to political leaders is a purchased privilege based on contributions or connections to big donors. Competition for the financial resources needed to win an election requires connections and deal making, satirically referred to as power politics.

In contrast, a participatory form of democracy "maintains that what makes for good leaders also makes for good citizens" (Cohen & Arato, 1992, p. 7). Active participation is a paramount virtue, in both leading and being lead. The lessons of Horton and Freire have become the foundation of popular adult education. The role of the adult educator is to serve as the public catalyst toward increased and more dynamic democratic participation. In this type of democracy the common good takes precedence over self-aggrandizement and self-enrichment. Using an analogy from Gutierrez's *A Theology of Liberation* (1973), the breaking of the bread during communion is the realization of shared sacrifice with one's community. Within this context, individual salvation has little meaning. Rather, salvation is a shared experience within community. This metaphor within the adult education context is broader than the Catholic experience. The effect of the social gospel on Horton and the effect of liberation theology on Freire are well documented. The context of community and the mundane lives of everyday people give purpose to popular education. In the postmodern experience of secular North American life, the town meeting and other similar forms of democratic decision making within community provide an important arena for today's popular education.

If citizens fail to participate, democracy fails and the elite model of government prevails. Although voting remains central to participatory democracy, more is required of every adult citizen. Although the elite model assumes that the "everyday" citizen is unable to comprehend the complexities of any modern, technological society, the participatory model insists that everyone is obligated to engage in the democratic process regardless of how complex the issues become. Dewey (1966) described the ideal democracy as having two elements. The first is for people to recognize their "mutual interests as a factor in social control." The second is for people to be free to interact within groups. It is the negotiation that occurs within and between groups that creates a "change in habits" or a moderation of political perspective for the common good (p. 87).

Foucault (1982) argued that the power of the state is in its ability to individualize its citizens. This is accomplished through special interest voting strategies that subsume what Bellah et al. (1992) and others have termed the common good. At the core of the common good is Mills' (1963) concept of small democratic polities that evolve around common goals, values, and vision. Those homogeneous groups that originally settled as ethnic enclaves and later evolved into incorporated towns typically developed strong and effective polities. Even though these types of polities have limited political strength beyond their location, the evolution of larger and stronger polities cannot be achieved without the establishment of these local polities first. In other words, larger polities evolve as negotiated coalitions of smaller polities. In Iowa, for example, the Iowa State Association of Counties as an advocate for county rights has proven to be a worthy check and balance to state legislation that would centralize political decision making. This strategy as suggested by Foucault, Mills, and others as a balance to centralized power of the state, begins by challenging our tendency to become individualized through special interests politics. Again, the town meeting is the first step in individuals' coming together to make community decisions based on their common good.

THE RELATIONSHIP BETWEEN EDUCATOR AND COMMUNITY

The relationship between the outside facilitator and the community, although complex, must be analyzed. Within the tradition of participatory research, the relationship between the researcher and the community is pivotal to the success of the community's achieving social change. Is it possible for the outside resource person to remain totally neutral, maintaining a quasiprofessional role whose responsibility ends when he or she walks out the door? Is it equally as destructive for the facilitator to assume an "expert" position where the community defers to him or her whenever a decision has to be made? As an individual, it is relatively easy for me to maintain a distant relationship with the community I am working with. Living in another community, usually in a different county, allows me the physical distance to remain emotionally aloof. Yet, as an agent of IS extension, we have an office in every county with staff, ongoing programs, and an 80-year history in Iowa. More specifically, Extension to Communities has been providing Iowans' community development services for more than 20 years. Hence, as an organization we have a vested interest and familial relationship with every community in the state. As the Extension's community development specialist, I am intimately responsible and accountable to every community, regardless of my personal relationship to a particular community or its leadership. If I do not perform up to the expectation of citizens with whom I work, they have several avenues of recourse to express their disapproval or dissatisfaction.

As the outside facilitator I feel conflicted between my desire to remain objective and those subjective biases we all possess at some subconscious level in any political situation. Part of ISU Extension's mission statement is to provide "unbiased, research based information." Is it possible to maintain this level of objectivity? Should the facilitator strive to be objective; if so, how is this achieved? Obviously, when I receive a request for assistance I need to confront my personal feelings about the situation. This does not mean I should push my own personal agenda. If I anticipate a problem, I need to first share this with the steering committee. They may feel I am too close to the situation and they should therefore look for another facilitator, or they may feel it is not a problem. If they decide they would like to work with me, at least the potential conflict of interest is in the open. At the beginning of the town meeting, I may share some of my background with the audience so they know I am not hiding potential prejudices that may interfere with the process. As facilitator it is easy to direct the discussion, manipulate the audience, and therefore bias the outcome.

More than once I have politely refused the invitation and recommended a colleague who, in my opinion, would be more effective. Other times I have found myself to be so close to the issue that I found my biases would serve as a catalyst. For example, I have been invited to facilitate strategic planning processes for groups with which I share the same perspective. In situations like this, when the facilitator is in basic agreement with the community or organization on values and belief, the process can move much quicker through the consensus-building part, leaving more time for analysis and planning. Yet, it may be difficult for the facilitator in this type of situation to challenge basic assumptions held by the group and that may affect the final outcome of the planning.

The level of intimacy between the community development specialist and the community does not imply that he or she take responsibility to "create" a healthier and more viable community. Rather, limits on what we can and cannot do need to be established, if for no other reason than to keep ownership of all decisions within the community, which in the end will have to live with the consequences of any activity. Within the town meeting scenario, we can provide technical assistance in organizing and delivering a public decision-making process. We can also challenge basic assumptions and decisions if we are not too close to the issue. But we can never develop priorities and strategies independent of the residents who will ultimately be responsible.

ACCOUNTABILITY

In Iowa, ISU Extension usually provides this type of community education to rural communities as a free service, which is problematic. Experience suggests if the community does not have a financial investment in the process, there seems to be less commitment to follow through. More than once I have been invited back to work with a community organization a year or two after our first town meeting only to discover that nothing had been achieved since the first town meeting. Placing accountability within an issue-centered committee is a simple strategy toward developing an action plan following a town meeting. But there needs to be follow-up and oversight to insure the community achieves what it promises during the town meeting.

As families and individuals become busier with the demands of children, it is becoming harder to get people to participate in community activities. In modern society it is too easy to become detached from community. If the town meeting does not have tangible outcomes, we know it will be more difficult to get people to turn out for the next one. People need to see that their participation—giving up an evening or two—is going to lead to improvements.

The next step in the democratic process has to be in place before people leave the warmth of the auditorium for the cold winter night back to the seclusion of their homes. Everyone who participated in the town meeting needs to fully understand what the next steps will be toward addressing the issues they identified during the night. One part of accountability is to take all the ideas that were written on the newsprint and to type them out as minutes of the town meeting. Include the names of people who volunteered to serve on committees; mail them out to every participant as well as to the key organizations in town, such as the city council. The town meeting then becomes part of the public record. Another strategy for accountability, as mentioned earlier, is to have each committee provide a 6-month report of their progress. Inviting a news reporter from the local newspaper that serves the community to participate in the town meeting can also strengthen accountability. If participants see a news story about their meeting they often take their participation more serious. The power of the press works at all levels in our society, including remote rural communities.

FINAL THOUGHT

When I enter a gymnasium, my goal for the evening is usually to take the group through a process where they can first identify the top two or three problems facing the community and then begin to develop strategies that address these problems. This process, as described earlier, seeks to build a level of consensus within the community in a 2-hour meeting. Consensus may not always be an appropriate goal. In some instances conflict may be a necessary catalyst for change before developing consensus. For communities with limited resources, especially in financial and physical capital, consensus is required to preserve and use these limited resources judiciously. This can only be achieved once the community identifies its values and those symbols that everyone shares. Without establishing this common ground, special interest politics will only fragment the community.

REFERENCES

Bell, B., Gaventa, J., & Peters, J. (Eds.). (1990). *We make the road by walking: Conversations on education and social change with Myles Horton and Paulo Freire.* Philadelphia: Temple University Press.

Bellah, R. N., Madsen, R., Sullivan, W. M., Swindler, A., & Tipton, S. M. (1992). *The good society.* New York: Vantage Books.

Berry, W. (1987). *Home economics.* San Francisco: North Point Press.

Bleiker, H., & Bleiker, A. (1981). *Citizen participation handbook for public officials and other professional serving the public.* Laramie, WY: Institute for Participatory Planning.

Center for Rural Affairs. (1998). Annual reprint. Walthill, Nebraska.

Cohen, J. L., & Arato, A. (1992). *Civil society and political theory.* Cambridge, MA: The MIT Press.

Dewey, J. (1916, 1966). *Democracy and education.* New York: Macmillan.

Foucault, M. (1982). The subject and power. In H. L. Dreyfus & P. Rabinow (Eds.), *Micheal Foucault: Beyond structualism and hermeneutics* (pp. 208–226). Chicago: The University of Chicago Press.

Gajanayake, S., & Gajanayake, J. (1993). *A participatory training manual on community project development.* DeKalb, IL: Office of International Training, Northern Illinois University.

Gaventa, J. (1980). *Power and powerlessness: Quiescence and rebellion in an Appalachian valley.* Urbana, IL: University of Illinois Press.

Gaventa, J., Smith, B. E., & Willingham, A. (Eds.). (1990). *Communities in economic crisis: Appalachia and the South.* Philadelphia: Temple University Press.

Gutierrez, G. (1973). *A theology of liberation.* Maryknoll, NY: Orbis Books.

Lasch, C. (1979). *The culture of narcissism: American life in an age of diminishing expectations.* New York: Warner Books.

Mills, C. W. (1963). *Mass society and liberal education. Power, politics, and people.* New York: Oxford University Press.

Participatory Research: An Introduction (1982). New Delhi, India: Society for Participatory Research in Asia.

Putnam, R. D. (1993). The prosperous community: Social capital and public life. *The American Prospect, 13*, 35–42.

Putnam, R. D. (1995, October 2). Making connections. *The MacNeil/Lehrer news hour.* New York and Washington, DC: Public Broadcasting Service.

Ryan, V. D., Terry, A. L., & Besser, T. L. (1995, August). *Rural communities, structural capacity, and the importance of social capacity.* Paper presented at the Rural Sociological Meetings, Washington, DC.

Ryan, V. D., Terry, A. L., & Woebke, D. (1995). *Sigma: A profile of Iowa's rural communities.* Ames, IA: RDI-0101, College of Agriculture, Iowa State University.

Stanton, A. (1989). *Invitation to self management.* Middlesex, Great Britain: Dap Hand Press.

Strand, T. (1992). *The Dakota photo documentary project.* Paper presented at the 35th Annual Missouri Valley History Conference, Omaha, NE.

Tandon, R. (1988). Social transformation and participatory research. *Convergence, 21*, 2–3.

WORKPLACE

8

A Collaborative Committee Process in the Workplace

Mary Ellen Belfiore
Independent Consultant

Sue Folinsbee
Tri En Communications

We went beyond our hesitant relationships with each other. We developed a true partnership based on trust where everyone believed in what we were doing.[1]

This quote from a member of a workplace committee captures some of the meaningful growth and "refreshing" relationships that characterize the work of collaborative committees in workplace education. We use a collaborative process for developing a program for literacy or basic skills education in workplaces.[2] Our committee process involves the active participation and decision making of employees, management, and union. Our role is to build knowledge, skills, and experience in an organization by working through this participatory process with committee members so they can plan and sustain their own program of educational activities.

---

[1] Unless otherwise indicated, quotations used throughout the text are the comments of committee members documented in our needs-assessment reports, in committee meetings, or in follow-up research on the benefits of participating in collaborative committees (Belfiore, 1997). These quotations were collected and originally documented anonymously as they are shown here.

[2] We worked on these projects as consultants with the Workplace Education Centre of ABC CANADA, a nonprofit literacy foundation. The center operated from 1995 to 1998, with Sue Folinsbee as the Director of Workplace Education.

BASIC SKILLS

The terms *basic skills, foundation skills,* or *essential skills* are usually used in workplaces rather than the more generic term, *literacy.* Although the word *literacy* has a rich history and many layers of meaning, especially social analysis and action, workplace educators find the other terms attract more workers by broadening the scope of learning and connecting it to the workplace. Our definition of basic skills education includes: reading, writing, basic math, oral communication, English or French as a second language, and basic computer skills.

These basic skills can be supported through workplace education programs (classes, tutoring, seminars, etc.) or through integration into job-specific training. Other common initiatives that dovetail with basic skills education aim at improving overall communication in workplaces and enhancing job training. Some examples are instructing in clear writing workshops, establishing effective communication channels, offering consistent opportunities for employees to review workplace practice and contribute ideas for improvement, and developing within the organization knowledgeable and skilled job trainers. Our tools, simply stated, are education, training, and changing the ways things are done at a workplace, not just for line workers or front-line staff, but for employees at all levels.

WORKPLACE NEEDS ASSESSMENT:
A COMMITTEE PROJECT

We work with committees in companies, unions and sector councils to examine basic skills needs in the context of work, develop education action plans to meet those needs, and evaluate the programs and activities that take place. In this article, we focus on one aspect of our work—the workplace needs assessment (WNA). The WNA is a systematic way to identify an organization's educational needs with a focus on basic skills. We investigate the use and need for improved basic skills within the culture and context of the organization, paying attention to changes in the workplace, to relations and communications between all the players in a workplace, and to their commitment and investment in training.

A WNA offers both immediate and long-term benefits to an organization. Organizations frequently contact us when they are in the midst of change—technological, structural, or industry-wide. The WNA gives employees at all levels opportunities to understand these issues, give their perspectives, identify group and individual needs, point to areas of strength and improvement, and suggest ways to enhance their working life. The WNA helps organizations analyze their readiness for change by revealing employees' attitudes and practices regarding learning, management styles, communication, labor–management relations, equity, and current issues with which everyone is grappling. With that information, committees make recommendations for immediate actions, both educational and organizational, that will help employees get the learning and support they want and need to participate fully at work and in their own personal pursuits. For the long term, the WNA offers organizations their employees' visions for the future, their aspirations for involvement and development, their keen sense of what's needed for superior quality and job performance, and many suggestions for learning and training.

Our collaborative process relies on the understanding, determination and hard work of the workplace committee. Although we facilitate the process, the committee members are the decision makers, the planners for action, and the ones who set up basic skills programs and activities for their workplaces. While moving through the planning cycle over about a year, members gain many opportunities to develop their capacity for taking on the role normally assumed by a consultant or human resource personnel.

We feel strongly that a collaborative committee process is beneficial to the individuals, the organization, and the educational program. Our examples of WNAs in three organizations across the country point to specific benefits in particular contexts. More generally, the committee process develops a broad sense of ownership for the program, thus helping to ensure a longer lifespan. Because committee members are drawn from all levels and all interest groups, the process roots the knowledge, skills and understanding of the culture, and needs of an organization within its own employees. With this ownership, they become initiators at their workplace—presenting and supporting new ideas and practices as well as relating basic skills to other workplace issues.

The number of members for workplace committees depends on the size of the organization: number of employees, sites, and a regional or local or national base. In our examples, a citywide committee had 14 members, a national organization had 13 members, and a local company had 7 members. To share perspectives and get buy-in from the whole organization, we stress the importance of having representatives from different levels and groups. Senior management is matched by union leadership; line workers or frontline staff from different departments are at the table with office staff and supervisors.

We need members who have the power to make decisions and others who have the connections to interest employees in the needs assessment and ultimately in learning. We need experienced people who have participated in committees at work or in their communities as well as those who have interest and enthusiasm but no experience. The committees reflect the diversity of the organization in its people and its voices.

The committees work through the following steps in a WNA:

- understanding the role, variety, and extensive use of basic skills at work and in personal life;
- setting goals for the WNA and naming their project;
- deciding on issues to investigate in their WNA;
- scheduling focus groups and individual interviews;
- promoting the needs assessment to all levels of employees and making arrangements for the consultants to speak to everyone who is interested;
- reading the WNA report prepared by the consultant and making recommendations for educational programs and other related activities;
- presenting the findings and recommendations to other key stakeholders; and
- preparing an action plan and carrying out initial short-term recommendations.

The committees usually work on a WNA for about 3 months in a small or medium organization and 6 to 9 months in national organizations with many sites to visit. Their work is intense and time consuming during this period; the process requires full participation, analytical thinking, attentive listening, creative spirits, belief and trust in colleagues, and plenty of enthusiasm.

EXAMPLES OF COLLABORATIVE COMMITTEES IN CANADA

The three examples of committee work that follow show how the WNA process can be shaped by the committee to fit the organization or community represented and how the committee gets buy-in from all the interest groups. The recommendations made by these committees also illustrate how a participatory process enables participants to set their own priorities for action that will benefit employees, the company, and the union.

Lethbridge Community Training Partnership: On-A-Team Committee

In our work with the Lethbridge Community Training Partnership we were part of a community initiative that spanned public, private, and nonprofit organizations in one city. The partnership, which is still active in offering training communitywide, is made up of six organizations that share a desire to enhance team-based work. As one member described his experience, "What is unique about the community initiative is that it is a core group of people who came together with a common vision, representing different organizations."

The committee wanted to investigate two important questions: Can we pool our resources and save money? Can we benefit from training with others? (Mabell & Thurston, 1997). The answers to these questions began with organizational needs assessments (ONA)[3] in all six organizations to "identify common and/or unique organizational and individual needs which, when addressed, will foster the development of effective teams" (p. D1).

Our interest in this project, which focused on team training rather than basic skills education, was threefold: which basic skills participants would identify in relation to team-based work; how basic skills could be integrated across diverse organizations; how the ONA could bring the organizations together and serve as a model for ongoing collaborative work. The ONA offered these six organizations their own intensive team experience.

> The energy of the [different] groups made the total committee more powerful than the individual groups. The committee process really re-enforced the need for community participation and support throughout the entire program.

> [The process] brings unity with organizations of all shapes and sizes.

> Learning a new approach was an incredible opportunity. Personally a new beginning for me.

This extraordinary committee, so energetic and so committed to its community investment, faced some significant hurdles. To begin with, the six organizations varied not only in sector affiliation but also in size, ranging from small business to the municipality of Lethbridge. Some were unionized and others were not. The organizations also had different conceptions of team-based work as well as different levels of development of team environments. Employees within the organizations also had their own views of team, not always consistent with their employers' views. Through the ONA process, committee members realized teams would not look uniform across the organizations, and training would have to appeal to employees with diverse ideas and practices around team-based work. Given the different perceptions and operations in the six organizations, it was important to determine how each one could meet its needs in this diverse group and still remain committed to a partnership.

The committee members tackled these issues by adapting the ONA process to their context to ensure their focus was maintained and their original

---

[3]Organizational needs assessment (ONA) is another name for workplace needs assessment. At the time of this project, we used the term ONA.

questions answered. The committee asked for individual needs assessment reports for each of the organizations as well as an overall report for the partnership. Although this process was time consuming, it provided both levels with relevant information: confidential information for individual organizations to determine their own training programs based on needs and interests and a generic report guiding the partnership in their first workshops for community wide training.

Keeping in mind their central role in community planning, the committee decided to use the ONA as a learning and mentoring opportunity for themselves. Most of the members as managers, counselors, trainers, and union executives had a wealth of experience participating in projects and working with committees in their own organizations. Several of them decided to go one step further through the ONA process and take the responsibility for leading focus groups and conducting interviews. We offered a brief training session in theory, observation, and practice before they began their data collection in organizations other than their own. In a week of intensive information gathering, our consultants and committee members worked with the six organizations asking employees about many aspects of team-based work.

Although much work was completed with the data collection, the committee still had significant planning ahead of them: making recommendations and an action plan from the findings of the overall ONA; going back to their own organizations with their individual results and getting buy-in for the overall recommendations; and planning a few pilot workshops for the partnership. As two committee members said, "It takes time . . . and perseverance. . . . From everyone's perspective it seems forever but we were working full out."

That dedicated work earned high praise when the committee began offering its community-organized training programs: "The first time people in government, industry and the volunteer sector have pooled their resources and trained together." "Partners from different sectors coming together. . . . They became a learning team themselves." The On-A-Team committee continues to offer employees "custom-designed training experiences which build on what participants already know" (Mabell & Thurston, 1997).

Alcan and the Canadian Auto Workers:
The PEP Committee

Our second example is from northwestern British Columbia where Alcan smelters and the Canadian Auto Workers (CAW) set up a joint union–management committee called the Personal Education Program (PEP). Whereas the Lethbridge project presented challenges in overcoming multiple sites and diversity of views and needs, here the equality of union and management in all aspects of the project was paramount. From the outset, the CAW wanted to be equal partners. Their key to establishing that equality was having "functional authority" in all aspects of working together, that is, equal authority to act. For our own future consultancy work, this project was a model for true joint committee work in any unionized workplace.

The Kitimat Skills Centre, a provincially sponsored learning center for preemployment, work-related, and community-based learning, invited us to assist them in working with the CAW and Alcan to investigate the need for basic skills education. With pleasure and some trepidation, we embarked on the project realizing our partners were prominent players in industry and in the union movement. Although they had different perspectives on issues, they maintained a mutual respect for each other's right to be different. After our initial meeting in Kitimat to explain the committee process, both union and management representatives went back to their constituencies to confer before recommending that the project proceed. Once approval was granted, the committee decided that recommending a letter of understanding and a dispute-resolution mechanism would be part of their mandate. These first steps demonstrated to us how a strong, formal union–management process would shape our work together.

At first, this formality of procedure gave us a sense that this project would be a tough one. Although at times it was hard going, in the end the PEP project proved to be one of the strongest and easiest to facilitate precisely because of these formal structures. The PEP committee was not only committed to offering education, it was also solidly principled and always prepared. Although both union and management could agree on the process and the goal of access to basic education, they had different reasons for joining together. The name, Personal Education Program, carried the union's desire for their members to achieve their own personal goals for education in math, reading, writing, computers, and oral communication. Management could accept this direction and hoped to see improved skills at the workplace and in working relations.

Although we facilitated sessions, the PEP committee led them. They set the agenda for each meeting, came fully prepared for participating, and accomplished each step thoroughly and carefully. They had productive ideas, asked hard questions, and demanded sound answers. Their method ensured equality in each decision and action taken. With each subsequent meeting, trust grew among the members and we noticed smoother working relations as the process drew people together.

> The workplace needs assessment was a big learning experience for me. Usually we just do it with management. Bang! Going through the process has to be done and now we can see the future.

> We needed everyone's support. The whole process brought us together. It's so rare for a committee to be all on the same page.

We went beyond our hesitant relationships with each other. We developed a true partnership based on trust where everyone believed in what we were doing.

The committee also had to build trust in the workforce for this initiative. They spoke to all the workers and staff in small groups and individually, almost 2,000 people, to advertise the needs assessment process and the goals of the project. This extraordinary effort brought out 188 volunteers to the focus groups. The focus groups were shortened to accommodate everyone, which made the time together that much more intense and purposeful. This type of joint effort depends on the full support of all partners, which was gained through the dedicated work of the committee members.

The Kitimat Skills Centre was an important resource in our process. The center's director used the needs assessment as an opportunity to learn about and participate in a collaborative committee process. As with the Lethbridge project, he assisted in the data collection for the WNA. The center worked with the committee and coordinated the training for them. For example, they provided instructors for the five pilots that began after the needs assessment and approval of the recommendations.

The committee's recommendations are exemplary in that they provide a set of principles as a foundation for all future PEP programming. Based on principles for good practice in adult education, PEP's guiding principles promote lifelong learning, equity in access, recognition of achievement, and firm support for learning from union, management, and participants. All the partners involved in PEP, including the instructors, sign the statement of principles and agree to carry out the mission of the project. The committee also recommended that PEP be raised to a standing committee status to gain permanence and enable it to "oversee the development, implementation, and evaluation of PEP."

The project began with five pilots in basic skills education on 100% company time. After completion and evaluation of the pilots, the company agreed to a new round of funding for PEP programming.

North American Warehousing

North American Warehousing[4] is a warehousing, logistics, and distributing service for grocery products. The WNA for this company was a large-scale needs-assessment project, covering several provinces in western and central Canada as well as a U.S. site. The size of the organization at that time (more than 500 employees working at 27 sites in North America with 9 un-

---

[4]The identity of the company in this case is disguised. The name and certain identifying features have been changed with the knowledge of the company.

ions and employee associations), a bilingual workforce, and the different divisions and departments within the company made this project exciting, challenging, and at times overwhelming. The enthusiastic committee of 13 employees, representing most of the geographic regions covered by the company, planned and carried out a WNA involving 160 employees from 21 sites.

Members of the committee represented middle management, unions–employee associations, unionized workers, and staff in the two divisions of the company and in the two languages, English and French. Although senior management was formally part of the committee, their participation and support was not fully realized because of the history of the project and their lack of understanding of the real value of basic skills education for the company.

The history of the project is worth mentioning briefly because it illuminates how complete a participatory process has to be to succeed. North American Warehousing was implementing a new computer system when their outside consultant recommended they investigate the need for basic skills upgrading. The human resources department followed up on the recommendation and thus the collaborative process began. It is important to know that basic skills training was never part of the corporate strategy of the company, but rather a recommendation from the consultant, followed up by the human resource department without the full understanding and buy-in from senior management. Ultimately, their absence led to difficulties in maintaining the strength of the full committee and in implementing some of the recommendations.

The committee connected their WNA to the newly formed goals of the company, which emphasized employee involvement and training. The goal of the needs assessment was to "identify personal and work-related training needs and to recommend skills training programs and activities. This training will assist employees at all levels in our goal to become a well-trained, motivated, and empowering team." The collaborative approach tied in with the philosophy of training and involvement that the new chief executive officer brought to the company. The committee members, powered by renewed energy, enthusiasm, and commitment, wanted to make a difference in the lives of their coworkers, and in the company and union by working together.

With so many sites to cover, each member took on the responsibility for advertising and planning the needs assessment at one or more sites. In addition, some committee members drafted the information and invitation letters to employees, and others prepared and presented the plan to senior management. Because employee participation in the WNA was voluntary, every member made presentations at their own sites to inform employees and encourage them to join this phase of the project. In our evaluation of the committee process, members looked back on this intensive, 3-month period of organizing and visiting sites, and they commented on the communication skills they learned:

> I'd never spoken in a room with more than five people. Now there were forty-six.

> Management noticed a big improvement on my part when I stood up and gave presentations.

> For the long term I learned how to let people say what they need to say and how to pay attention at the conscious level.

Others mentioned their gains in confidence and responsibility, their efforts in group collaboration, and their understanding of the role, power, and practice of employee participation.

Even more important were the opportunities that committee members had to work together as equals, discovering common issues, understanding perspectives across all levels of the company and across the continent, and creating a national action plan for all employees. The two national committee meetings we facilitated and the many local meetings held by the members forged an identity for the committee and a deep respect for each other:

> We became a lot more aware of all the problems across the country. Things brought up at the table were very illuminating for all of us.

> We were all equals at the table. Not that [the company] always works that way but sometimes it's good to work that way.

> Everyone came from different sites and aspects of the company. People brought their own riches. We all gave our insights and helped everyone understand the big picture.

At the first meeting to review the report and make recommendations, committee members began with their overall reactions to the report, what they learned and what was confirmed. Then, they broke into groups to focus on different topics in the report—communications, training, basic skills, distributions of the findings—and to draft recommendations. Each group presented their recommendations to the whole group for revisions and final approval. Finally, they developed an action plan that prioritized the recommendations and the steps necessary to carry them out. The final version of the report incorporated the committee's recommendations and their action plans. Our role was not to hand the committee ready-made recommendations, but rather to help them formulate their own.

Their recommendations and action plans emphasized improvements in communication throughout the entire organization as well as education and training to meet new demands in technology, company growth, and employee responsibilities. Carrying out such plans in a large and still hierarchical organization was a slow, step-by-step process. Gains made at the head office had to be duplicated or adapted at sites across the country. Committee members at different sites took on various initiatives. One promoted job training specific to his facility; another worked on a basic skills program in reading, writing, and basic computer training; after a time, the company as a whole instituted a computer-purchase program.

Although the company continued to incorporate the collaborative process into more of its operations, basic skills education did not become part of the corporate strategy nationwide. One factor was their corporate history and business management, which determine priorities for funding and ongoing support. For example, forklifts for warehouse operations are a budget priority that can be easily understood. The committee made consistent efforts to keep senior management informed of its plans and decisions. But those efforts could not fully communicate what they learned through the experience, insights, and shared learning of their committee work. The members were highly focused and committed because of their growing understanding of the key role of basic skills and communication. Unfortunately, at that time, senior management did not share this understanding and therefore could not give the committee its full support for continuation of the committee's activities.

For a time, the overall committee and its work were in limbo, yet individual members continued to effect change at a local level. They continued to work on communication and education and training initiatives at their sites, participated on company committees for improving communication, got promoted to positions of greater responsibility, and even took the committee process out into their community work. One committee member with a long record of community involvement initiated the planning process with a government workplace agency to set up a basic skills program for employees at a community sports complex and obtained a grant for program development. One member described the effect of the collaborative process:

> The committee has a life as long or as short as you choose. . . . They don't have to do it all. . . . They can be a resource and make a difference in a variety of locations.

THE CIRCUMSTANCES UNDER WHICH
A COLLABORATIVE COMMITTEE PROCESS
IS APPROPRIATE

We have presented three diverse cases where it was appropriate to use the collaborative committee process. Although we clearly favor this process, we acknowledge it is useful to think of collaboration on a continuum and that collaboration only works successfully under certain conditions. Whereas many organizations we work with are moving toward a more participatory form of work organization, there are still many that have traditional, hierarchical decision-making structures.

We now discuss both the conditions under which the collaborative committee process can be attempted and the conditions that should be put in place to ensure the process is successful. First, there must be a desire on the part of the decision makers and other stakeholders to undertake a collaborative process. For many of our projects, this means ensuring that senior management, supervisors, and workers support the concept of a collaborative process. In unionized workplaces, the union must be on board. This condition was aptly illustrated through the PEP project case study. Supporting collaboration means those who hold the decision-making power must be willing to share it. Second, there must be enough trust for parties to work together even though they may have some different hopes and goals for the result of the committee process. In addition, the participating organization must be willing to invest the necessary human resources and time for the project to be successful. Finally, the organization must be willing to communicate about the process with its employees clearly, consistently, and continuously.

We have found that if any condition is absent, the collaborative process is severely compromised. For example, the success of the collaborative committee process is directly related to the commitment of the interest groups involved in the project. If committee members do not have enough time to invest in the process, its effectiveness is greatly hampered. We have had situations where all the conditions were met but, halfway through a project, a significant workplace change was introduced. For example, in one situation a new shift at the workplace was introduced. The energy of many of the committee members was focused on this change, taking away the resources needed for the project. In other situations, a strike temporarily derailed the project. Sometimes, in the final analysis, senior management is unwilling to share the decision-making power with workers even though they had agreed to in the initial stages.

The collaborative committee process is challenging one. Careful planning and ensuring clear expectations with our clients is the key to success. Even so, situations are likely to arise that we could not have predicted even with the best planning process. We offer some practical, concrete guidelines to help educators working with the collaborative committee process gear for success. Let's assume that initially the conditions we described have been met. Here is a set of guidelines to follow to ensure the process is a success:

• Provide awareness for the project partners in many ways as to the steps and realities of the collaborative process. Plan for several initial presentations with the client and provide ongoing information. For example, it would be helpful to provide the new client with cases studies from other organizations as well as references from clients who have been through the process. We think it is important not to assume that clients clearly understand the collaborative committee process after only one or two meetings. It is also important to continually help committees see where they are in the process, what has been accomplished so far, and what still has to be done.

• Investigate the history of labor relations in the organization. How have labor relations played out over the years? Have they improved or deteriorated? What types of joint initiatives have previously taken place? Even if none has taken place, is there the goodwill and the right environment to proceed? Many of our projects represent the first joint initiative in an organization. We think an essential or basic skills initiative is a good area for joint committees to start with. Basic skills is usually an area that all interest groups see a need for even though they may have different reasons for supporting such an initiative.

• Investigate the culture of the organization. Where does it fall on a continuum of traditional versus participatory decision-making processes? What policies and organizational practices support your assumptions about where the culture fits?

• Be clear about who needs to be on the committee and the time each step will take. Ensure that a member of the senior management team and the union executive are on the committee. We have found that often because of workload and other priorities, people in these roles resist being on the committee. A compromise might be that the senior management representative attends during the start up and that a process is put in place to ensure that he or she is continually updated and attends meetings at strategic crossroads. In addition, try to ensure a mix of experienced and inexperienced people on the committee. One of the goals of the collaborative process is to build the capacity of workplaces to manage their own projects. Experienced people can assist less experienced committee members. Remember that assigned tasks need to be appropriate to the skill level of committee members and their role in an organization.

• Ensure that you provide team building and awareness sessions for the committee. Ensure that members set guidelines for how they will work together as well as a process for resolving conflicts.

• Set out an agreement as to the roles and responsibilities of the educational consultant and the organization regarding the committee process. Ensure that both parties sign the agreement.

We have provided both the preconditions and some practical guidelines for ensuring a successful collaborative process. If an organization is unable to meet the preconditions or agree to some of the recommendations, we do not recommend using the full collaborative committee approach as outlined in this chapter. We recommend a more traditional approach to setting up education programs using aspects of collaboration where necessary and appropriate.

RESEARCH ON THE BENEFITS OF PARTICIPATING IN COLLABORATIVE COMMITTEES

After working with numerous committees in a wide variety of organizations, we looked more closely at how committee participation builds capacity in organizations and individuals to meet ongoing change through carefully planned action. Our approach aims at "leaving a legacy," as one member described it, so we asked what common benefits were evident across organizations and committee members. Belfiore's (1997) research on these benefits is a descriptive piece on the positive effects of committee membership.[5]

We distinguish between committee members who had experience on committees either at work or in their community activities and those who had little or no experience. An unexpected trend in the results is that the more related experience people have, the more they learn in the collaborative process. One member said "that the experienced people have a base and are more receptive." Experienced members can reflect on their past practice so they can deepen their understanding of how this process works. They can also integrate important elements of our collaborative work in their own context. In contrast, those new to any type of committee work make some first steps in acquiring skills and becoming aware of how their organization operates.

The two most frequently mentioned benefits are as follows:

- an increase in knowledge and skills for developing projects, and
- working with others in a new style of teamwork.

"Developing a project from scratch and putting issues and tasks in order," or "an opportunity to rethink the whole operation" or a chance to learn "how to organize nationwide" illustrate the skills and knowledge some experienced members gain through participation. These members can see how they can use or adapt the model in their current or future work. Other members point to specific skills they learned such as interviewing, leading

---

[5]This section is adapted from the research report (Belfiore, 1997).

focus groups, making presentations, running meetings, resolving conflict, and delegating responsibility.

The teamwork that develops through the collaborative process can at times overcome traditional adversarial relationships to work on a common goal—education opportunities for fellow employees and a chance to improve personally and collectively. Members describe how they meet as equals for committee work and have opportunities to work with colleagues they would not normally associate with or may not even know despite being part of the same organization. Their work helps them learn how to deal with different opinions, formed by different knowledge and experience of the same issues. In fact, committee members report that the breadth and experience within the group are its most valuable resources. "It's the mix that makes it all work." In some cases, this communal support on a single cause can transform individuals and relationships; in other cases people develop tolerance to get the job done. In all cases, people "grow and learn."

Committee members also mention the personal benefits they gain, especially the "tremendous boost of confidence" from participating in and completing a worthwhile project. They become aware of more issues within their organization by interacting with people from different levels, departments, and sites. Experienced members comment on how literacy, for instance, and the broader basic skills are brought to the fore. These members can integrate this new knowledge into what they already know not only about their organization but also about their communities.

In addition to the actual basic skills education programs that usually result from a WNA, organizations and communities benefit from the collaborative process itself. Committee members pass on their excitement and experiences with the process to other colleagues and to their community activities. They initiate a committee-style approach to addressing other issues as well as use steps of the process in other projects. Committee members report the growth of a different culture in organizations, more respect for peer training, participatory approaches to evaluation procedures and audits, as well as more interest in expanding the scope and audience for basic skills education.

Collaborative work in organizations has its distinctive challenges, of course: a different kind of teamwork, time and perseverance needed to see a project through to completion, and negotiating the hierarchy of a large organization. Despite these challenges, and sometimes because of them, committee members not only look back on a valuable experience but also look to the future for more creative uses of a collaborative approach.

> You learn to work with others and learn that there is always a solution somewhere.

> It's been a wonderful for me. I wouldn't have missed it for the world.

IMPROVING THE COLLABORATIVE PROCESS

Because our collaborative process is an ongoing educational endeavor, we want to be attentive to steps in the process in which members might need more support in knowledge and skills to carry out their work. Overall, we find that some committee members, especially hourly workers, are sometimes at a disadvantage and would benefit from a preparatory seminar on committee work with an emphasis on roles, shared decision making, and group action. In contrast, staff, management, and union leadership usually come to the table with some experience in these areas because of their responsibilities in organizations. We would like to see strong, confident voices from everyone on the committee so they can fully represent and outreach to their constituency. With more confidence and improved skills, we believe these workers (unionized or nonunionized) would also be able to see more personal benefits through their participation on the committee.

Oral presentation skills as well as conflict resolution are two areas where many committee members could benefit from additional practice and reflection. In our committee meetings, members make a conscious effort to distribute the work of leading small groups and reporting back orally. Although these activities provide some practice time, we do not use them for feedback and revision for improving oral presentation skills. And, although we offer committees opportunities to practice the presentations they will make to their coworkers, usually we only review the content and organization of their outlines. Conscious practice for a presentation is foreign to most members, but even one session with peers commenting and supporting each other would offer another opportunity to build skills and solidarity.

Conflict resolution skills are beneficial for any committee working together on an intensive project but especially in organizations where relations have been characterized by mistrust, hostility, and insecurity. These skills are also useful as members try to make important decisions, and plan and take action together. For instance, one committee working through a WNA had to make decisions about the number of people who could leave the factory floor at one time to enroll in a basic skills program. Two of the committee members did most of the negotiating between union and management and made decisions without getting back to the group. This derailment of the group decision-making process angered members to the point that some mediation was necessary. With more of their own skills in resolving conflicts and more attention to process, the committee members could have avoided this disruption.

Beyond actual committee work, the members can also advance and expand the use of basic skills education in their organization if they become more knowledgeable about the varieties of instruction available. At present, most workplace instructors are underused because committee members and management and union representatives are not fully aware of the many possibilities for integrating them into the workplace. Not only can basic skills be integrated into company training and union education programs, but instructors can also help prepare employees for organizational change.

As consultants, we promote an asset-based approach to all education and training. This positive approach builds on the knowledge, skills, and experiences of the workforce to engage them in ongoing learning. Our needs-assessment process is planned and carried out largely by employees on the committee who are asked to participate precisely because of what they bring to the process. The assessment is also based entirely on the ideas and perspectives of all the employees interviewed. The committee's recommendations are firmly rooted in the expressed wishes of the employees in the workplace. Yet, our process needs to go further and deeper. To date, our WNAs have emphasized the needs of an organization and its employees. Although we try to understand and capture the culture of an organization in relation to communication, education, and training, we have not explored in depth the assets and resources that both individuals and organizations bring to the endeavor. This foundation of experience and support is an important element in enriching our work and preparing the ground for successful, respectful, and well-developed workplace education programs.

REFERENCES

Belfiore, M. E. (1997). *The benefits of participating in collaborative committees*. Toronto, Canada: ABC CANADA.

Folinsbee, S., & Jurmo, P. (1994a). *Collaborative workplace development: An overview*. Toronto, Canada: ABC CANADA.

Folinsbee, S., & Jurmo, P. (1994b). *Collaborative needs assessment: A handbook for workplace development planners*. Toronto, Canada: ABC CANADA. °

Mabell, D., & Thurston, B. (1997, August 23). New tricks from old dogs. *The Lethbridge Herald*, p. D1.

9

Participatory Workplace Education: Resisting Fear-Driven Models

Andrea Nash
New England Literacy Resource Center/World Education

The workplace is a complex teaching context. Like the rest of the world, it is full of contradictions and mixed messages. Employers acknowledge that their outmoded ways of organizing work have kept workers from developing their potential, but blame workers for not having the skills needed for the workplace of the 21st century. The new culture of work teams offers workers long-awaited opportunities to make decisions, but allows them little authority to carry them out. And companies tell workers that participation in education programs is an important show of worker initiative, but offer few or inconsistent opportunities for workers to demonstrate or be rewarded for what they learn. Each of these examples spells disappointment for workers, as employer promises turn out to be, essentially, more rhetoric than substance.

Publications by the business community suggest that employers *want* a more participatory (though not democratic) workplace, if only workers could contribute the right skills and attitudes. And they *want* to remain at their present sites rather than relocating, if only workers could get their skills "up to speed" quickly enough. Never mind that for the last 50 years workers have been actively discouraged from using most of the mental skills employers now covet, or that education programs are usually offered, maximally, 4 hours a week, with permission to attend classes often dependant on production schedules (in manufacturing) or floor coverage (in health care). This ideology primes workers to feel responsible for their own job insecurity and grateful for not being left behind.

Where unions are present to challenge this rhetoric, workers can more effectively resist the exploitative messages. When such forums don't exist, however, and workers are immersed in images of themselves as unskilled, lacking in self-esteem, and poor at communicating, workers can begin to wonder about their own abilities and potential. This self-doubt, seeded by employers' "patient" attempts to bring workers up to speed erodes the confidence needed to challenge the ideology and the status quo it protects.

One of the problems with this damaging view of worker inadequacy is that it doesn't account for the workplace as an environment that can encourage or inhibit the way workers learn and use skills. A close look at shop floors shows that workers are creative in learning and performing their jobs, resourceful in circumventing language and literacy barriers, and deliberate in their choices of when and how to use their skills. Ethnographic research has shown that workers often possess more skills than they are willing or able to demonstrate, and that many skills they do use go unrecognized by employers (Darrah, 1997; Gowen, 1992; Hull, 1997b). Skills may go unnoticed because workers, over time, specialize in certain areas and informally divide tasks among themselves. Though each may have the knowledge needed to perform many jobs, they may have few opportunities to demonstrate that ability. Sometimes specialization (or seniority) brings workers special status that others are reluctant to challenge by showing that they, too, are skilled in a particular area. In addition, individuals develop their own strategies for approaching their work, methods that may not be recognized by managers as being equally effective ways of accomplishing their tasks. In short, workplace ethnographies raise questions about the worker deficit rhetoric by pointing out workplace constraints that prevent workers from using and expanding the skills and knowledge they already have.

The other problem is that, according to this model, the only route to "empowerment" is through individual assimilation into company values and vision of one's future. It assumes employers know what's best for workers and can be trusted to set a direction that will be healthy for company and worker alike. But we know that history doesn't bear this out, and that demonstrations of worker loyalty do not forestall downsizing, lay-offs, relocation, or the ever-increasing wage gap between workers and management. When a small manufacturing company in southeastern Massachusetts was recently bought and relocated overseas, dedicated participation in the education program did not save workers from having to work double overtime, building inventory in preparation for their own lay-offs. The new workplace is looking for employees that are willing to adapt to constant change ("lifelong learning") and accept an uncertain future. As Gee put it, workers are expected to be "eager to stay, but ready to leave"(Gee, Hall, & Lankshear, 1996, p. 19).

An education program in this setting can do one of two things. It can perpetuate an ideology that defines the central problem as a workforce skills deficit, cultivating in workers a sense of indebtedness and inadequacy. Or it can support an approach of critical inquiry about work, the workplace, and the nature of the workplace education program (How does (or doesn't) the workplace function well? What knowledge and skills are valued in the workplace? What function might it serve to portray workers as the cause of economic stagnation? and so on), taking into account the competing perspectives on all of these questions.

Although necessary job-related skills can be developed through either approach, a participatory approach offers the added possibility for workers to study the messages and practices that have undermined their progress, and assert their own definition of workplace improvement. First, let's look at what the dominant model offers.

THE FUNCTIONAL-CONTEXT APPROACH

Most programs follow the educational model that prevails in the literature, that is, the functional context approach, which centers on teaching the immediate and localized work skills (functions) that employers feel are needed in a particular work setting (context). The specific job-related skills differ from program to program, but they are all defined primarily by the needs of the employer and the future the employer envisions for the organization. To the extent that there is union or government collaboration or both, the stakeholders identify their overlapping interests (health and safety, for instance) and leave areas where they don't agree outside the scope of the program. The shared goal of being part of (if you are the worker) or employing (if you are the employer) a more highly skilled workforce is seen as the unifying factor that supercedes labor–management differences.

In the classroom, teaching is made relevant by tying it directly to on-the-job applications and daily work demands. Lessons might actively engage workers in linking what they already know to new work challenges. In this sense, the curriculum is typically student centered, drawing on worker experiences and building on strengths to develop new skills. Where there's an emphasis on practicing teamwork and problem solving, workers might also have opportunities to make suggestions about certain aspects of their own jobs. Workers generally value the chance to practice job-related skills in these traditional programs, and they appreciate the supportive encouragement they get from teachers.

When a company rewards learning by offering genuine opportunities for promotion and other incentives, these programs provide an essential service. In my experience, however, few companies have integrated their education programs into a larger human resource development effort to upgrade and promote wage workers. Fewer still have developed career or skill ladders that allow workers to take clear educational steps along a career path. (This is a strength, however, of many union-based programs.)

Furthermore, because the functional context approach focuses on workers without similar attention to workplaces, it fails to consider several important factors that influence the success and credibility of a workplace program:

1. Job security does not reside in a particular set of job skills. Those that are needed today may be obsolete tomorrow, and even highly skilled workers are vulnerable to corporate trends (nurses, for example, in today's world of managed care).

2. There are risks to participating in employer-run education programs. Without a union, workers can't be sure whether to trust on-site education as an opportunity to demonstrate their commitment to learning new skills, or suspect it as a process for identifying and weeding out the undereducated. Because this is not unheard of, it's important to protect the confidentiality of student records and insure there are no repercussions for participating or not participating in a program.

3. Literacy is not inherently liberating. When the primary materials for literacy instruction are work-related texts (directions, forms, timesheets, task logs, etc.), literacy becomes a means of self-monitoring—keeping track of one's own activities for the employer—rather than self-direction and autonomy.

However, people do need skills upgrading, for work and life. How can we make sure workers acquire the practical skills they need and want as we explore our understanding of the factors that shape our work futures? How do we provide opportunities to practice the skills needed to fit in as well as the skills needed to critique and transform? How can we all take responsibility for our development without accepting the myth that our access to gratifying work is completely up to us?

A PARTICIPATORY APPROACH

A participatory approach is based on the belief that the purpose of education is to expand the ability of people to become the shapers of their worlds by analyzing the social forces that have historically limited their options. As they do this, they begin to envision a new role for themselves and to identify the skills they will need to develop for this role. It incorporates both a collaborative *process,* which involves students in defining their own needs and negotiating the curriculum, and a *content* focus on understanding one's experience within a larger social context to be better prepared to act upon that context. This is not an assumption that people don't already think critically, but that making ever-new connections between our experiences and others', past and present, provides a fuller picture and clearer understanding from which to make decisions.

The participatory approach differs from a functional context approach in that it doesn't presuppose a particular solution (skills) to a predefined problem (workers). It asks participants to name the problem and cocreate an educational plan that will help them address it. And although the two often get confused, or perhaps collapsed, a participatory model also differs from a student-centered approach in that, along with an inclusive process, it focuses on critical analysis. Student-centered lessons elicit and validate student experiences and knowledge. Observations of and reflection on one's own learning is often an area of study. Participatory teaching applies this same thoughtful process to the social relations of daily life.

Consider this example. A popular student-centered lesson I know asks the class to construct a flowchart of how materials are produced at their factory. The lesson builds on the knowledge people bring, but goes beyond that to fill in gaps in their understanding—the details of certain processes or what the front office does, for example. It gives people a new perspective on how their work fits into a larger picture of the manufacturing process. This lesson often results in workers guiding others through the factory, demonstrating their expanded awareness of the work process by describing how each department should treat the next one as its customer by providing the best service possible and sharing responsibility for product quality. There's no doubt the lesson helps workers understand their surroundings and builds confidence, and it could stand alone as a successful student-centered lesson.

A participatory model would likely add a step to this, inviting workers to raise questions or comment on what they have discovered about the way the work is organized. This might lead to further investigation or to a discussion of why the work process is organized the way it is. What or whose priorities does it reflect? What are *their* work priorities and how would the work be designed differently for those? These activities support the discovery of what exists, but also creates space to imagine alternatives.

But is the participatory approach a realistic possibility for the workplace? Almost every workplace educator I know trying to do this kind of work describes himself or herself as "sneaking" it into the curriculum; many talk of downplaying certain lessons in their teaching reports or feeling they need to give them a different "spin." And the limited class time makes the thorough study of anything extremely difficult, especially when students

have expectations of traditional coursework and hopes of measurable outcomes. Given who foots the bill for much of this education, what really are
the opportunities for applying a participatory approach? I suggest that if we
practice our own theory and examine the workplace as a setting that presents both barriers and possibilities, we'll discover many unexpected opportunities. Mindful of the delicate context we're working in, we can apply
the principles of participatory practice in the following ways:

1. Use every opportunity to inquire about how the workplace runs and
how it affects our lives. Investigate the ordinary. Practice asking questions
and getting them answered. The questions may not necessarily derive from a
particular workplace problem. In fact, many teachers note that workers resist bringing such problems to the classroom either because they do not feel
safe in that group or, sometimes, because they are already looking up and
out to a future that does not include that workplace. Asking questions about
one's environment, however, serves adults wherever they go. Some useful
starting points, besides those that workers raise, include the following:

- Why does management think you need this class? What abilities do you
  have that management doesn't know about?
- Who has access to information and how do you get it (formal and informal routes)?
- What's a "good" job here? How do you define that?
- How do you get promoted here (the official and unofficial routes)?
- What is the history of this workplace? (Create a timeline of the organization, charting the size of the workforce, its ethnic make-up, organizational changes, etc.)
- Make a map the workplace (tracing the work process, noting the demo-
  graphics of who works in which areas, marking health and safety dangers, etc.)

2. Seek to make and understand connections. These might be between individual and collective experience, specific concerns and the larger context,
actions and consequences, or teachers and students as workers, who are in
many ways struggling with the same issues of marginalized, insecure work. I
share an example of this from some work I did with new practitioners. I was
trying to generate discussion about the worker identity we share with our
students. Adapting an activity from Simon, Dippo, and Schenke (1992), I
asked each person to think of a job they'd had and to list what they would
have needed to become more productive in that job. I then asked them to
sort the list into the items that related to their own changes and skill development ("more training," "a better attitude," "reading my training materials,"
etc.) and items that described other kinds of changes ("more information

from the company," "more feedback on my work," "end of capitalism," "a more comfortable workspace," etc.). When we came back to share and discuss the lists, we found that individual changes accounted for only about 25% to 30% of those needed. We used our observations as a way to begin talking about our own roles in emphasizing education as the primary means to an improved worklife, when our own experiences were telling us something else. How could we more consciously use those experiences to inform our teaching, make connections, and build relationships with students?

3. Use the participatory approach flexibly, always trying to carry forward its purpose rather than its method. Many practitioners get stuck equating participatory education with a particular set of steps that result in certain kinds of public action. Many teachers, myself included, have spent years either hurrying toward premature actions of one kind or another, or apologizing for lessons that merely ended in a new awareness of a workplace dynamic. To hurry the process can backfire, however, leaving workers to carry out a teacher-fueled agenda and, perhaps, take risks that have not been properly weighed. This is in no way to ignore the fact that acting in the world and examining what results is a terrific learning process. But, contrary to some interpretations of the approach, I believe that getting to an explicit public action is not as central as developing a depth of understanding that can support informed action whenever it becomes appropriate.

4. Prioritize worker goals to learn concrete skills. Work with them to recognize and articulate the skills they are learning during nontraditional lessons. Some practitioners end each class with a group recap of the ways they have practiced language and literacy, problem solving, and "team" skills.

THE PROCESS IN ACTION

In the stories below, we see some of the possibilities of teaching with a participatory approach. In each of the three examples, workers became engaged in redefining the meaning of a problematic situation and, in so doing, redefining themselves in relation to their work, their colleagues, and their employers.

The first lesson comes from an advanced ESOL class in a unionized manufacturing company, taught by Adam Bolonsky. He reports that "the lesson was designed in response to a class request to learn more about the jobs in the front office and, also, in response to a management request that students meet front office managers in the hopes of opening better channels of communication between line workers and management" (Massachusetts Workplace Literacy Consortium, 1996, p. 21). To start off, the group invited the marketing director to their class to interview her about her job. During the interview, she described her work in jargon that confused some students and frustrated others. After she left, the group discussed their reactions to what they referred to as "inside language," some with that angry edge that comes from feeling stupid or inadequate. The more they talked about it (what it is, why it's used, and when they themselves use it), the more they saw it as a tool that could be used, purposefully, to include or exclude. They concluded that when they hear inside language they should ask themselves, "Is the person using it because it is the language he or she uses everyday? Or is the person using it because he or she wants to keep me on the outside?" (Massachusetts Workplace Literacy Consortium, 1996, p. 21). Their perspective on the manager's language use shifted from a view of it as an oral mastery that reminded them of the education they lacked to a view of it as a social discourse that serves many purposes other than communication. This understanding opened up a much wider array of options in dealing with it. Bolonsky says, "Some students want others to learn to speak in plain English, yet are unsure of how to make that wish clear or even what plain English is; other students want to learn how to translate inside language but are unsure of how to do so; still others want to learn those discourses which separate them from the jobs, privileges, and goals they desire" (p. 21). Rather than thinking about language as something you have in varying amounts, the workers started talking about language as a process that mediates relationships, a tool the manager may have used to create distance. And understanding more clearly how language can be used to privilege some groups and diminish others, the workers saw choices in how to respond. In their acknowledgment of the value of their "plain English," we can see how they reclaimed their own language patterns as they prepared to approach more confidently the company's "inside language."

In the second example, some hospital workers have come to their ESOL class with a familiar Monday complaint. They say they have too much work to do because the weekend shift hasn't been pulling its weight. Their teacher, Amy Battisti, responded by writing up a catalyst dialogue about supermarket workers in a similar situation. After one reading, the workers began relating the scene to their own experience, creating additional characters, and dramatizing what they believed would happen next. As they discussed it further, they realized the problem was primarily in the way work was being organized, divided, and waylaid. The focus moved off of allegedly lazy workers and onto an organizational issue, which suggested vastly different responses and solutions.

Rather than going with the workers' initial assessment of the situation, the teacher prompted the group to look at the issue in a bigger context, discussing who had the authority to plan and divide work, and how the lines of communication worked. In the end, they determined that efforts to change the work system were beyond what they wanted to take on at that point and chose not to take any public action. They had, though, redefined the issue from one that divided them as workers to one that supported their solidarity. Their discussion enabled them to examine the environment that nurtured these conflicts and to see it as a place to look when other issues arose.

I quote the last example from Sharon Carey's (1998) reflection on her "Writing for Communication" course. It illustrates the authority students begin to take over their lives when presented with the opportunity:

> I use a lot of literature in my classroom as a way to open doors and comfortably discuss workplace issues, so I looked for literature that dealt with fences, walls, barriers. We studied Robert Frost's "Mending Wall" . . . and read a scene from "Fences" by August Wilson. . . .
>
> Everyone wrote a story about a barrier that prevented or enabled her/him from doing something that she/he wanted to do. Then we looked specifically at walls in the workplace. People imagined the walls they meet everyday—visible and invisible. Then we talked about the walls that we wanted to build or wanted to take down, and why. Once we started taking walls down we were ready to deal with specific talk of the merger. A huge wall between two hospitals was coming down and none of the workers were happy about it, but there was nothing that anyone could do to stop it, so we decided to study it. We did a compare and contrast chart. We looked at the differences and the similarities of the two places and tried to anticipate problems that might occur when two very different places become one. We wrote out questions about downsizing and reorganizing to ask supervisors and union representatives. We shared valuable information with one another and corrected a lot of misinformation. We laughed a lot.
>
> The next day, a student brought in a card with a Chinese character drawn on it which, translated, meant "crisis as opportunity." Despite their fears, the workers began to explore the merger as something potentially positive. They decided to put together a simple list of strategies that could give people a measure of control and self-direction during a time of great change. Out of this came, after many discussions, "Our Merger Survival Handbook." It included:
>
> 1. Remember the saying "crisis as opportunity" and keep a positive attitude and an open mind.
> 2. Gather information by asking questions rather than listening to gossip and rumors.
> 3. Become valuable to the workplace:
>   - let people know you're willing to try new things,
>   - inventory your skills,
>   - identify what new skills might be needed in the workplace and learn them (especially computer skills) or let people know you're willing and able to learn them, and
>   - brush up your basic skills in reading, writing, speaking, and math.
> 4. Update your resume and practice cover letters.

5. Start networking—call friends to find out what's out there and keep an eye open for job opportunities. (p. 2)

The workers were proud of their product and distributed the handbooks at their annual achievement ceremony, as well as through the union newsletter.

During this unit, students grew beyond their positions as victims of change to become leaders in their workplaces. Their recommendations may appear to have accommodated management's needs, but I see them as practical suggestions that make it loud and clear that workers owe no loyalty to this organization. Their enlarged perspectives allowed them to create alternatives and plan for the future, even as they were anxious about the present. They didn't change the situation, but they changed their relationship to it, feeling less in its grasp and better equipped to take care of themselves and each other.

CONCLUSION

A participatory model is welcome in few workplace settings. Practitioners are often only able to weave it in, intermittently, with more traditional approaches. But this is true outside of workplace education as well, even though the language of "empowerment" and "student directedness" is everywhere. Adult education is generally oriented to preparing people to uncritically participate in the current work, school, and political systems. Many argue this is what adults say they want. Participatory education will continue to ask deeper questions to find out if this is *all* they want.

ACKNOWLEDGMENTS

At the time of this writing, Amy Battisti and Sharon Carey worked for the Worker Education Program of SEIU Local 285. Adam Bolonsky worked for Jewish Vocational Service. Many thanks for their permission to use their work in this article.

REFERENCES

Carey, S. (1998). *Curriculum highlights from the field of workplace education*. Unpublished lessons collected for the Massachusetts Department of Education. Massachusetts Workplace Literacy Consortium, Boston.

Darrah, C. (1997). Complicating the concept of skill requirements: Scenes from a workplace. In G. Hull (Ed.), *Changing work, changing workers: Critical perspectives on language, literacy, and skills* (pp. 249–272). Albany, NY: State University of New York Press.

Gee, J., Hull, G., & Lankshear, C. (1996). *The new work order.* Boulder, CO: Westview Press.

Gowen, S. (1992). *The politics of workplace literacy: A case study.* New York: Teachers College Press.

Hull, G. (Ed.). (1997a). *Changing work, changing workers: Critical perspectives on language, literacy, and skills.* Albany, NY: State University of New York Press.

Hull G. (1997b). Hearing other voices: A critical assessment of popular views on literacy and work. In G. Hull (Ed.), *Changing work, changing workers: Critical perspectives on language, literacy, and skills* (pp. 3–39). Albany, NY: State University of New York Press.

Massachusetts Workplace Literacy Consortium. (1996). *Curriculum highlights from the field of workplace education.* Malden, MA: Massachusetts Department of Education.

Nash, A. (1993). *Curriculum models for workplace education.* Malden, MA: Massachusetts Department of Education.

Simon, R., Dippo, D., & Schenke, A. (1992). *Learning work: A critical pedagogy of work education.* New York: Bergin and Garvey.

10

From Where We Live, How Far Can We See?

Gary Pharness
The Hastings Institute, Inc.

PLAYERS AND PIECES

British Columbia Buildings Corporation (BCBC) is a Crown Corporation of the Province of British Columbia. Its purpose is to provide working space for the many provincial ministries and agencies. In most instances, the Corporation owns the buildings in which government staff are housed; in other cases, it leases space or builds new structures. It presently manages more than 3,500 buildings provincewide.

The BCBC workforce is representative of that found in real estate: property management, property analyst, marketing, rentals, law, electrical, plumbing, and carpentry trades, administration, landscape, and security. It also provides community services in earthquake and disaster preparedness; environmental consultation; and coresponsibility and participation on various boards; i.e., Riverview Hospital. BCBC is often documented to be one of Canada's 100 Best Corporations.

BCBC is a part of the Hastings Institute, Inc., Workplace Language Partnership. Other partners are Vancouver School Board, various locals of Canadian Union of Public Employees, especially 1004, 2950, 15, and the University of British Columbia. Within the BCBC context, the British Columbia Government Employees Union is a strong and supportive partner. In common, all of these partners have large, diverse, and many layered, multi-skilled workforces carrying out all manner of modern work.

The Hastings Institute, Inc., established in 1989, is a private, not-for-profit corporation owned by the City of Vancouver. The Board of Directors is composed of the mayor and four members of the city council. It assists the City of Vancouver, especially the Equal Employment Opportunity Program, in delivering specialized training for city departments and outside clients. The kind of training the Hastings Institute makes available to its user base of government, agency, and private sector clients focuses on workplace issues of harassment, diversity, and intervention. Language is viewed as an issue of equity, fitting within the overall Hastings mandate. Hastings' training meets the needs of senior-, mid-, and entry-level staff. Participants in various training venues represent a wide range of fields: technical, professional, administration, clerical, trades, and labor.

OPENING MOVES

In the final years of this century, many North American corporations evaluated and assessed the literacy skills of their employees because, as employers, they see these skills as an important factor in their strategy to compete locally, nationally, and globally. Consequently, business is nurturing its human capital as an asset, understanding the cost to service its employee skill needs is not a liability but rather an investment in the future well-being of the company.

The following account represents BCBC's efforts toward achieving a more inclusive literacy within its workplaces. These efforts move from building and enriching employee literacy to acknowledging and understanding corporate and employee diversity, then connecting this personal and corporate literacy to the community in a proactive way, placing literacy as the foundation of social change. This way of using basic skills training to encourage learning and change in workplace cultures is not an option for most literacy providers because the ideals of literacy, the expectations of business, and the limitations of funding are in conflict.

This conflict occurs because most often employers present workplace literacy programs to employees in the form of a challenge: learning the purpose of keeping employed, helping the employer remain competitive or achieve market competitiveness, and increasing employee skills to adapt to new technologies.

For many workplace literacy providers, their work requires only that they adopt the rhetoric of their business employer or client, then adapt Adult Basic Education (ABE) materials to the needs of the workplace. These programs are the employee's needs viewed from the employer's perspective. Consequently, the workplace is awash with literacy audits, needs assessment, preskill testing, specific job instruction, and posttesting. All of this reinforces several superficial notions about literacy. The low point in this kind of thinking about employee literacy is when educational providers and employers fail to understand how little literacy is achieved by employees working in the wastelands of prescriptive programs that sanitize worker experience and neutralize worker thinking. (Sanitation and neutralization of worker thinking can happen within the context of something as innocuous as policy for confidentiality. Given that some employees require and want confidentiality for personal barriers, this aspect of confidentiality is understandable; however, less than reasonable is the employer response to confidentiality issues that declares overall confidentiality: personal as well as the work literacy program. This hushing of the program subtlety patronizes the employees strength to identify what needs confidentiality; keeps the decision-making powers with the employer; and distorts and silences the development of employee voice, which is one hallmark of literacy. Simply, how many human resource managers hide training initiatives such as total quality, customer service, and safety behind confidentiality?)

Much of this measurement and inventorying of employee basic skills is readily available to astute and engaged managers. Working managers using informal assessment tools—listening, discussing, and observing—know the strengths and weaknesses of their workers. Therefore, they need only build or enrich a learning culture in specific worksites.

Literacy, as practiced in these sterile business managed learning environments, is beginning to change, as can be seen in some workplace literacy initiatives. None of this is meant to take away from the programs and older learning structures that did help many employees improve their skills and gain advancement or better their employment prospects. However, new literacy opportunities exist for those who design and implement workplace literacy programs to come together to create a fresh vision for basic skills and literacy programs in the business arena. As in business, we as literacy workers must nurture the assets of literacy and invest human capital in strategies practical and motivating to our clients.

LITERACY FOR SPECIAL MARKETS

BCBC is one corporation that has been slowly and subtly reshaping its idea of literacy through becoming more literate about itself, its employees, and its place in the larger community. In doing this it has evolved into a special markets literacy client, a client whose literacy needs have broadened over time.

As a corporate entity, BCBC is not unlike other corporations and individuals that often give something back to the community where they have been successful. In most instances this giving back to the community is not a hands-on experience for the company or its employees. More often, the giving back manifests itself in the form of a check. BCBC is a hands-on kind of company. It works hard to achieve a high standard of efficiency for and service to its many provincial clients. It gives its employees many learning opportunities and community projects to realize personal achievement.

This story about literacy in a special market is told to us more accurately by those within the corporation. It is best to start at the beginning. In this way we can see how one corporation first tackled (looked at) basic skills needs of employees, then faced issues of corporate literacy.

In early summer 1991, some managers within the BCBC met to explore learning models that could help employees gain or increase their language communication skills for both work and home. At the time, few models existed that could accommodate and deliver to a diversely skilled and peopled workforce with any degree of economy of scale.

GETTING LITERACY ON THE BOARD AT BCBC

By the fall of 1991, BCBC was ready to offer its first literacy classes to any of its employees who wished to improve their language skills. Employees identified their particular needs such as reading, writing, listening, speaking, and numeracy. Some of these needs reflected workplace requirements and others focused on home and school literacy. Consequently, some employees worked on writing, others tackled the GED, and some worked on numeracy. However, all participants wrote pieces about their lives, work, and hopes as well as memos, reports, and so on, and read and discussed this writing during each session. The employees' diversity divided along the lines of age, gender, position, ethnicity, and so on.

Hans Wenger, property manager of the largest property unit in the corporation, wrote his thoughts about that time, starting this story:

> About late summer of 1991, as part of our business plan, I wanted to provide my people access to some basic program that would give them skills that they could apply to their every day life. Little did I know, at the time, that this basic program, Language Training, would turn out to be a great success some three years later.

In this beginning to a larger written comment, Hans seemed to be intimating that he viewed literacy as the primary building block for success in everyday life. Later in the same text, he wrote:

> These stories are not the result of some complicated, convoluted, or intense teacher based program, but, rather the outcome of what happens when em-

ployees are given the chance to learn in their work environment. Yes; to learn; to discover about one's inner self; to discover one's inner voice.

Looking back, Hans was setting the stage for BCBC to let its framework for literacy grow to include issues of diversity that in time would include not only personal and corporate literacy about diversity, but also ways to make all of this corporately confined literacy more inclusive for and accessible to those outside of the corporation and the corporation's mainstream focus.

Another passage from Hans who attended the first language training program shows how his notion about skills improvement differed substantially from what most of his peers, at the time, were thinking. To illustrate, this excerpt shows in a significant way how management expectations can direct workplace language programs toward more far-reaching personal and corporate outcomes than can be achieved through the purchase of basic skills training thinly disguised from its everyday ABE roots:

> The elements for this to happen, apart from the right physical environment, revolve around self. One must trust self and others. One must see what one wants. One must be prepared to take a risk. Risk is most difficult to accept and therefore the most critical. The risk of allowing others to see the real you, to know your real feeling, to know your desires, passions, and secrets that remain camouflaged behind the great facade. Yes, the risks are great, however, the rewards are greater.

This passage fairly well sums up the importance of creating a wellspring of vision from which various literacies and skills can draw to build more literate work environments. In these pieces, we see Hans putting his personal literacy on the table with that of his workforce. He finished reflectively by simply writing:

> I have gathered many fond memories over the years of giving leadership to the people that I have had the privilege to work with. However, my memory of choice, without a doubt, will be about the people whose words I read and learned from in our first workplace language groups. After all, they are the ones that trusted in self and others; they are the ones with vision; and they are the ones who took the risk.

Hans' words marked the beginning of a long evolution for employees and employer from basic skills literacy to corporate literacy about difficult questions such as, "In what ways can we give something back to the community we live and work in?"

This question and its answer shows the fundamental connection that exists between literacy and the community. Neither literacy nor the community are well served through acts of exclusion. It is in the act of inclusion of the many voices we hear around us at work and in the community that we begin to see ourselves and how we fit into this larger scene. In giving opportunity for literacy to its employees, BCBC started on its journey of listening to the voices within the workforce—voices that had gone unnoticed and unheard and isolated, often for decades. In this listening, the corporation heard stories it had not heard before. These stories instructed the corporation in learning about the struggles and successes of its employees and how, as people, they live.

This personal and corporate experience melded into a collective history growing from everyday life. Before this dynamic change, trades employees shared little contact or conversation with the cleaners, and both of these groups worked segregated from others in the corporation.

BCBC President and CEO Dennis Truss put it the following way:

> The Workplace Language Program in BCBC has been very successful in not only drawing people out, but also in bringing people together from different occupations and parts of the corporation.

This point also shows one way of recognizing and building on the diversity within the corporation. Large workplaces most often exist as collections of isolated and disconnected pieces of the whole.

The CEO added his thoughts on the changes at BCBC:

> Communication and understanding language are essential to the well-being of BCBC, and this language program has certainly made a major contribution toward achievement of our goals.

Although BCBC is in the business of securing space and services associated with real estate operations for provincial government offices in British Columbia, the CEO offered some insight into how the corporation values literacy overall:

> Until now, some of the more tangible indications of the Corporation's success have been related to our buildings and services we provide; the language program shows something of the people within BCBC and is another solid indication of what makes us the organization we are.

Having writing opportunities available for all employees gives voice to the corporation in ways not as easily accessible in more conventional and structured workplace language settings. The usual argument for not having a broadly based workplace program is that it fails to address the specific language needs of individual employees consistent with our understanding of instruction, application, and assessment. It is likely that this belief stems more from not having tried building literacy on a larger foundation than from genuine validation arising out of practice. Therefore, it is surprising and encouraging to see the following passage written by the director of human resources for BCBC, Grant Close. Succinctly, along with the two earlier voices, Grant answered the "bottom line" question thrown out by many managers exploring the feasibility of implementing basic skills programs in the workplace:

> In the Language Program, these stories, vignettes and poems as well as the work related documents are slices of our employees' lives as they explore and grow through their experience with this program. By topic and tone, in this writing, there is a process here that achieves advances that are both substantial and measurable.

The comments to this point express how some BCBC staff viewed the language project after 3 years of employee involvement. To express these views, these staff members wrote out their thoughts, which is a significant way of substantiating and valuing literacy. Other BCBC staff also wrote about the program over the 3 years.

In the following piece, Steve Ketola, a building service worker, seemed to be experiencing an epiphany about a part of his life's experience:

> My writing has been appreciated. The concept of team work and effect is highly focused in the classroom. We are developing positive attitudes toward each other.

This is an epiphany for the corporation as well because in reading and hearing the stories of its employees, the corporation began to see itself as a story. In seeing its own story, BCBC understood and saw that the story changed with differing points of view. This recognition helped the corporation recognize how a fundamental framework for training in one area could be used to stage, extend, and enrich training about other issues and policies.

This connection to story also happened for employees. At the start many employees referred to themselves in the third person. In most cases, this initial hesitancy on the part of employee learners to connect to and reveal who they were and their vulnerabilities associated with such personal revelations stemmed from fear. Rick Smith started his writing in this manner in November 1991. In time Rick used writing, including first person narrative, to express the functions of his job as an environmental control officer within the corporation and to share his motorhome adventures.

By February 1992, Rick was writing about his resolution of problems focusing on individual voice. He began the following piece reflectively and ended with the self-recognition that in writing "He has found . . ."

The Power of Writing

One-on-one, he is an effective communicator. But in a group, the reverse is usually true; although he is a very good listener. When he talks many don't really listen and some people cut him off in mid-sentence and tell their own story. He gets frustrated, and his pride is hurt. "Oh, what the hell, why bother trying? he says to himself dejectedly, and he clams up. But he really does want others to hear what he has to say!

One day he gets an opportunity to join a Writing Class at work. He has always been interested in writing, but had never done anything about it. Joining the large group, he begins to write: a small poem is created; stories are told about his younger days. What a difference! Now, when he "talks" to the group, the others not only pay attention to what he is saying and don't interrupt, but are genuinely interested.

He invites feedback about his writing. The others ask about parts not understood, and he receives helpful, positive suggestions for improvement, and encouragement and support to continue.

As his writing improves, his confidence grows. Can some measure of success in this medium help in other areas in life? Yes. He sees it beginning to happen. And he tells himself to keep trying to be more effective when talking in other groups.

Meanwhile, he savors the sweet taste of the personal approval given to him as he talks through his writing.

He has found a powerful way in which to communicate; not only for relating tales about his youth, but also as a way to express his hopes and dreams, his plans and ideas, and his joys and frustrations.

Oh, the power of writing!

Later, after several revisions Rick had this piece and one other published in the "Voices" section of the *Vancouver Sun*.

Another writer, Libby McAusland, wrote about returning to the library in Victoria 10 years after finishing school. She listed the physical changes that have taken place over the 10 years. She checked out her first romance novel and said, "I would definitely read another novel of that kind."

Libby at this point in her writing discovered something more important about herself that seems to have come from writing about experiences.

As I reflected again, I realized that I had changed as much as the library. No longer did I fear the entry to the library, but I actually looked forward to the enjoyment it contained! At the start of language skills the confidence was not there to accomplish this. Now it's just natural.

Libby showed how she is literate about the library and about her own self-confidence. She has achieved success in an area of her life that until then she had felt uncomfortable.

In another piece, Bill McKenna wrote about a language not his first language but that of his grandmother. Bill's tone and feeling spoke to each of us, even those having only heard English since birth.

Language

Cultus, schklep, camoot, these are a few words of a language that has been lost to me and my family. My maternal grandmother was a respected elder of the Hat Creek Band, members of the Shushwap People. Alice Yerxi passed away when I was very young, and I treasure my memories of a weathered looking but beautiful woman who always had time for a small boy. She would talk to me for hours, about our family and would tell her favorite stories always using those wonderful but hard to understand words. After Grandma was gone I never heard anyone speaking our language. The importance of our heritage seemed to be lost in the business of life. To have and to be able to pass on the knowledge and history of our language to my children would fill the emptiness I now feel. I'm lucky that a few distant friends still know our language. At every opportunity I talk to them, to learn what I can.

This is a beautiful introduction to cultural and family perspective. And, again, writing is shown informing the writer.

The Workplace Hazardous Materials Information Systems training seldom excites employees. At best, it motivates people to be more aware of safety issues and more competent in working with dangerous materials. The following gives us opportunity to see the surprising way a coworker viewed it through less than bureaucratic eyes:

Workplace: I hear there's work going on in this place. Whoever spread that foul rumour is out of here.

Hazardous: Check out the hazards on the main floor Secretarial Pool. Whiplash and eye strain.

Material: The "material" on the dietary wagons is very colourful; and take the '60s groovy threads the patients are wearing. Some nice material there, too.

Information: Have you ever wondered why staff get the information before supervisors? A while back there was a demonstration, high speed buffing machine for cleaners to try out. This was a very nice machine: lightweight, fold down handle, 2000rmp vacuum for picking up dust off the pad. After about ten minutes of operation I was winging tiles off the floor at 2000 rmp. After pulling up the handle I saw a metal panel with "Operation Instructions." Before operating, read manual. I guess you have to buy the machine to get the manual.

Systems: The institution here has miles of different systems. Phone, water, heating, etc. Explanation of these systems is complicated, taking years of schooling to understand theory and practical application. To me the bottom line is if one of these systems breaks down you're knee deep in "shit."

The result of these early workplace language groups at the BCBC River-view Hospital site, Victoria Head Office site, and Prince George site was the introduction of viewpoints from across the corporation and from across the job strata. The corporation realized it had much to learn from its employees, and both parties started to trust what they could learn from each other.

Although it is difficult to describe the day-to-day work of the employees attending workplace language groups at various BCBC sites (Victoria, Prince George; Woodlands, and Riverview), the following excerpts from the different locations give some idea of what employees thought and wrote about. This was a long process of discovery about personal literacy, about work, and about meaning. Much of this thinking shows up later more re-fined in the ordinary thoughts and acts of diversity sessions.

Libby McAusland, property analyst, wrote in the fall of 1993:

> I finally admitted to myself it was time to work on my literacy skills. I'm not placing blame. In the school system I was educated in phonics was considered unimportant and was left out of the program. My punctuation is okay, not great. My sentence structure and spelling are appalling. I admire people with an even balance of all communication skills. It's mainly up to me. I'm exploring my weaknesses. The challenge is small compared to the one of admitting my problem which isn't going to go away on its own.

Laundry worker, Arne Pitkanen, wanted to improve his occupational standing. He didn't like courses and there was not any certificate for attending the workplace language groups.

> Courses, courses, courses, how many more courses do I take? This language course will help me. This Thursday is my day off and I will come in for 3 hours because of the benefits.

John, a cleaner, wrote:

> When I see negative corrections on my paper, it does not enhance my already poor opinion of my own writing. In this situation, my first day at the program, everything becomes different and in another perspective. What I do right is en-couraged and this gives me a positive thought to build more and more con-structive ideas upon.

And, he clearly answered the question, "How do I see myself through the corrections and revisions of others?"

Throughout the workplace, at all sites, and from participants and non-participants in the language groups, all employees said they wanted to be treated respectfully and fairly. John Isberg cautioned those of us having heavy pencils wanting to remake his thoughts into ours. In a companion piece he wrote:

Over coffee this morning, Bobby, my workmate, said, "Write about co-operation and consideration." "I'll try," I said.

Cooperation is how we deal with other people; consideration is how we feel about those people. . . . The important thing in all this is that co-operation and consideration always reverts back to the individual. Every individual has to be willing to bend a little to achieve the common betterment. How is this achieved? Look inside. Have you cultivated feelings that tell what is right or wrong? We must learn to act on what we feel is right for the betterment of ourselves, the other person, the group or the community. Why not give it a try!

Sometimes during discussions about important issues, those taking part lose sight of what is essential, getting sidetracked by considerations taken into their arguments without having any clues as to why they are doing so. John's thinking is straightforward. His authority probably comes from his position of awareness of self-power and not from appointed or entitled power. John also has pointed to the direction in which language training would move.

PLAYING THE GAME TOGETHER

Recognizing the benefits of the language sessions over a few years, BCBC undertook an optional strategy for developing and delivering training by welcoming and understanding diversity issues in early 1994. The first diversity sessions centered around conventional approaches. The initial training sessions given throughout the corporation had for objectives the raising of employee awareness about the history of human rights legislation around issues of diversity.

The second sessions given throughout the corporation engaged employees in various role-play scenarios, most often involving a "critical incident." Over several months BCBC completed much of this training. What became apparent early on was how the anticipated outcomes for change in employee behavior failed to manifest itself. In some instances, reports of incidents of harassment, discrimination, and racism increased. Although fairly insignificant in numbers, and expected, it was disturbing all the same to see an increase in complaints after training.

Challenged to achieve diversity training, BCBC considered how it could help employees accept corporate policy and provincial legislation without its workforce feeling like it was being forced to take a bad, unknown medicine. The direction to take became clear when the organization identified how diversity shared many of the same characteristics as literacy. This clarification of common characteristics showed the people charged with delivering diversity training how it might be more successful to tackle diversity issues more as issues of literacy, using the framework of language training.

For BCBC, diversity training now eased seamlessly into diversity work, comfortably engaged in emergent strategies that took into consideration the personal literacy of BCBC employees.

By accident or design, the language groups built the foundations on which BCBC could now strengthen the framework of its diversity initiatives. A few lines here describe the shape of diversity training at this point in the evolving literate corporation.

The mix of work culture and individual history reflected in the BCBC employee pool provided a valuable resource from which to draw to move from diversity training to diversity work. This indigenous resource was used to support the notion that literacy is about making connections, and the connections to be made need to be grounded in the immediate and historical lives of learners. Seen from this perspective, the substance of diversity training is the life experiences of employees. Learners were asked to become aware of how their experience connected to diversity policy and human rights legislation. An added dimension essential to this learning included using voices from literature and nonfiction to supplement the voices of experience with which employees could make connections, which, in turn, raised their depth of awareness of social and personal racism, discrimination, equity, and harassment.

The writing of personal historical experience and the reading of literature and nonfiction by employees posed real issues of congruency for many BCBC employees. When this happened employees engaged in critical thinking about personal acts of discrimination, racism, and so on, and about individual accountability. At the discussion level, employees faced not only their own stories around the issues but the stories of other writers who had struggled with the same issues. For the first time in BCBC diversity workshops, employees had the opportunity to write and talk about personal experience with issues rather than responding to an agenda prepared by workshop facilitators. In these participatory workshops, diversity issues took on genuine shape and meaning, not impression, vague thought, or fleeting observation. In this instance, over 2 days employees could truly ask themselves, "What do I really think about racism and why?" and answer it based on personal experience. This is the most important thing, this way of seeing who we are by thinking about it and then writing. This process, in some instances, brought about a resurgence of employee attention, commitment, and vigorous action to diversity issues. For many, this bringing together of private story and public literature built a collaboration of support and understanding.

In the diversity training it is important that employees make a commitment to individual growth and development with an understanding of the importance of how corporate culture and community culture influence employee processes. In the workplace language groups, employees learned how to talk about collaboration and shared goals. Individual literacy growth and acquisition of diversity perspectives by employees in these groups brought about significant change in the overall corporate culture. The experience of change coupled with that of talking things through helped employees engage in diversity training, which focused on personal incidents of inclusion and exclusion. As well, employees through discussion and writing identified simple acts they could undertake to bring about change in racism, discrimination, employment equity, and harassment in the workplace, at home, and in their communities.

One way to get a picture of the diversity workshops is to look at comments by participants:

> Most participants liked the open and comfortable atmosphere of the meetings, left feeling informed and thought the facilitator instructed the workshop.

> It was great to be a part of the training and to get a better understanding of diversity. Also, I feel more comfortable and more involved after sharing information about myself and committing myself to this.

> The facilitator was knowledgeable, easy going and shared like the rest of us.

> Introductions were a highlight because there was no time limit. People really shared how they felt about the issues and this meant so much more than "Hi, I'm Warren."

> It was wonderful to use current, real life and real work issues.

> We drew many conclusions about how we understand and don't understand each other at work and in the community.

> The process was very human because all of us participated by speaking and sharing our writing.

> I like the facilitator's idea of franchising diversity, but he could be right out to lunch here.

Certainly not everyone agreed with the facilitator.

Some participants' comments questioned the workshop structure, then realized their engagement with issues had determined the structure:

> And, the facilitator helped us to draw specific examples and ideas together to make sense of our different experiences and values.

The comments helped all of us who were a part of the diversity workshops to make sense out of the interaction of policy, personal experience, and societal expectations in the workplace. It also showed how employees use experience and their personal literacy to solve issues and problems in the workplace when trusted to do so.

Some commented they would have liked more case studies, others suggested a text book, and some would have liked a strictly timed format. One thought, "A more entertaining facilitator." Another felt a warm-up class was needed.

Many of the comments show the agreements and conflicts experienced when people get together to build meaning from words. In this instance, the words came from BCBC policy, human rights legislation, and personal experience. The personal experience broadened the language base on which participants needed to conceptualize experience and meaning, whereas policy and legislative language narrowed the possibilities for thinking.

Congruency, unlike assimilation by choice, invites employees to participate actively in training that allows personal choice of movement between noncongruent positions. To illustrate, the corporate policy stated employees could not harass each other without expecting consequences. In writing personal experience, employees could identify where they were in relation to policy. If the employees' position was not congruent with the expectations of company policy or the laws of human rights legislation, they had to face some choices. Much like congruency in triangles, employees can place their experience and personal behavior like an overlay on the policy or law and choose to adjust toward congruency. This adjustment can take place in small behavioral changes with an identified outcome determined in advance, or it can be accomplished quickly. This becoming congruent was purposeful and comprehensible to the corporation and its employees. It was the framework for giving voice and achievement to what for many was only the empty rhetoric of training for training without connection to the lives of those who would and who have brought change to their worksites.

In taking personal inventory of how they are or are not congruent with societal expectations, employees gain a clearer picture of how they fit into the world where they live. The writing and reading about issues of diversity helped BCBC to see how it fits into the communities where it works.

Over time this raising of awareness, this building responsibility and accountability for personal and corporate literacy as a means to improve working and personal life became inclusive in that these new literacies of others' issues challenged all employees to find ways to bring others into their corporate or personal world, or to take individuals and corporations beyond their recognized boundaries.

WHO ARE THESE NEW PEOPLE AT OUR GAME

To further develop and build on its commitment to diversity issues, BCBC began to explore ways to introduce a concrete model of diversity to its employees. Discussion started on what a specialized model would look like. At first, discussion focused on what would be the targeted populations and whether this diversity initiative would consider only groups identifiable as diverse.

Recognizing the need to enlarge notions around inclusivity, the discussion participants decided to target youth at risk, which takes in a cross-section of youth, thereby preventing ghettoization and, consequently, strengthening project participants by showing diversity in youth experience. This move toward a stronger model of inclusiveness was viewed as diversity plus.

A few common threads running through the discussions were corporate commitment to the initiative; the desirability of building an initiative that considered the needs people have around work, that is, physical condition, lifestyle, literacy, and numeracy skills; the critical function of the kinds of work to be developed for program participants; and how this initiative could, if successful, sustain itself. The thrust of this initiative was to develop a diversity strategy that used job creation for youth to put into practice some of the concepts that support and sustain the leadership role imbedded in the BCBC organization.

This suggests as well as confirms the fundamental changing role of organizations, be they public or private. The nurturing of the status quo within the organization may feel comfortable, but it will not nurture the organization or ensure its long-term success. The new benchmark of successful organizations will be determined by their ability to innovate and increase effectiveness.

Many corporations perceive change to mean, "We're not doing it right," and many employees perceive change to mean, "I'm not doing it right." Change is a process as is culture. Change in workplace culture is not an isolated event or setting because it exists within the larger contexts of community, nation, and world. As such, it invites us to remove the temporary threats of failure and success, right and wrong.

Within the corporation, many influences inhibit and enable change. Together, these two qualities determine readiness. Readiness is crucial to success. BCBC at the beginning of what came to be known as the "Generation Y" project was ready to bring something different into its work culture that might effect some change in corporate and employee behavior and attitude.

As the following demonstrates, it is the people, in all cases, within the corporation who give leadership. In leadership, and indeed in most decisions about implementing change, the direction of the change reflects the thinking of the person or people behind it. Grant Close spoke outside of the usual human resource management parameters:

> I see a lot of applications for the jobs we have at BCBC. In fact, I can hire from the cream for any job posted. However, I have concerns about those youth who don't fit into this pattern of achievement and success. I wonder how

youth with bad histories, few skills and fewer contacts will gain access, if ever, to a mainstream work environment. This is some of my thinking around the proposed Generation "Y" project.

In sum, corporations as well as their employees learn by talking about ideas. BCBC talked within its walls until it discovered what it wanted to do with its diversity learning. Overall, it focused on how to bring different people into the corporation for a time in a way that reflected BCBC's values, beliefs, and processes. This focus showed how the present framework supported the corporation, and it was agreed that this framework could serve as the structure for the Generation Y project.

This discussion process also brought to light not only how to organize the project, but also when and why particular strategies for participant success should be applied. To be most effective, the project needed to draw on the information about work that BCBC had on hand. In this exploration and discovery process to find the direction to take with diversity, BCBC was being instructed within the process. Generation Y is not the corporation's ultimate goal; it is one goal along the continuum of literacy.

WHERE IS THIS GAME GOING?

BCBC sought to create an employment and learning program for at-risk youth. This objective was important to the corporation; therefore, several discussions followed that drew on the collective experience of staff having much interaction in real-world business.

Before the first session of the Generation Y project, BCBC did not have a model. To get started it had to have a detailed plan because it was important to all parties to make the project work, especially because the project represented exploration into and commitment to uncharted territory.

As a name for this diversity and employment project, Generation Y began as a fun description. Now, after 5 years, the Generation Y project holds a solid position in the minds of BCBC staff.

To start, the most important step was to contact and inform groups working with youth about Generation Y. Working with BCBC, we reached as many people as possible, all the while trying to explain as clearly as possible that BCBC wanted youth at risk because it wished to bring diversity into the corporation and it wanted to extend opportunity, in the form of real work, to people who for the most part would not get such an offer. In the end, we interviewed 16 youth for 10 positions.

Learning throughout the first session, we found the need to limit the number of organizations we contacted. Several attempts were needed to find a way to bring the youth we wanted into the program. However, by the second session, using focused face-to-face meetings with people working with at-risk youth and drawing on what was learned in the first session, the Generation Y project finally started working as planned.

The on-site work aspects of the Generation Y program meets all conditions and expectations of what participants can expect to find in other workplaces with other employers. It has a 35-hour work week, with days starting at 7:30 a.m. and ending at 3:00 p.m. Unlike in many job-creation schemes, the work of Generation Y participants is real work. There is a 3-day work component on work generally performed by the corporation. These 3 days are spent as part of the BCBC workforce in gardening, recycling or heating, or ventilation and air conditioning. The youth work as part of a crew, experiencing cooperation and teamwork in real work situation with the support and guidance of BCBC coworkers, supervisors, and managers. BCBC staff acknowledge the importance of the work and recognize the efforts of these new faces in the organization. In addition, 2 days are spent in the classroom to learn how to develop and use strategies to deal with personal and workplace issues. For example, many of these youth have never obtained or been able to hold a steady job because of an inability to consult and negotiate with authority figures. The classroom sessions give them opportunity to discuss options and appropriate behavior with peers, supervisors, and instructors.

Toward the end of the first year—with the project beginning to look like a project, with much support from all involved staff, and with most participants working well—BCBC staff could see where the language, diversity, and job creation initiatives were going. The general thought behind Generation Y shaped up in this way: design Generation Y to address an increasingly pervasive social challenge; provide employment for youth between 16 and 31 who are at risk of never being fully employed because of difficulties they have had early in life with issues such as substance abuse, parental abandonment, dropping out, trouble with the law, and so on; and attempt to help at-risk youth, often so-called "street kids," acquire the skills and confidence necessary to integrate into the workforce and the community. Then, give these youth a program that addresses their learning and financial needs.

Simply, as a practical application, BCBC invited some at-risk-youth to discuss how they might fit into the BCBC work culture. From this point, this collaboration at partnering brought people together to participate in working and learning processes. As well, staff expected participants to develop integrative skills and to function in systems (composed of people, equipment, timelines, regulations, administrative functions, goals, etc.). This expectation guided participants to develop the transferable, generic skills needed for most jobs, regardless of their application. Along with the notion of integration, these new employees learned to make distinctions between reading for knowing and reading for doing.

Helping youth make all or most of these connections helps them visualize change in their attitudes and performances. These connections speak to the hearts of learners when learners connect the idea, problem, or experience to their life experience. This strategy helps learners bridge their understanding of personal experience to more formalized learning.

How much we try to control, intervene in, and time manage change is a critical concern for the facilitator. If instructors or facilitators control the discussion or change, they soon acquire ownership. To intervene in discussion and change is to police and take away personal responsibility and authority over others' actions and life. To manage the discussion period or change distorts the process, denying participants the time to think problems through and thus denying the youth at risk the opportunity to discover the answers to problems such as taking responsibility, being accountable, effecting personal change, and building self-esteem. Often, resolution around these issues is contrived and artificially constructed by teachers who wittingly or unwittingly corrupt personal learning processes. Much of what happens in discussions and change depends on how we see ourselves as people, then teachers.

NOTHING EXISTS ALONE

Generation Y as a project calls on the strengths of many within the organization. For the participants, the project asks that they be willing to put forward all they have to give to make themselves, and the project, successful. To fully participate, BCBC staff and Generation Y participants must engage the notion that work and daily life are linked together. Obviously, it is difficult to accommodate all the disrupting personal issues and behaviors in the workplace; however, this recognition of the links that make up individuals is crucial to implementing and making Generation Y, and participants, successful. As the following discussion demonstrates, participants have knowledge and insight into issues in ways that are often overlooked in teaching efforts to find causes for unresolved issues and unacceptable behaviors.

The learning (literacy) needed here for the Generation Y person is taking ownership of personal responsibility and identifying areas for taking responsibility. Mostly, they learn there is a difference in how they feel about being responsible when it is of their own choosing and not imposed by external authority. Once this is worked through in oral and written ways, participants can begin to see how personal responsibility transfers to the requirements of the workplace. This process differs for all Generation Y individuals because each has rejected responsibility for his or her life in personal contexts.

People change as they begin to see why they rejected taking responsibility. This change is reflected in their workplace behavior such as punctuality, less absenteeism, more enthusiasm and motivation, increased engagement and interaction with coworkers, and greater self-esteem, bringing about usable and willing confidence. Like discipline, responsibility becomes less problematic when teachers have something to say that is connected to their learners' lives and young workers have opportunities to show personal acts of responsibility in ways that are visible and constructive.

For many Generation Y participants, writing represents "doing something for teachers." In time, youth and older workers come to see writing as the visual record of their thinking. When this happens writing is no longer a burdensome chore placed on individuals to please or satisfy a host of people or expectations. When writing undergoes this transformation within the minds of Generation Y participants, they quickly see it for the tool it is and use it to solve work and personal issues. Writing becomes a tool drawing attention to its many uses and allowing and requiring participants to try out this new tool, however they see fit.

Writing in many instances gives employees the opportunity to explore their thoughts, feelings, and actions. For some, their thoughts are acknowledged for the first time as beliefs or values that hold an important place in their everyday lives. Others discover through writing that their life has changed, improved, or taken a different turn. Writing, reading, and discussing these thoughts, feelings, and actions of employees, by employees, is a public way of recognizing how we are more alike than not, how we learn collaboratively when we share the process of learning, and how we are connected in our learning by powerful external forces such as the collective histories of our life cultures.

All of this writing falls into the area of literacy as it is generally defined. Because it is not teacher or employer directed, some educators see it as unfocused or not sufficiently specific to build, improve, or change employees' literacy skills.

What is evident at BCBC, be it the earlier language programs, the diversity workshops, or the Generation Y project, is that the participants clearly show their writing is being used to develop personal and work literacies that help each of them to function better at work while developing personal skills and realizing individual potential. Participants seem to be advancing their understanding of self, learning, work issues, societal structures, and expectations, and in doing so these individuals are taking responsible positions in their overall culture. Sometimes the position taken is tentative at best, but taken all the same; at other times it is strong and vibrant; and in some instances the position is steady.

One participant, Rob, wrote, "A few employees of BCBC consider members of the Generation Y program to be inexperienced, untrustworthy street punks who don't deserve equal treatment." However, David saw it differently, "My co-workers make me feel so at home. They have helped to raise my self-esteem. Not to mention they teach me something everyday." Together these two writers raise the issue of how clearly the workplace presents itself to newcomers. Have the staff changed in how they see the Generation Y workers?

As well, Vickie agreed with David, "I'm getting along well. I enjoy getting up every morning at 5 a.m. I'm going to work with people I like working with." On the other hand Brian, talking about other participants, was frustrated. "Our personalities clash. After trying to communicate and openly discussing our differences, we tend to solve our problems. At least for the time being."

Chris Somogyi joined Generation Y at its very beginning. In the 6 months he spent at BCBC he spoke of fighting, drugging and stealing. He also wrote several poems:"Tattoos," "My Dad," "Car Thief," "Mom," and "Slaughter of the Innocents"(Dunblane, Scotland). Chris showed how one young Canadian easily moved between criminal and mainstream culture, without reflecting on their differences or their influence on him. Chris wrote about daily concerns:

> In the beginning the class days were very monotonous. No one looked forward to coming. The work was dull, repetitive and made for children in grade 3. My point of view. Once the project was up and running there was more substance. Now Mondays and Fridays are our favourite days except for payday.

Looking back after 3 months of working and not missing one day, Caleb Henyu confidently confided to the reader,

> Since the start of work I've actually begun to save some cash in the bank, which is a first for me. What else is real cool too is that now we've got lots of food at our house, so now we don't gotta go to the food lines no more, which leaves more for everybody else there. Yup, nothing like an honest job.

An honest job is one purpose of the Generation Y project. Grant Close, the director of human resources, also wrote about sharing resources.

> These youth are not the people I usually see. It is important for us as a corporation to put something back into the community and to show these young people something positive about corporations.

Working in a corporation gives young people a strong internal structure that in most ways is not as yielding as school. This work structure is important to youth who do not have discipline or structure in their lives. In positive contexts, work gives meaning beyond service and product to all players.

Wayne Rothenberger, on-site human resources staff, said, "I see the youth working in all kinds of weather, see the blisters on their hands and I see them gardening and doing heavy work. It is not charity." In other words, from this manager's viewpoint, it is not conventional job creation.

Again, Grant said, "The work needed doing. We have social responsibility. However, and, most importantly, I've found that everyone who gets involved with the Generation 'Y' youth gets something back. Sometimes, even friendship; we've found this project is not as costly as not doing it."

The structure of the specific work, the structure of the social order, and the nature of relationships are all a part of the Generation Y work and learning environment.

Arif, a participant in the third Generation 'Y' session, said, "This is the longest I've done something other than prison time. I like hugs and smiles and knowing my family feels safe when I'm around."

Another participant, Jamie, found the foundation for personal change during the first month, saying, "I'd not dealt with important issues in my life. Here I went from nothing to what was important in six months. I feel much better."

Matthew, in the same session, said, "I needed something. I wore the same shirt and pants for 2 months. I passed 4 of 5 GED tests."

Talking about and listening to each other's experience, be it work or personal, requires taking the time writing about their lives. Actively reflecting on work and life experience demands levels of concentration few have in the beginning. Participants seem to acquire focus fairly quickly; then, the hard work of consulting together and singly to get the "right" meaning begins. Most employees in the BCBC language, diversity, and Generation Y projects show this effort to "make sense" of experience time and again.

And despite some very real problems with their past personal experience, Generation Y participants revisit it to discover meaning about their lives. Generally, participants who stay 6 months begin to see themselves moving beyond the context of their past attitudes and behaviors.

Although still shaggy in appearance, unruly in behavior, and less than well-trained to perform at command, the Generation Y project moves forward expectantly. What benefits it will bring to participants and the corporation over time is more measurable now than in the beginning; the costs are comparable to summer and co-op employment at BCBC and the other British Columbia Crown corporations. Tracking most participants to date and seeing what they are doing after leaving BCBC encourages BCBC to continue Generation Y.

By monitoring past participants' working lives, we are finding out that most have settled into mainstream employment or are continuing their schooling. Three have started landscape services in which they are succeeding. None has gone back to doing time in prison. One dropped out of a good job as a youth counselor and started using drugs again. Two participants work with youth services within the provincial government framework. So far the figures are a good sign that Generation Y is achieving what it set out to do.

Job creation possesses enough of both ambivalence and opacity to distort or destroy the most clearly planned objectives. In the Generation Y project as we've been looking over the individual Generation 'Y' outcomes at the midway and final weeks of each project, where everyone is anxious to know the degree of success, and just before the start-up of the next Generation Y project, we question again our assumptions, our questions, our observations, and, most important, our purpose for all of this.

Clear to everyone is the notion that it is a mistake to dismiss the experience of youth at risk, to ignore it as aberrant, and to exclude it from mainstream workplaces. Clearly, if employers have the means to bring these youth into their organization, if even only for a short time, the benefits will become obvious quickly.

The voices of these youth inform the workplace about people living in different cultures, with oppositional values to the mainstream; however, given time, these youth help themselves to much of what is good about work and workplaces. In doing so, they show that the real problem, and the continuing sickness for humanity, is individual and collective acts of exclusion.

From this formative and dynamic core of the Generation Y project, BCBC is preparing to begin another Generation Y in Victoria, British Columbia. It will be different from the one in Vancouver; it will grow and mature in predictable and unexpected ways. And, sometime, in a year or so, everyone involved in this new project will begin to see how little knowledge they really had to start, how much they truly have gained, and how these starting points are always the beginnings of emergent literacy for each person participating in projects of this kind.

INSTITUTIONS

11

Learning Democracy/Democratizing Learning: Participatory Graduate Education

Elena Bront de Avila
Theresa Caron
Patricia Anderson Flanagan
Denise Frer
Thomas Heaney
Nancy Hyland
Susan Kerstein
Christine Kowalski
Eugene Rinaldi
National-Louis University

All learning is a quest for greater participation. We each seek to name our world, to influence decisions that shape our lives, to speak with an audible and credible voice. Students, no less than their teachers, seek control over the educational milieu that brings them together. The agendas of students and their teachers are similar in many ways, perhaps in most ways, but there are differences as well, and therein lies the struggle for democracy in the classroom.

There is a strong tradition of democracy in adult education with historical roots in the writings of Lindeman (1961). But higher education is not adult education. However much well-intentioned faculty attempt to infuse their professorial roles with the best practices and principles of adult education, there remain systemic and cultural barriers to democracy embedded in academic discourse and practice.

This chapter is the story of one attempt to minimize the antidemocratic culture of higher education and maximize the democratic and participatory interplay between students and teachers in a doctoral program.

ADULT EDUCATION AND DEMOCRACY

Participation can mean marching to another's drum. That might satisfy the feet, but does not participation of the mind mean calling the tune? The highest order of participation involves both decision making and action. At its core, adult education is participatory in this latter sense, historically grounded in voluntary collaboration and democratic purpose.

Lindeman, a founder of the "adult education movement" in the United States during the 1920s, promoted adult education practice on the principle that democracy demands an informed public (Lindeman, 1961). Education is critical to the development of reasoned and shared decision making, especially for adults, who throughout their life struggle to participate in social and economic decisions affecting their lives. The effectiveness of widespread participation in decision making, such as democracy requires, demands ongoing and timely strategies for adults to reflect on and learn from their experiences and the experiences of others. For Lindeman, what distinguished adult education from other learning activities is that it is internal to the democratic struggle. Its absence leaves critical decisions in the hands of an educated elite, promotes a cult of experts, and erodes the democratic social order.

This vision of adult education practice inexorably linked to the project of democracy has frequently floundered on the shoals of expediency. Educators of adults have often been called to reproduce inequities, train people to acquiesce to the decisions of others, and adapt learners to the requirements of systems and institutions without question. These latter educators seek participation too; they seek learners who will march to another's drum.

PARTICIPATORY GRADUATE EDUCATION:
AN OXYMORON?

Almost 6 years ago, a group of adult education faculty at National-Louis University began to plan a new doctoral program that would, so they envisioned, reflect the critical edge of a democratic practice and embody adult education principles. There were then, and continue to be now, many ambiguities and possible contradictions in that vision. What happens to the themes of voluntary participation and democracy when transposed into an institution of "higher" learning? Can adult education, as a field of graduate study, find academic legitimacy in pedagogical forms that contradict its own practice? Or is a democratic practice of adult education possible within graduate programs that are increasingly the guardians at the gate of adult education discourse?

Without prejudging the answers to these difficult questions, the faculty realized that embedded within democratic practice there are always the contradictions of power and constraint and especially in a credentializing, academic program. Experiments in democracy are always circles within circles, subgroups within larger groups, tribes surrounded by warring nations, nations within a global political economy. In its purest sense—government by, with, and for the people—there can be no democracy until there is democracy for all. Which is to say that all experiments in democracy are a compromise. This is undoubtedly true in relation to a cohort of learners (which attempts to be self-governed) within a university (which, despite lip service to collegiality, too often does not).

Voices are never equal, even in a democracy. Assumptions of knowledge and skill are likely to determine influence and power, even within a self-governing cohort. The question here for faculty was the extent to which their own professorial voices would be privileged. And are there means by which the voice of students can be strengthened in negotiations with faculty over curriculum and academic policy?

For example, in this new program an attempt to democratize student evaluation was advanced in multiple opportunities for rewriting the many papers required within the curriculum. All writing is considered a draft, subject to frequent reviews by peers, as well as by faculty, and reworked on the basis of this critique. Nonetheless, some students perceived this rewriting as punitive, an instance of faculty exercising its privileged position by requiring additional work.

Although differences in opinion about outcomes persist at the university, the commitment to create an adult education doctorate consistent in its content and procedures with the democratic practice of adult education has been unwavering. If adult education as a field of practice is to reclaim its themes of voluntary participation and democracy, then adult education as a field of study must reinvent those processes by which adult educators are developed and nurtured. The challenges posed in the previous paragraphs, however, were a constant reminder in discussions among faculty and between faculty and students that democratic participation in graduate education is complex and fraught with difficulty. Whether the barriers to democracy in the graduate classroom are insurmountable remains to be seen.

THE PROGRAM BEGINS

In the summer of 1996, a cohort of 21 students and 6 faculty initiated their experiment in postsecondary education—a doctoral program in adult education that would be both participatory and democratic. At the center of its design is a Cohort Council, created and named by the students, which meets independently of the faculty and negotiates with faculty on matters of curriculum and policy. The participants represent the rural and urban United States, Canada, South America, and Eastern European countries, a cross-section of adult educators and practitioners who brought a legacy of personal, cultural, and social experiences. These adults have, over time, evidenced a unique mix of qualities that has enabled them to engage the perspectives of others and to live with ambiguity. One member of our group is an activist and educator from Chicago's Puerto Rican community; two are native Colombian educators. Another is a diplomat representing the cultural interests of Taiwan in the midwest. Yet another directs adult education for a provincial government in Canada and is active in revitalizing her nation's network of adult educators. Several work in a corporate setting, others work as academic administrators, one is in the federal medical domain, and another is in a state social welfare agency.

Our differences have been frequently brought to the surface in both written and verbal life histories, which we have freely shared. Our qualities of creativity, imagination, tolerance, respect, humor, passion, and skepticism are threads in the cloth that drape our bodies during this journey. Our time together has challenged us to build cross-cultural understanding through democratic processes in the hope that we might embody the "spirit of democracy" and support one another's transformation through learning. Our adventure is both professional and personal, demanding our collaborative engagement in fostering social change and reflecting our desire to not only improve individual practice but to significantly benefit the world through our critical exploration of "self."

Before the inaugural Summer Institute (June 1996), an earlier weekend seminar and interview were required for admission into the program. The intent of this "admissions" weekend was to mirror the collaborative, democratic process the program was hoped to achieve. Like democracy itself, the weekend proved to be replete with joy, hope, anxiety, silence, voice, and struggle. At times it appeared the balance of power in this higher education program could be equalized; at other times, especially during the personal interview, it was impossible to escape the power that faculty wielded, despite their democratic assurances. Students were formally interrogated by a panel of at least two professors whose mode of questioning left some students confused and fearful, their experience being far different from the solidarity established between students and faculty on the weekend.

This issue of faculty power was frequently heard in the critique by some students who sought greater involvement in the planning of each syllabus. Promotional material for the program stated that the roles of student and faculty would gradually converge. At the beginning, however, each syllabus was presented, usually a month before the class began, but with little opportunity for students to comprehend, much less deliberate on alternatives. The faculty responded to early demands for full participation in the preparation of syllabi with an appeal to the logistics of planning, which took place months in advance. "How can students plan a course without first knowing its content?" the faculty asked. "But how can the students participate in defining their own learning without such participation?" students countered. Both activities and assignments were regularly negotiated between students and faculty. Students saw their positions reflected in the curriculum, but the broader issue of who defines the core—the parameters within which activities and assignments are determined—remained unresolved until the program's third year, at which time the role of faculty and student did in fact converge.

The willingness of faculty to acknowledge this power imbalance was first evidenced at the inaugural Summer Institute. Faculty proposed that the students organize a "steering committee," its function being to allow students to strengthen their collective voice and provide a vehicle for ongoing dialogue between cohort and faculty. This structure had been suggested by the work of Shor in his efforts to negotiate power with students at the City University of New York (Shor, 1996). The faculty asked students to discuss this proposal on their own without the faculty present.

The students collectively and almost unanimously decided that representation of the whole group by a few members on a steering committee did not sufficiently represent the students' voices. No one wished to be left out of the decision-making process. Each student preferred to be fully engaged in the dialogue and subsequent reporting of results directly to the faculty in the form of recommendations, requests, and collective decisions.

One of the first democratic decisions made by the students was to be called the Cohort Council rather than a steering committee. The birth of the Cohort Council would, in the student view, better foster democratic processes. At very least it would provide a mechanism where potentially all voices could be heard by the faculty. This has been especially important when the council's views have been divided and students have been unable to reach a unanimous collective agreement. The Cohort Council allows that all voices be heard with anonymity unless an individual wishes his or her personal view to be disclosed.

The creation of the Cohort Council has been appealing in concept but difficult in practice. Some members chose to set themselves outside its structure and, although they had the individual right to do so, they disturbed the maturation process of the fledgling council. Furthermore, the withdrawal of a few led some members of the cohort to distrust the intentions of these self-proclaimed "outsiders." As novices in democracy, a few were quick to impute motives, to confuse judgments with observations—in short, to exhibit the usual factors that plague collaboration and participation. In retrospect, the decision by a few to withdraw from the council has limited the potential for each member of the cohort to fully experience democracy and the deconstruction of power with each other and ultimately with the faculty.

STRENGTH IN DIVERSITY

And so, with the formation of the Cohort Council, the journey for learning began. What was it that could bring 21 people from a multiplicity of careers and backgrounds—people with varying agendas and political commitments—to one place in which they would delve deeply into themselves and their practices? The answer at first glance may appear to be the prestige and market value of a doctoral degree, but it is much more complicated than that; it involves a willingness to reexamine the commitments underlying our practice and a common desire to better understand who we are and what we are capable of becoming. It is less a securing of professional status and more an opening of one's self to the responsibilities of a vocation (Collins, 1991).

In the second semester the students divided into subgroups to critically analyze several theoretical frames for looking at adult education practice. One group examined the "learning organization," another "perspective transformation." A third group undertook a study of "adult education for social change" spanning the United States and Canada. Within a few short months, the perspectives of several students in each of these groups turned 180 degrees. Their self-understanding and their vision of who they were becoming had to be rewritten.

For those transformed by the process of learning, the aim of their collaboration has not been the proclamation of diversity, but discovery of commitments that unite. Whether we find ourselves in a corporate environment influenced by expectations of profit and systemic efficiency, in an educational environment surrounded by demands for standardization and objective outcomes, or in a community service environment frustrated by a diversity of needs and the lack of funding to address them, we have discovered much in common. The fact that we are racially and ethnically diverse, that geographically we represent both rural and urban experience, and that politically we include the bureaucrat and the activist, adds to the common experience as opposed to lessening it. As Brookfield (1987, p. 87) stated, "True education is a social process" and we have begun our engagement with this process by creating our own collective learning community. Ultimately, the program is about citizenship and our role in the lifeworld, finding the socially redeeming merit in our practice. As stated by Boggs (1991, p. 46), "Clearly, the education that is necessary to successfully fulfill the rights and obligations of citizenship should not be left to chance."

STRUGGLING FOR DEMOCRACY

Ultimately, the program design is about democratic practice and our role of nurturing democracy in a world marked by unequal relations of power, conflict, and systemic barriers to choice. In our program, which has embedded in it all the contradictions of the lifeworld, we have been united in the exploration and testing of borders. The Cohort Council has increasingly been united in testing its power over faculty and over university policies, confronting the faculty—a counterforce—who band together, at times, to protect pedagogical elements they perceive to be central to the program. For example, the council pushed for a relaxation of attendance requirements to the point of making classes optional, whereas the faculty defended our already infrequent meetings as critical to collaborative learning. Our lifeworld in this program is not simply given; it is the subject of constant negotiation and struggle in the face of relations of power, which are systemically unequal. As a site of democratic practice, the university is ultimately flawed. But in this, the university is no more flawed than the greater society. Democracy is always exercised in the midst of struggle and conflict, and in the face of power.

Our program responds to this challenge through its intent and frequently—at times, painfully—through its practice. Critical reflection is foundational to this practice. Many hours of class time, small and large peer meetings, and consultations with and among faculty have been committed to negotiating areas of disagreement and attempting to work within and around faculty power. At the beginning, faculty naively assumed they could easily forego their power and privilege, ceding to a collective process of decision making that included students as full participants. In many instances this has been possible, but not in all. It is the exceptions, of course, that claim the greatest attention and energy of the cohort.

For example, as we approached the final year of the program, the Cohort Council was invited to compile issues and themes for the third Summer Institute. The faculty team assigned to the institute worked with these recommendations and incorporated all of them in a draft syllabus, all except one that required all faculty advisors be present on the Chicago campus. It was impossible to meet this request in that half the faculty was assigned to a second doctoral cohort at another site almost 100 miles distant. Logistics not withstanding, acrimony and expressions of frustration from a few students continued for weeks.

Although a few students have experienced the Cohort Council's inability to effect every one of its decisions as a breakdown of democracy, others have recognized that compromise among competing interests is a characteristic of democratic practice. Through moments of tension we collectively and individually have become aware of not only the process in which we were engaged, but also the role each was expected to play and the influence each of us had on the other. The interdependence between program and lifeworld is manifested in our understanding of the factors that support and destroy democratic participation. In our quest for democratic participation, students and faculty press forward, making the road by walking it, one weekend session at a time; enduring frustration at times; and building on what we have learned and what we have achieved.

EVOLVING WORLDVIEW AND PARTICIPATION

Coming together as teachers and learners, we each brought our worldview, our meanings about participation and democracy, meanings forged in the traditions of family, the university, and local and global political structures. For some of us, participation and democracy were words that once inspired, but were now void of meaning. The systems that shape and, at times, determine our worldview often inhibit the challenge and possibility of democracy. So we came together, some in disbelief, some skeptical, most of us unaware that in this time and space—in our cohort—democratic participation was to be taken seriously and was to be a conscious and persistent component within the program that might transform our understandings of the possible.

The cohort has been a new dance. Not knowing the steps, we stretched the limits of our humanity and opened our minds to unknown nuances of democratic participation. We took its lived definition and meanings; we compared, contrasted, and acted toward it; and we translated it to our new reality. The Cohort Council has functioned without a formal structure and without any defined leadership roles. Agenda setting and decision making have been everyone's responsibility and nobody's. Agendas tend to form around individual self-interest and it is not unusual for a decision of the council to reflect the will of only one or two members. In addition, we have been not one, but two democracies: the Cohort Council and the faculty. Each group tries to make decisions democratically. That some of those decisions affect the other group, which has not been involved in the decision making, has been a source of frequent frustration. Although our commitment to negotiate our differences has lessened the domination of one group over the other, it has not eliminated conflict.

Interpretations became more intricate when we, as worldviewers, came in contact with each other's meanings through the sometimes tumultuous debates of the Cohort Council. Not all disagreements are between students and faculty. There have been frequent disagreements within the council, and some students claim their voices are consistently ignored in that forum. To know about the possibilities of democratic participation we have to participate democratically. Democracy has become both the content and the process of our learning. Each of us has the opportunity and responsibility to raise a voice on rules, regulations, structures, and procedures of the doctoral program. We observe and learn from our own interventions, and we risk the possible negative reactions of our peers to those interventions.

The possibility to raise our voice and critically reflect has developed our capacity to become conscious of ways our worldview is reflected in our practice and in our lives. Personal meanings have been transformed and new frameworks of understanding created. Although it has been difficult to identify and clarify power issues or to stay the path, the Cohort Council and negotiations with faculty have placed democratic participation on center stage, pushing us to expand limited worldviews with which we came and re-think our relationships with each other and with the world. Faculty power is clear when it is invoked. The power exercised by students is more subtle, as when the council, speaking with one voice, collectively withholds consent and limits faculty's power to act. Occasionally, scheduled units of coursework have been preempted by the persistent demands of council re-negotiations.

COLLECTIVE LEARNING

It is easy to espouse a theory of democratic participation; it is more difficult to live it. At risk in the practice of democracy is not only the dissolution of the individual in a collective decision, but faith in and commitment to de-mocracy itself. It is only through collaboration that we can provide a coher-ent narrative of democratic participation, but as we discovered, collabora-tion is never free from individual values and attitudes; the latter are framed by multiple realities present in our worldviews. Collaboration does not im-ply personal control over the situation but an openness to transact, ex-change, and become exposed to change.

The variety of human worldviews brought to our doctoral program has not threatened democratic participation. Both students and faculty came with divergent perspectives on the meaning of collaboration. Our doctoral program exposed us to startling impetuosity, to regimes of communication and power much different from what many of us had previously experi-enced. We learned that collaboration cannot endure much human abuse, and collaboration is not chaos in which anything goes and each person is free to act out without thought of others.

Some students and a few faculty have felt alienated by the tensions con-sequent to our differences. When students expressed their discomfort with conditions on the Chicago campus by issuing an ultimatum that they would no longer meet there, the faculty-director of the program was angered that no attempt had been made to negotiate a resolution of difficulties, which both faculty and students admitted existed. At another time, students, having negotiated a plan of action with one group of faculty concerning the meeting time of the Cohort Council, expressed anger and frustration that another faculty team, which did not know of the prior agreement, recommended changing the meeting time. Yes, we learned that democratic participation demands collaboration, but also that collaboration needs respect, flexibility, and timing to survive.

We also learned that the melding of diverse points of view in democratic decision making requires critical reflection, an intellectual and emotional exercise unfamiliar to some. If democratic participation is to be lived as an ongoing struggle for a never-to-be-attained ideal, a deeper understanding concerning what the process entails, its characteristics and benchmarks, is necessary. This is possible only through critical reflection. Critical reflection implies contemplating and openly discussing individual quests, inquietudes, assumptions, and identifying their consequences on our actions. Critical reflection cannot take place ignoring the universe of preconceptions and expectations, the visions and commitments that each of us brought to the program. We have learned that individuals engaging in critical reflection can understand and support democratic participation; they can live with its compromises and endure its sacrifices. Those unable to engage in critical reflection have been far more likely to miss the subtlety of the process, less likely to have patience with time-consuming deliberations or to be accepting of outcomes that fall short of their own aims.

At the beginning of this journey, students participated in collaborative projects. From this first step, most continued onto productive and creative problem solving by employing the principles of critique and active participation. They became communities of interested persons actively participating in cooperative inquiry of epistemological questions and problems. These beginnings are framed in a deep level of personal commitment that flowered into fused personal relationships, creating solidarity that now sustains these students for the long haul. We have all come to realize we can energize our weary spirits both individually and collectively by sharing responsibility for our learning.

Our common struggle to identify a curriculum relevant to all might be an unrealizable "pie-in-the-sky" goal, but this goal, which requires negotiation between faculty and students, is not only emotionally and intellectually demanding. It is the ideal on which our practice as adult educators is fashioned. Teachers align themselves with learners to maintain a collegial environment by sharing, cooperating, and assisting in the learning experiences. At such times, students pursue the challenges of shared decision making. At other times, however, students find it easier to cede power to faculty, especially when faculty are perceived in a position to reject their academic work.

The faculty serve as relevant and productive adult educators by planning learning activities, negotiating subjects, discussing issues of differences openly, and respectfully challenging each others' viewpoints, while demonstrating respect for the work of all colleagues. Students see that critical discourse is possible and their lifeworld is not a singular universe. As a communication tool (and another attempt to reduce the imbalance between faculty and students) a Critical Incident Questionnaire (CIQ) has been used frequently. It is an anonymous evaluation form, the results of which are summarized and distributed to the entire cohort so that everyone can to keep a finger on the pulse of the group and know both its shared concerns and its differences.

Although at times an effective mechanism, systemic forces and personal interpretation occasionally thwart its potential to inform constructive and rational action. When faculty informed students that occasionally judgmental comments directed to individuals in the group had been omitted from summaries of the CIQ, many students were angered. To assure accurate and full reporting, including attacks on individuals, students thereafter assumed responsibility for compiling results of the CIQ.

The variety of cultures within our group keeps all of us outside our familiar comfort zones. We have learned that multiple and often contradictory voices must be heard, and that participation is painful. But in moving out of self into the larger world, new dimensions and layers of self are discovered, old biases are discarded, and both students and faculty aspire to transform narrow perspectives into a more expansive, holistic vision that respectfully includes everyone.

The cohort is continuously exploring and changing. Its voice becomes stronger through shared discovery and history. All are encouraged to speak, but some choose silence to make their statement. Each member is strongest by balancing the power needed for his or her role within the group against the power ceded to others. At this time, one can be certain that participatory education, lived in a tradition of democratic practice, continues to challenge students and faculty to pursue the mission of adult education and dream of wisdom.

BARRIERS TO DEMOCRACY

In the pursuit of wisdom, there are restraints and limitations, especially in our attempt to develop a democratic process within the academic environment. Some of the barriers that hinder the democratic process are also, in another way, strengths. These barriers and strengths are diversity of cultures, ethnicity, language, race, communication, learning style, and age. The more obvious barriers are programmatic, geographic, and power differentials. They become barriers when miscommunication occurs between the speaker and the listener, causing tension, anger, and loss of trust.

A particularly painful example of a breakdown of trust occurred in a conflict over the scheduling of classes. The university calendar, published in advance of the program, called for students to meet the second weekend 8 months during the year and the first 2 weeks in June. Unfortunately, two of the scheduled meeting dates fell on the holiest days of the Jewish year, Rosh Hashanah and Yom Kippur. A Jewish student brought this to the attention of faculty and learned the published schedule could be changed only if the cohort could agree to an alternative date.

When presented to the Cohort Council, some students stated that this only affected one student and that everyone's time was being wasted in discussing the problem. Others stated that the program could not be expected to accommodate every minority group's religious needs. After lengthy discussion, the council agreed in principle to reschedule the class, but no alternative date was proposed. Months later, several students had already made commitments based on the original calendar. The published schedule prevailed and the class met on the Yom Kippur weekend.

During the second year, the same lockstep "every second weekend" schedule resulted in classes being scheduled not only on Friday evening of Jewish Passover, but on Good Friday and Easter Sunday as well. Given our inability or unwillingness to adjust class time to the legitimately expressed religious concerns of one student, the Christian majority found itself stymied by its own precedents. How does one accommodate diversity issues such as this? More important, although we talk about sensitivity to diversity, when real issues arise we are forced to look back on a history of ignoring them or reducing them to individual problems.

A bitter lesson has been learned. Words that echo the importance of honoring the traditions of others have a hollow sound. Institutional inattentiveness to religious, ethnic, family, or racial values reflects insensitivity totally inconsistent with an espoused commitment to multiculturalism. The council's and the faculty's inability to remedy this inattentiveness is a reminder that in democratic participation, words have no power or meaning unless paired with action.

Perhaps we are a first child of fledgling parents—bold, opinionated, but also insecure. We are easily embarrassed by our foibles, but proud to break away, frequently without reflecting on our clumsiness. At times, our newness permeates our exchanges and clouds our interactions. Issues that strike at the heart of our being—race, gender, age, religious convictions—have been before us, in our face, but just beyond reach. We are impatient with our status as beginners, but at the same time have recognized that it is only through painful years of growth and struggle that democracy is learned and practiced.

NEGOTIATING IN THE FACE OF POWER

Without doubt, the power differential between faculty and students remains a most formidable barrier to democratic participation. Who makes decisions and how are decisions made? Through the pass/no-grade system, faculty have the power to make major decisions affecting each student's status within the program. The faculty, despite their other roles and dispositions, are agents of a powerful institution that dispenses degrees and, through its academic departments, determines what knowledge and skills are required if one is to be recognized as a "doctor" within the field. Appeals to the demands of accrediting agencies and academic policy not withstanding, resistance to student-initiated change is deep seated in historical and political understandings of the university.

Given this presence of institutional power, embedded in the practice of faculty who are its agent, it is no wonder that students fear they are not being heard or understood. This results in some students withdrawing in silence and others increasing the decibels and frequency of their interventions within and outside the Cohort Council. Participation is difficult for all, a constant challenge demanding persistence and courage. At times, the compelling strength of personalities and learned behaviors from past educational experiences dominates dialogue, leaving us in competitive rivalry. At other times, despite these many barriers, a collective voice is spoken and heard. Traditions are rewritten, policies rethought, and democracy—in those wonderful moments—is more than merely a vision.

UNFINISHED BUSINESS

During the first Summer Institute both faculty and students engaged in critical reflection and explored ways of challenging one another without being judgmental, being critical of assumptions without impugning intentions or attacking individuals. This was modeled in an approach to dialogue in which we attended as much to process as we did to content, especially in the discussion of difficult issues such as race, gender, class, and culture. Because such discussions engender significant emotional responses, faculty provided and modeled in their own interaction strategies that insisted on both individual and group respect while engaging in critical discourse. The entire group adopted these strategies that first summer, expecting they would serve as an informal "code of discourse" throughout the program.

This expectation was frustrated, however, by a dilemma that emerged in the second semester. A faculty member whom students had met in the early days of their program, but who had been absent during most of the Summer Institute, returned to teach as a member of the faculty team in the fall. This faculty member, not having been part of the "strategy development" for critical discourse the previous semester, found himself subject to a "code" that conflicted with his disposition, temperament, and beliefs. A struggle over normative expectations in our day-to-day interactions ensued, and the presumptive authority of the dissenting faculty member held firm.

Each weekend session seemed to bring new emotional exchanges that escalated from disagreements on culture and the meanings of "respectful discourse" to issues of race, gender, and the power of individual faculty. The presence of this dynamic so early in the journey was detrimental to the intent of the program—democratic participation—and led to a virtual paralysis in authentic dialogue that all strove to attain, but that had suddenly become so elusive.

This critical incident early in our mutual history brought three questions to the foreground, each of which remains our unfinished business today. How can we, without agreed-upon rules of discourse to guide us, embrace one another in respect as coparticipants while informing our dialogue with challenge and critique? How can we develop such rules, or even common understanding, without compromising cultural and racial norms? Finally, how can we overcome the inequities imposed by faculty power?

Two years later, we find our intensive critical exchanges occasionally peppered with hurtful and judgmental comments, less so now, but occasional disrespect is more obvious as we mature in our understandings of democracy and see more clearly the ideal that eludes us. Recapturing a spirit of trust in open dialogue on issues of race, gender, class, and power remains painful. The cohort and faculty continue to seek out or create moments in which power is negotiated, but progress is slow. Windows of possibility are sometimes shut abruptly through inattention. It is small comfort that in most of our lifeworld the attempt to combine critical discourse with respectful collaboration is simply not attempted and therefore the frustrations we continue to experience in the cohort are absent.

Democratic participation requires energy and commitment. The presence of these qualities in both cohort and faculty is the minimal foundation on which the bridge between honest critique and mutual respect can be built. This bridge building is our unfinished business.

SOME EARLY CONCLUSIONS

We have come to understand that democracy is, in its purest form, unattainable. Our ability to influence decisions affecting our day-to-day life is frequently limited by the complexity of systems in which those decisions are made and the real or imagined need for expediency within those systems.

Furthermore, democratic communities such as we hope to build in our doctoral program are always enclaves within larger communities that are less participatory, less democratic. Any program founded on the promise of democratic participation is a challenge to those less participatory institutions of which it is part. On the borders of our democratic practice, at the point of interface with the university, it is the art of compromise, as much a source of frustration as it is of achievement, that is the lifeblood of our frequent and recurring negotiations.

Democracy is a pursuit, never a state of being. It is the gradual and persevering struggle to participate to the fullest extent of our abilities in decisions that affect us. Democratic practice always exists in the face of contradictions both from without and from within. From without, democracy is confronted by layers of nondemocratic practice. From within, it is confronted by our inability or our unwillingness to take responsibility for situations or comprehend the basis on which decisions are to be made.

As faculty and students engaged in a struggle for democracy, we have attempted through this chapter to summarize our personal reflections on our experiences—the pain as well as moments of exuberance. Indeed, the process of bringing words to these pages as a collaborative group of nine has been another vehicle for us to continue to clarify and expand our knowledge of both the possibilities and limitations of living democratically. Within the vulnerability of sharing our strengths and weaknesses, we challenge ourselves and our readers to persevere in a commitment to transform the world, democratically.

REFERENCES

Boggs, D. (1991). *Adult civic education*. Springfield: Charles C. Thomas.

Brookfield, S. (1987). *Developing critical thinkers: Challenging adults to explore alternative ways of thinking and acting*. San Francisco: Jossey-Bass.

Collins, M. (1991). *Adult education as vocation: A critical role for the adult educator*. London: Routledge.

Lindeman, E. (1961). *The meaning of adult education*. Montreal: Harvest House.

Shor, I. (1996). *When students have power: Negotiating authority in a critical pedagogy*. Chicago: The University of Chicago Press.

12

Possibilities for Participatory Education Through Prisoners' Own Educational Practices

Howard S. Davidson
University of Manitoba

> *The Archambault guys demand . . . that facilities be provided . . . for writing, producing and editing a paper, which is to be . . . produced by the prisoners, [and] is to be free of all censorship by the staff of the prison.*
>
> *To us, talking about education means talking about the chance to acquire an intellectual and practical formation that increases understanding and decreases alienation from things, from reality and from life. A step toward a liberated spirit.*
>
> *The Archambault guys demand . . . the immediate opening of a special class for illiterate prisoners. Other prisoners will run these classes . . . [and] there is to be no limit imposed on the number of prisoners who may take these courses.*
>
> (cited in Gosselin, 1982, pp. 191, 195)

The great difficulty one faces in writing about participatory education and prisoners is appearing to be impartial about crime and criminals. This is especially true today when fear of crime waves and support for "get tough on crime" politics has become so fashionable. An analysis of prisoners that does not presuppose a host of negative stereotypes is presumed to be romantic at best, certainly unrealistic, if not loathsome. The negative myths surrounding subordinate but not deviant groups (e.g., the working poor) are not so restrictive. But speak of prisoners—a word that connotes images of violence and manipulation (i.e., the "con")—and one assumes that social policies should carry some element of coerciveness. The tolerable limit of conventional debate is to argue that rehabilitative programs for prisoners should be more therapeutic than punitive. Any discussion that stretches this limit must first refute popular assumptions that policies for deviants are expected to be coercive and to involve sanctions, force, and even sterilization and death (Schneider & Ingram, 1993, p. 339). As if to address the subject of this chapter, Schneider and Ingram noted that deviant groups are "discouraged from organizing, and subjected to the authority of others—including experts—rather than helped to form their own self-regulatory organizations" (p. 339).

Thus, the opening passage to this chapter, which appeared in the manifesto of striking prisoners at Archambault Penitentiary (Quebec) in 1976, may appear pretentious to some and actually insolent to others. Yet demands such as these and their connection to a history of prisoners' own educational practices is the subject of this chapter.

Centering on these practices does not equate to dismissing individual responsibility for egocentric criminal acts, nor does it romanticize prisoners as primitive rebels. This chapter recognizes that becoming a prisoner is a process intimately connected to the social conditions that constitute what activities are defined by the modern state as criminal, who gets arrested for these activities, who is found guilty and sentenced to prison, and who gets recycled through the criminal justice system repeatedly until held indefinitely (Pfohl, 1985; Reiman, 1990). Juan Rivera (1995), cofounder of a prisoner-organized educational practice in New York, said that prisoners:

> reeducate themselves so that upon release they can take up their lives in a way that will benefit themselves and their communities.... [They] come to see that criminal behaviour is *not* harmful to the power structure, but that it is destructive to communities and the people who live in them, most of whom are Latino or black. (p. 160)

Attending to prisoners' organized practices does not presuppose that all prisoners want to engage in them. Contrary to popular belief, most prisoners are serving sentences of fewer than 3 months and are unlikely to organize participatory education. Among those serving longer sentences, many are disinterested in education and participate in schooling only because they are coerced into doing so; others are convinced the official curriculum is desirable, and in any case "that is how things are." Still others believe prisoners cannot learn anything constructive from other prisoners. Racism and fatalism are serious barriers (Rivera, 1995, p. 168). Tersely put, just as it is naive to assume that oppressed people everywhere are eagerly looking to organize democratic educational practices (Shor & Freire, 1987, pp. 24–30), it is no less credulous to assume that all prisoners identify with the demands of the Archambault guys and the participatory models discussed in this chapter. The focus here is on a minority of prisoners who do.

I argue that possibilities for participatory education do not exist within the constraints of officially sanctioned prison schools. Efforts in this direction have led to occasional, highly compromised practices that have been short lived and dependent on the commitments and good will of outsiders and prison officials (Baker, 1985; Boudin, 1993; Kasinsky, 1977; Murton, 1976). In contexts where people are labeled deficient and delinquent, and staff have an official mandate to rehabilitate (i.e., to normalize) them, participatory models do not grapple well with the asymmetrical power relations operating within and upon the setting. Therefore, instead of considering efforts to democratize prison schools, this chapter explores possibilities for participatory education outside these classrooms in prisoners' own educational practices, and it encourages outside educators (i.e., nonprisoners typically but not always working for prison schools) to form alliances with them.[1]

This exploration is based on a few published studies, many written by prisoners and former prisoners. In reviewing these accounts, I adopt the perspective of Cervero, Wilson, and others that program planning must be examined within the context of "historically developing and structurally organized relationships of power, which may either constrain or enable . . . [planners] to negotiate the interests of all people affected" (Cervero & Wilson, 1994, p. 5; Collins, 1991; Forester, 1993). In this case, I examine how these power relations have affected the social space in which prisoners plan, teach, and learn. Because the purpose of this study is to encourage a critical alliance between outsiders and prisoner educators, I pay close attention to the roles outside educators and prison schools have played in constraining or enabling prisoners to negotiate their practices.

I believe that in the foreseeable future adult educators cannot formulate anything more than the most highly compromised participatory models within officially sanctioned prison schools. The presumptions underlying the curricula of prison schools, and the instrumental uses of those schools by prison authorities, preclude them from being sites for any meaningful participatory education. This may not rule out the necessity of strategic collaborations with prison schools, but it does recognize that these pacts are problematic arrangements between antagonistic forces. There are forceful reasons for taking this antireformist position. It is important to discuss these reasons here because this chapter makes a strong argument in favor of forming alliances with prisoners' educational practices instead of attempting to reform the conventional classroom.

---

[1]Although the features of an alliance cannot be formulated abstractly in the absence of praxis, it implies the ally does not presume to speak for the prisoners' educational needs. It suggests a commitment to a critical reading of reality, to problematizing the selection of content and methods, and to interrogating the authority of authoritative and experienced knowledge (Freire, 1996; Giroux, 1997; hooks, 1994).

THE POVERTY OF CORRECTIONAL EDUCATION
AS PARTICIPATORY EDUCATION

The central supposition of the correctional ethos is that criminal activity may be attributed to criminals' poorly developed sense of empathy or moral judgment, an incapacity to make socially acceptable choices when faced with adversity, and a failure to own the right package of intellectual skills that enable a person to work and support a family or oneself. In this discourse of deficiencies, education is touted as a panacea for correcting criminal behavior because it can improve job opportunities by teaching entry-level work skills and functional literacy, develop moral reasoning, and correct problem-solving techniques through cognitive skills training programs (Blinn, 1995; Duguid, 1993; Fabiano, 1991; Samenow, 1991). A liberal view of correctional education superficially acknowledges social conditions influencing who is imprisoned and may object to an obsession with correctionalism (Werner, 1990, p. 75), but these concerns are quickly set aside to get on with a less behaviorist variant of the correctional project (e.g., "the importance of [prisoners] making informed choices hinges on the development of empathy"; Duguid, 1992, p. 41). A senior official for a company that operates the privatized educational programs in Canada's federal prisons adopted a Piagetian focus (Wright, 1997):

> Promoting moral development in the correctional classroom through moral discursive practices can be enhanced with neo-Piagetian cognitive development strategies; Vygotskian social-cultural approaches; strategic, experimentally mediated, process-oriented and transformationally driven educational practices. (p. 20)

In an earlier period, the liberal variant was more simply put. In 1981, Morin understood the aim of prison education to be autonomy and self-actualization: "learning to become and learning to know oneself" (Morin, 1981, p. 33). Duguid, arguably the most influential contributor to a liberal, humanistic discourse, called for prison education to be "sensitive to context, by accepting a link with individual development and by a focus on empowerment and engagement" (Duguid, 1992, p. 43). But under continuous pressure from the punitive, conservative ideologies of prison staff and politicians, advocates of the liberal discourse have been pushed into defending the very presence of schooling in prisons by demonstrating its ability to reduce recidivism and keep prisoners manageable. One consequence of this pressure is that notable proponents of the liberal discourse have either abandoned the field or become advocates for coupling a humanistic discourse to cognitive skills training to assist in parole decision making. The fundamental normative underpinning of this ethos is not to further humanistic values; instead, schooling becomes a means to further the stability and predictability of the prisoner before and after release. Education is about making people tractable; thus, both liberal and conservative educators unite in evaluating the effect of schooling on recidivism rates.[2]

The question that concerns us here is: Should progressive educators focus their energies on revitalizing whatever vestiges remain of a humanistic discourse in the prison classroom, or opt for a radically different strategy by critically engaging prisoners' own educational practices?

If participatory education implies "the democratization of the programmatic organization of content, the democratization of teaching—in other words, the democratization of curriculum" (Freire, 1996, p. 116), if it is a model that takes into account the repressive conditions that label and marginalize particular groups of people and struggles to formulate practices that may move them out of and beyond their subordinated positions, if it is this or something approximating this, then it is utopian to believe the prison school can house participatory models. The correctional ethos has set its sights on fitting prisoners into the existing contemporary society. Nowhere in its discourse does it offer or even link itself to a sustained critique of that society and its effect on who is imprisoned and for what reasons. Functional literacy and cognitive skills curriculum are about learning to cope with the status quo without adopting deviant behavior. In Freirian terms, the correctional ethos is quintessentially a discourse for the domestication of prisoners, not their politicization. If it were not so, the prison school and the discourse on correctional education would necessarily place at the center of its concerns how to "redefine education from the perspective of the subordinate classes" (Torres, 1993, p. 125). No evidence from within this ethos suggests even recognition of a serious need to examine *with* prisoner-students the relationships among literacy, poverty, racism, sexism, and the experience of being incarcerated.

We live in an era of incarceration unparalleled in North American history. In the United States "between 1980 and 1994 the total number of people held in federal and state prisons and local jails almost tripled—increasing from 502,886 to 1,483,410 (Bureau of Justice Statistics, 1995, p. 1).[3] After Russia, the United States has the highest incarceration rate per capita in the world. The magnitude of imprisonment in Canada is significantly less than in the United States; nonetheless, Canada has the third highest incar-

---

[2] The executive director of the Correctional Education Association wrote, "At this time, when the cost-effectiveness of programming is of major concern to everyone in the criminal justice field, the value and importance of evaluating the effect of education on recidivism rate and on the rate of employment for released offenders cannot be overlooked" (Tracy & Steurer, 1995, p. 161; also see Harer, 1995).

[3] In 1993, 2.6% of the U.S. population (i.e., 5 million adults) were either on parole, probation, or in prison; an increase of 3 million in 12 years (U.S. Department of Justice, 1996, p. 1).

ceration rate among the major industrialized countries, with 148,000 people under custody or in community corrections programs in 1993 compared with 110,117 in 1983, an increase of 34% over the 10-year period (Foran & Reed, 1996, p. 294).

The relationship among poverty, racism, and imprisonment is readily apparent from the overrepresentation of people of color. In the United States, 60% of state and federal prisoners in 1990 were Black or Latino(a) (Buck, 1994, p. 337). Blacks constitute about 12% of the population, but their incarceration rate in state prisons exceeds the White rate by almost seven to one (U.S. Department of Justice, 1996, p. 1). In Canada, Aboriginal people are about 3.8% of the Canadian population but account for 12% of the federal prison population and 17% of the provincial prison population (Foran & Reed, 1996, p. 298).

The disproportion of people of color to Whites occurs in part because poverty and unemployment breed criminal activity, but discriminatory criminal justice practices are a serious contributing factor. As offenders move through the criminal justice system, educated middle and upper class offenders are released or diverted to nonpenal sanctions, and the undereducated poor, especially poor people of color, are sentenced. Criminal activity seems to occur ubiquitously across class and racial boundaries, but crimes committed by visible minorities living in low-income districts are more likely to be noticed by police and to result in arrests than the same criminal activity in middle class districts. Once arrested, indigent defendants with limited education are more likely to be convicted, to receive longer sentences, and to be denied probation or parole than middle class defendants charged for similar offenses (Reiman, 1990, p. 96).[4]

Hence, prisons are filled with the undereducated poor, which explains rates of illiteracy in prisons, estimated to be between 40% and 60% (Williamson, 1992, p.15). Overcrowding has surpassed crisis proportions in the United States, and the vast amount of funds needed to construct and service prisons has created multinational corporations with vested interests in high incarceration rates (Christie, 1994). There is a resurgence in the use of prisoners' labor to defer operation costs, and there is a growing body of evidence that prisons have become miniature fascist states. In Canada, the Arbour Commission's recent investigation of incidents at Kingston Prison for Women is replete with references to "cruel, inhumane, and degrading" treatment (Arbour, 1996, p. 81), the "absence of a culture [among staff] respectful of individual rights" (p. 93), and managerial strategies and staff practices that directly contravene applicable law and policy (p. 54).

---

[4] The National Institute on Drug Abuse estimates that 12% of drug users are Black but 44% of those arrested for possession are Black (Buck, 1994, p. 338). The *Manchester Guardian* reported a British government study showing Blacks in Britain are eight times more likely to be stopped and investigated by police than Whites (Campbell, 1998, p. 8).

In this context, prison school policy has followed a predictable pattern. When negatively constructed groups receive considerable public attention, social policy follows political expediencies and practices become more coercive (Schneider & Ingram, 1993, p. 338). By 1996, 21 state prison systems and the federal prisons in the United States had introduced mandatory school attendance regulations. Prisoners labeled illiterate must attend school as a prerequisite to working in prisons at paid jobs, transferring to lower security, and obtaining parole consideration (Barton & Coley, 1996, p. 21). The Correctional Service of Canada (CSC) and National Parole Board adopted a similar mandatory policy in the late 1980s by making "satisfactory performance by inmates in ABE [adult basic education] programs . . . a major consideration in determining parole release" (National conference, 1987, p. 8). Today, CSC has integrated literacy and cognitive skills training into a "correctional planning process" that provides "incentives for offenders to participate in programs designed to overcome their criminal behaviour" (Correctional Services Canada, 1994, p. 28). CSC claims that this programming reduces the risk of recidivism and thus makes those who participate in them eligible for lower security classification, release to community correction programs (e.g., halfway houses), and parole consideration. Refusing to participate or failing to achieve prescribed standards leaves one at the higher security level (Davidson, 1998). In this context any consideration of a mandatory correctional education housing democratic curricula is ludicrous.

Alongside such mandatory policies, schooling continues to be supported by prison administrators and their associations to keep prisoners manageable by keeping them occupied and dependent on the system's rewards and punishments. In the first hundred years of the penitentiary, hard labor combined with corporal punishment were the primary means for managing prisoners' time and offsetting costs through the sale of prison labor. However, with the onset of corporate capitalism in the late 19th century, small manufacturing operations that leased or contracted prison labor became targets for unions and corporations that objected to competition from cheap labor. Between 1888 and the 1930s, prison industries were banned or restricted by legislation. Schooling was promoted as one of several substitutes for prison labor to keep prisoners occupied and involved in seemingly useful activity (Davidson, 1991, pp. 119–140).[5]

This history is continuous with the present. In 1989, when the prison population was exploding and overcrowding, racial gangs, health issues, and suicide rates increased markedly, the American Corrections Asso-

---

[5]Before World War I and during the 1930s when prison overcrowding reached crisis proportions but prison labor was effectively curtailed, major gains were made by reformers advocating for education as a rehabilitative panacea (Schlossman & Spillane, 1992; Werner, 1990, pp. 1–55).

ciation promoted literacy education to wardens by arguing that once "offenders become accustomed to functioning in the more structured environment of the classroom, they are often more amenable to engaging in other structured activities" (American Correctional Association Program Committee, 1989, p. 6), and although "the immediate benefit of improved literacy levels of . . . offenders may have little impact on overall institution operation, *the net effect of education . . . is to enhance supervision and security in the correctional setting* [italics added]" (p. 7). In 1992 this position was reiterated by the education director for the Federal Bureau of Prisons (BOP; McCollum, 1993):

> The BOP's commitment to literacy is based on many factors, not the least of which is the hoped for post-release success of individual offenders. But aside from this important consideration are two additional factors: the positive use of time while incarcerated and the impact of positive programming on the prison's internal climate. . . . The increase in the number confined has led to severe crowding that can contribute, in the absence of positive use of time, to dangerous tension levels. Staff and inmates alike suffer when inmate idleness is excessive. (p. 27)

This instrumentality permeates every aspect of officially sanctioned schooling. As a means to reduce idleness by keeping prisoners occupied in classrooms, participatory education can be nothing more than a thinly disguised form of cooptation that serves only to make prisoners compliant. Advocates for reforming the prison school may argue that within this instrumental context and correctional ethos, space exists to carve out participatory models. Typically, this involves some form of peer tutoring (Boudin 1993; Collins & Niemi, 1989; Kerka, 1995; Steurer, 1991). I would not deny that isolated incidents can appear, but the energy it takes to constitute and sustain them would be far better spent engaging an alternative form of education that is neither correctional nor instrumental. The second part of this chapter explores a history of prisoner-organized educational activities as that alternative.

PRISONERS' OWN EDUCATIONAL PRACTICES

The earliest account of these practices dates back to the 1700s and was more a form of participatory governance than education. Prisoners of London's King's Bench prison had organized a "sophisticated . . . economy as well as a complex organ of self-government, notably the so-called prison 'college'" (Innes, 1983, p. 251). The college defined itself as a "corporation or fellowship" that conducted administrative and disciplinary procedures based on social organizations familiar to their times (e.g., municipal corporations and guilds). In 1729, rules provided for a room of "devotion or conversation" and as a place to "settle affairs of common concern" (p. 280). Over its history there were numerous challenges to the college's authority by prisoners and outsiders, but Innes argued that it maintained a high degree of harmony and order in the prison, and it allowed prisoners to speak with a common voice to magistrates and marshals.

Its existence depended on the weakness of state authority. There were no public funds or local government support for the King's Bench prison. Only a marshal and a few "turnkeys" regulated it, and these officers confined their surveillance to the prison's perimeter (Innes, 1983, p. 268). For the most part, guards were interested in avoiding trouble and "pacifying the prisoners in the interest of peace and quiet" (p. 272). Under these conditions the prisoners' authority extended over considerable social space, and the college became a complex entity.

Although the college fell victim as much to the moral entrepreneurship of prison reformers as the growth of state authority, these entrepreneurs had considerable influence on practices of imprisonment (Garland, 1990). To them, prisons were slovenly environments seething with moral debauchery. Prisoners were atavistic beings whose bodies, emotions, morals, and intellects required the disciplining mechanisms of solitude, religious and literacy education, and hard labor.

Outside of the considerable influence that the writing of John Howard had on reformers' ideologies, he had little direct effect on prison policy. But in combination with trouble in England's colonies and rebellion at home (including militant antidebtor prisoners' campaigns), major transformations took place in systems of punishment during this period. Transporting prisoners to penal colonies and prison hulks gave way in time to the first silent regimes of the penitentiaries. In this transformation, independent prisoner organizations like the college were crushed and rehabilitative-surveillance practices came into effect.

Howard is seen as one of the first "correctional education heros" in the literature's historiography. Speaking on behalf of his colleagues in the field, Roberts (1985) concluded that Howard gave correctional education "standards to meet" that "pointed [it] in the right direction." Fondly, he quoted Howard: "Let them be managed with calmness, yet with steadiness; show them that you have humanity, and that you aim to make them useful members of society" (cited in Roberts, 1985, p. 138). This ethos differs noticeably from Innes' (1983) interpretation of the purposes of the college:

> College officials contributed as much as anyone to *making the prison a livable environment*. [italics added] Moreover, when the mass of prisoners were

moved by great passion against the prison regime or against the law of debt, the college *provided them with a forum and with certain traditions of collective action which helped to shape their behaviour* [italics added]. (p. 286)

Making the prison experience livable and providing prisoners with a collective voice to affect their lives are objectives concomitant with a participatory education. For Howard it was unthinkable to recognize prisoners' knowledge as having value and these objectives, coming as it did from atavistic beings. A historiography of correctional education rooted in the celebration of Howard's worldview does not permit the educator to begin with the learner's common sense, strive to understand its meaning, and attempt to transcend it to achieve a more critical, historical consciousness. For the most part, we must say that the reformers' worldview dominated the discourse of correctional schooling. If prisoners' organizations continued to exist in the silence regimes of the 19th-century penitentiaries, they were so suppressed or so secret that they have escaped any notice in major studies on penal history. This repressive influence of correctional educators on prisoners' educational practices continues to the present.

PRISONERS' SCHOOLS AND RADICAL POLITICS

In the early 1900s, the dramatic growth of corporate capitalism in North America exploited millions of immigrants from southern and central Europe. The conditions in which these people worked and lived contributed to the popularity of radical political parties and industrial unions (Gutman, 1976). Militant political activities and strikes were suppressed by deporting and imprisoning the leaders. A growing number of socialists and anarchists were incarcerated, and they carried their political campaigns into prisons. Articles on the politics of prisons in class struggle written by prisoners and outsiders were featured frequently in the radical literature (e.g., "A Voice," 1919).

Penal regimes insisted on censoring this literature and efforts to organize prisoners. Along with censorship, isolation was essential for control. However, in overcrowded prisons, where individuals had to mingle to work and live, censorship and isolation were hard to sustain. In the endless struggle for social space between keepers and kept, the latter managed to gain enough power to operate clandestine networks that brought this literature inside and circulated it widely (Legere, 1914, p. 338). These networks should be included in a history of prisoner organized education.

Legere, who participated in these clandestine networks at Auburn prison, New York, in 1913, became a teacher in the prison school. How this happened he does not say. Nor does he tell us why it was that in 1913 censorship was sufficiently relaxed to allow this literature to be used openly in class. But Legere described the prison school as a "center of revolutionary Socialist and industrial union propaganda" and he mentioned a "library" of radical literature (p. 340).

Legere was writing to alert radicals to what he believed was the insidious role of a progressive educational and managerial reform that was popular among liberals and (ironically) some socialists. Thomas Mott Osborne's Mutual Welfare Leagues are famous in the discourse of correctional education for their use of participatory democratic methods to teach prisoners to become self-governing citizens (Scharf & Hickey, 1977). But Legere warned that Osborne's method was anything but democratic when it came to the influence of socialists and anarchists. The league's elected officers collaborated with Osborne in censoring radical literature, keeping radicals from teaching in the prison school, and banning them from occupying elected offices in its self-governing bodies (Legere, 1914).

Based on other research, Legere's claims about the league are plausible. Before becoming a prison reformer, Osborne was a leading figure in New York's Democratic Party and had a history of confrontations with socialists. Indeed, the leagues were part of a larger self-government movement that used participatory democracy in schools and factories to be rid of "the dangers of Bolshevism in this country" (Frank, 1919, p. 33). Participatory democracy was a compromise: In exchange for sharing a modicum of power with workers, students, and prisoners, progressives hoped to avoid the growth of industrial unions, anarchism, and communism in response to considerable "labor unrest" (Davidson, 1995, 1997).

Today, among the advocates of moral development and cognitive skills training, Osborne is another "correctional education hero" and the leagues are celebrated as "an organization that operationalized the highest democratic ideals . . . a remarkably effective prison management system" (Muth & Gehring, 1986, p. 14). Osborne's currency in the modern discourse rests on his success in applying a participatory model as a tool for effective management and citizenship education. There is no interest in the repressive influences this model had on prisoners' own educational practices, or the links between Osborne's methods and the use of self-government in factories and schools to stem the growth of radical political consciousness and more militant solutions to labor and social unrest (Davidson, 1991). This complex, but essentially repressive, influence by outside adult educators on prisoners' own educational practices is also characteristic of the relations that prevailed between correctional educators and the California radical prison movement in the 1960s and 1970s.

Dating back to the "bibliotherapy" program at San Quentin in the 1950s, teachers and librarians censored radical literature and prevented prisoners from writing and publishing commentaries on prison and crime (Cummins,

1994, pp. 21–52). Prisoners accused the school of serving as a form of surveillance and prison management. Some teachers resisted these roles and supported Black Muslims' efforts to take control of the curriculum, especially in ethnic studies. In most cases, however, teachers and students clashed over course content and class governance.

As they became disillusioned with the objectives of treatment and educational programs, prisoners' political activity was radicalized. This "led to a proliferation of secret inmate study groups intended ... to subvert San Quentin's official education system" (Cummins, 1994, p. 91). John Irwin, sociologist and former California prisoner, described what the study groups were doing:

> These were mostly whites, a couple of Chicanos, and one black. As the weeks went on they started defining it ["what was happening"], saying, "No, it wasn't race. The administration turned it into race." They were becoming more politically conscious, and they started reviewing history a little bit. So then a couple guys in the group started going around and helping organize for a strike. (cited in Cummins, 1994, p. 91)

Legislated and court ordered relaxation of censorship in the 1960s opened the prison to an array of radical literature that provided essential materials for these clandestine activities. Officially sanctioned "convict self-improvement groups" became book lending and political study networks that provoked considerable discontent from authorities. As these groups became more radical and better organized, the prison administration moved against them. But these groups were minor players in prisoner organized education compared with the "covert political education department[s]" of radical organizations.

In 1971 the Black Panthers and Black Guerrilla Family (BGF) operated "secret Marxist political education groups, which included instruction in basic literacy skills and production of rudimentary textbooks, along with discussion of revolutionary theory and practical tips on bomb making and gang war" (Cummins, 1994, p. 136). The *Communist Manifesto* was rewritten in plain language as a literacy reader. Students read Eldridge Cleaver, Che Guevara, Marx, and George Jackson. The Black Cultural Group organized circulating libraries and political study sessions that used Mao's works to inform self-criticism.

In his last major work, Freire (1996) cautioned that "in the domain of socioeconomic structures, the most critical knowledge of reality, which we acquire through the unveiling of that reality, does not of itself alone effect a change in reality" (p. 30). Historical consciousness must be related to concrete struggles for liberation. Cummins (1994) argued that the political movements in California's prisons were too isolated from political struggle on the outside and as a consequence became unrealistic. Prisoners believed their politicization was part of an imminent revolution; meanwhile, militant Black groups on the outside were being suppressed and becoming sectarian. The New Left, itself in disarray, failed to critique egotistical criminal activity or to confront a romanticized image of the prisoner as rebel. Cummins went so far as to question the authenticity of prisoners' politicization. For example, BGF and organizations like it relied on exploitive underground prison economies for their power base (Cummins, 1994, pp. 128–186).[6]

By contrast, the educational practices of Irish Republican political prisoners were intimately connected to an advanced political struggle. Dana and McMonagle (1997) opened their description of these practices noting:

> One of the crucial steps in gaining freedom is forming a system of self-education where the ideas of a revolutionary movement can be developed, tested through discussion and passed on to others within the movement. In the case of the Irish Republican movement, a good deal of this education takes place within the ... prison, among political prisoners. (p. 67)

When Republicans were first interned in 1971 as political prisoners, those who knew Gaelic and Gaelic history taught others with little interference from guards. In 1976, the British government withdrew their prisoner-of-war (POW) status and treated them as criminals. They resisted this by refusing to wear prisoner uniforms, wrapping themselves in blankets ("blanket protests") and going on hunger strikes. According to Dana and McMonagle (1997), during this period they:

> discovered that they could still educate one another, but now by shouting to their neighbours through doors, out windows or along water pipes. In this way a slow process was established where all men in a wing could share information by repeating it along the line until everyone was included. ... Without the availability of books, classrooms or even anything but the crudest of writing materials, each man became equally responsible for contributing his own knowledge to the best of his ability. (p. 69)

Like the clandestine reading of radical literature reported by Legere, this is prisoner-organized education in a more constrained form. Nonetheless, it seems to remain essentially democratic and highly participatory.

After 5 years of protest, the British government conceded to Republicans' demands for POW status. In the "communal lifestyle" that emerged,

---

[6]Further research should investigate the educational role of prisoners' Native Brotherhoods, Lifers' groups, and organizations for Prison Justice Day (Gaucher, 1990/1991; Infinity Lifers Group, 1988/1989). For critiques on prisoners' political activism see Cummins (1994), Gaucher (1993), and Ratner and Cartwright (1990).

they established educational practices. A required course for "those considering themselves political prisoners" was on the history of Republicans in Long Kesh prison "because it examines the importance of the struggle inside the H-Blocks, helping to define what being an Irish Republican POW is all about" (Dana & McMonagle, 1997, p. 70). Irish language was taught in beginner and advanced courses. The methods of instruction were peer tutoring and more structured learning. For example, a class called Historical Analysis was guided by a draft outline of modern Irish history written by a POW. Each week eight students took responsibility for assigning related readings:

> Draw[ing] up a number of points to discuss, as well as formulate questions to ask the others as a way to initiate discussion. The group then examines the topic from all sides, trying to determine what happened, why the event happened the way it did, and engaging in debate to decide if the Republican movement could have done anything differently and what lessons can be learned from the event. (p. 72)

Unfortunately, this account does not mention any links between the POWs and outside educators, nor does Hammond's (1996) study of Salvadoran political prisoners' educational practices or Sbarbaro's (1995a) notes on the *intifada*. The tone and temper of these studies suggest that little or no relationship occurred; indeed, it is likely that schools run by outsiders did not exist in El Salvador and Palestine. Nonetheless, a supportive connection between these educational practices and outside educators is found in cooperative efforts to publish accounts of these experiences and thus make them known to a wider audience.

PRISON WRITING AS PARTICIPATORY EDUCATION

It is plausible to assume that informal educational activities in the fullest sense were associated with the oral literature of African slaves and Black prisoners in North America. Slaves' songs and stories never sung or told in the presence of Whites preserved "subjugated knowledges" (Foucault cited in Giroux, 1997, p. 105) about their bondage, sustained the yearning to rebel, and gave explicit information on how and where to escape (Franklin, 1982, pp. 73–123). On the history of prisoners' oral and written literature, Franklin wrote:

> The prison system rested solidly on the belief that convicts were not human beings. . . . So the spectacle of prisoners actually publishing books which were being received as literary achievements or intelligent social analysis [e.g.

Robert E. Burns, Edna O'Brien, Chester Himes, Malcolm Brady, Victor Serge]
... was fundamentally threatening, ... for the practices of the modern prison
system ... like slavery, could not last if society recognized its victims as intel-
ligent human beings. (p. 161)[7]

As an example of organized educational activity centered on publication,
none is better than the Canadian penal press. This press was linked to an
international exchange network, the International Penal Press, that included Asian, Latin American, North American, and European publications.
It consists of prisoners' newspapers and periodicals published for internal
and external circulation. In Canada alone, from 1951 to the late 1980s there
were more than 80 publications (Gaucher, 1989, pp. 5–6).

Evidence of the press exists from the 19th century. Gaucher attributed
its recent history in Canada to the relaxed restrictions on prisoner writing
that accompanied the reformist zeal of the postwar period. The earliest press
was supported by the commissioner of the federal prison system, but any
amicable relationship between editors and administrators was tenuous at
best. At the time, enthusiasm among prisoners for vocational training and a
general easing of restrictions led to the publication of articles that supported
programs and thus found favor with authorities. When individuals discovered these programs did not prepare them for jobs outside and parole
boards and administrations were using them to maintain compliance with institutional order, the contents of the press shifted to a more critical tone.

As tensions rose, editors and writers demanded the right to express
their views openly, which put them in direct conflict with authorities and
led to increased censorship. In the 1960s, editors continuously battled censorship and curtailed funding. Disruptions to production and circulation
pushed them into disarray, and the press shifted to reporting prison social
events, sports, and related "internal" matters.

Although divisive disputes over accommodating censors continuously
destabilized the penal press, a state of social disorganization brought about
by the constant transferring of prisoners to other institutions with higher
and lower security classifications "had the most debilitating effect on the
editorial continuity and regularity of publications" (Gaucher, 1989, p. 11). By
the mid-1960s, the majority had ceased publication or were in decline. Their
educational focus and connection to the public through widespread distribution, and their identification with the International Penal Press network
all but disappeared (p. 10).

---

[7]Mumia Abu-Jamal, a Black journalist and former member of Move, is perhaps the most celebrated, current example of the U. S. government holding a political prisoner under a death sentence. Jamal's writing from inside is published widely in the alternative press (Abu-Jamal, 1991,
1995). Under current regulations these and other publications are permitted inside prisons,
where they inform prisoners' discussion groups.

This was not the case for prisoners in the only prison for women in Canada's federal system. Consequently, an editorial board published *Tightwire* at the Prison for Women in Ontario from 1973 to 1989. *Tightwire* continued to fight censorship and published articles criticizing government task forces and crime legislation and exposing prison conditions (A Lifer, 1989). It was the only Canadian press that was linked to the International Penal Press network in the 1980s.

In the 1990s there was something of a resurgence of the penal press (e.g., *Inside the Bay, Stony Mountain Innovator, OutLook Magazine*), but the destabilizing forces that affected the continuity and regularity of publication and inhibited distribution persisted. The editor of *Out of Bounds*, published at William Head Institution (British Columbia), wrote in 1994 about the struggle with censorship:

> Now I need to apologize to our readers for the big ugly black marks that adorn one particular article in the last issue of our pithy little publication. Yes those nasty old censors nipped us in the electronically enhanced bud. Actually, I want to thank them for doing that because at times I forget where I am, I forget that I am in jail. (Editor, 1997, p. 4)

In addition to the penal press, an alternative press publishes articles by prisoners and former prisons on prison conditions and related political events. Typically, these are in the form of newspapers (e.g., *Prison News Service, The California Prisoner*). Occasionally, prisoner's research appears in academic journals (e.g., *Social Justice*). In 1988 a group of outside educators, prisoners and former prisoners, and activists established the *Journal of Prisoners on Prisons* to provide a more academic forum for the development of a body of published research by prisoners and former prisoners on the politics and experience of crime, punishment, and social justice. The journal is connected to prisoners by the composition of its editorial board, prisoners as guest editors, correspondence with subscribers, and editors' personal connections with contributors. By publishing from outside the prison, it has avoided prison censorship and the destabilizing influences of transfers and segregated punishment that plagued the penal press. The social space for editing, publishing, and distributing is the relatively autonomous university. Influences on academia are the time outsiders can donate to its biannual production, limited financing that inhibits effective promotion, and the logistics of working with prisoners and former prisoners on articles that emerge out of a complex, heavily stigmatized environment. Those who have edited issues of the journal understand that they are working with "critical ethnographies" (Gaucher, 1988), which makes the work of editing a dynamic, politicized, and participatory process.

Whereas the newspapers were targeted to prison rights activists, the journal used a format and editorial practice that made this research more acceptable in academia and thereby capable of influencing discourse in the social sciences.[8] Consequently, the journal is carried in numerous university libraries, cited in formal research, and used as readings in university classes. However, it also relates to prisoners' own educational practices as a means to give those practices a voice to the outside. Like the penal press, it too is an educational resource within those practices. In a letter to a member of the journal's editorial collective, the prisoner and political activist Lorenzo Stone-Bey (personal communication, June 9, 1997) commented on this influence:

> Yes, most prisoners organized education is what Prison officials call a Threat to security, Revolutionary, Gang involvement, etc and often the response is harassment, transfers from the institution to . . . the Super Max and Indefinite Segregation. Yet, we understand the importance of education and political education in particular so we do so without fear of the State Repression. We create our own librarys with the books and other material such as you send [i.e., the journal] and get copies when we can in order to circulate it.

On the one hand, educational programs have functioned to suppress prisoner writing. The "bibliotherapy" and school programs at San Quentin and Legere's version of the Mutual Welfare Leagues are examples. On the other hand, outsiders have worked with prisoners to promote this writing and to disseminate it among a wide, unconventional audience. This duality occurs in other forms of prisoner-organized education. It is particularly evident in the relationships between prisoner educators and prison higher education programs.

PRISONER ORGANIZED EDUCATION AND PRISON HIGHER EDUCATION

On-site, accredited university prison programs date back to the early 1960s (Gehring, 1997, p. 46). These programs were able to sustain a certain autonomy from the correctional ethos and penal authorities because they were constantly conforming to and contesting the expectations of two masters: university and prison administrations (Coffey, 1994; Jones & d'Errico, 1994). Several Canadian programs, for example, were set up as somewhat self-contained democratically run schools based on Kohlberg's "just community" model as a pedagogy for moral development, and individual teachers adopted popular

---

[8] For examples of formats similar to the *Journal of Prisoners on Prisons*, see *Prison Journal* and *Prison Writing*.

education methods. The programs' directors quickly adopted a liberal correctional ethos, seeing in the study of the humanities and social sciences a means to promote moral reasoning and thereby correct deviant behavior. They conducted studies to correlate participation in prison higher education with reduced recidivism to demonstrate to politicians and prison guards they were not "coddling prisoners" and misdirecting education tax dollars to the undeserved (Duguid, 1997a; Duguid & Hoekema, 1986).

For the most part, the university instructors did not identify themselves with correctional education or participate in the correctional ethos. They came into the prisons to teach their discipline and identified themselves with their roles at the university. Typically, they taught for little or no wages and found the experience rewarding. The students were mature, eager to participate in discussion, and grateful to have the opportunity to study. Linebaugh (1995) found campus students in the 1970s to be "countercultural, young, and inexperienced: dreamy, dopey, and disturbed. The prisoners . . . were both cynical and hopeful. They wanted to learn. As students these prisoners were accustomed to discipline; and they learned by challenging discipline" (p. 66). The experiences these educators had is exemplified in Heberle and Rose's (1994) comments on teaching political science curriculum:

> The perpetual sense of negotiation of rules and power structure and the intense fragile sense of stability makes everyone's embededness in a disciplined and conformist society more apparent in prison than on the outside, where the negotiations are more obscure, less overt, and in some ways, more insidious. For us, as students of politics, this was the most important difference between our experience teaching inmates and our experience teaching students on the outside. (p. 100; also see Thomas, 1995)

In courses on women's studies, critical criminology, marxism, literature, social history, and sociology, it was possible to carve out a space for participatory practices because teachers were sympathetic to this approach and prisoners demanded recognition of their experiences. If these demands and course content were not enough to promote participatory methods, then, as Heberle and Rose observed, the tenuous nature of the classes and the relation between prisoners' experiences and the subject matter made participatory education a possibility.[9]

Arguably the most extensive attempt at a participatory model was the Santa Cruz Women's Prison Project (SCWPP) that began in 1972 when Karlene Faith and her colleague Jeanne Gallick responded to women prisoners who "wanted to know about 'women's lib'" (Faith, 1995, p. 174). These two women developed a course called "Women and Society" and managed to get the University of California at Santa Cruz to accredit it. Between 1972 and 1976 SCWPP evolved into a "statewide educational, political, and cultural network which converged at the . . . [prison] most weekends for four years, involving hundreds of volunteers over time" (p. 175). Accredited courses and workshops were either initiated by the women or the women "were consulted about every decision concerning academic curriculum and cultural workshops; their priorities affected and often dictated the program direction. It was a collective investment" (p. 187) that struggled to operate outside the correctional ethos. Faith wrote, "Education for liberation and empowerment of confined groups, wherever and however it occurs, is an exercise in counter hegemony which calls for a more equitable and transformative share in social power and decision-making" (p. 190).

Throughout its history the program experienced moments of strong support from the warden, senior department officials, and politicians. It also suffered periods of intense resistance. The support allowed the program to expand; the resistance caused teaching staff to be harassed when entering the prison, learning materials to be subjected to surveillance and confiscation, courses to be disrupted by guards, and the entire program to be repeatedly canceled if only one instructor violated a prison rule. Although this merry-go-round of support and interference and a "combination of political and organizational shifts" (e.g., appointment of new wardens) explain, in part, the final demise of the project, Faith (1995) noted that "those of us coordinating SCWPP would have had to reduce our activity. After four years, many of us were close to burnout, and the logistical complications of commuting 500 miles for weekend work were taking a toll on our personal lives and pocketbooks" (pp. 185–186).

SCWPP was unique, but it existed within a framework of general support for prison higher education. By 1975, well before the growth of prison higher education in Canada, more than 300 colleges and universities in the United States operated programs involving more than 50,000 prisoners annually (Lawrence, 1994, p. 34). Testimonies cited by Faith (1995, p. 180), Sbarbaro (1995b, pp. 94–99), and others attest to prisoners' support for higher education.[10] In an article that strongly defended it, Attallah Salah-El (1992) wrote:

> In pragmatic terms, we must analyze existing "prison programs," meagre though they may be, to assess precisely how they work or do not work, while forming ourselves into political organizations to structure our recommenda-

---

[9]On her experience teaching a course in women's studies to male sex offenders, Holly Devor wrote: "I believe that this . . . class . . . was as successful as it was because the men who came to women's studies were highly motivated to learn. Their lives had been entirely restructured as a result of their criminal conviction; they had come to be among the most despicable members of society and they wanted to understand how they had gotten there and how to innoculate themselves against ever returning" (Devor, 1989, p. 149).

[10]For articles describing prisoners' support for prison higher education see Jones (1992), Lynes (1992), and Mason (1994).

tions. We need to gather and duplicate whatever is valuable and bring in persons to impart and interpret information and share experiences. (p. 47)

This critically reflexive approach to officially sanctioned programs describes the relation between a course in jailhouse lawyering organized by Julian Stone at Norfolk prison, Massachusetts, and prison higher education. Stone taught himself the law to appeal his death sentence. When death row was temporarily abolished in the United States in 1972, Stone began to promote legal education. At Norfolk prison, his idea for law classes was picked up by the prisoners' Legal Advisory Committee (Stone, 1995, p. 194). The course was divided into two classes. A basic class taught the jurisdictions of American courts and how to read law and do legal research. An advanced class taught students to prepare legal actions, to access and extract information from law books, and to prepare and serve court documents. Students were required to attend class, discuss readings, and pass oral and written tests. Those who passed the advanced class were issued certificates. Stone argued that these conventional methods, modeled on a university setting, were necessary for students to take the program seriously. The certificate, after all, designated a person qualified to give prisoners legal aide in fighting wrongful convictions, appeals, and civil suits.

Stone's program had an equivocal relation with professional outside educators. On the one hand, he thought it essential that it be kept apart from the prison school because "the principal would be in a position to dictate what materials would be used to teach the course, who would be suitable students, how the class would be organized, who would teach, and how students would be evaluated" (Stone, 1995, p. 194). At the same time, Stone fostered connections with law students in Boston's major universities. These connections legitimated the program, provided a resource for course content, and opened up possibilities for released jailhouse lawyers to obtain jobs as paralegals. Stone, like many students in his classes, participated in Boston University's prison higher education program. The courses and degrees complemented their legal studies. Moreover, it was through teaching the sociology of deviance in this program that I came into contact with Stone and, as a consequence of that contact, was able to publish his account of this program.

The prison higher education program that supported Stone's work is one of the few remaining in North America. In 1993 the Solicitor General of Canada cut funding for all on-site programs. The 1995 Crime Bill in the United States disqualified prisoners from obtaining Pell Grants to pay their tuition fees. These grants provided the financial resources for almost all university and college programs. Without them few have survived. Outside educators who rushed to the defense of prison higher education adopted the correctional ethos. Politicians were reminded that participation in university programs correlated with lower recidivism rates, and educators were encouraged to conduct more studies that would prove this point (Duguid, 1997a). Others placed considerable blame for the demise on the universities and colleges that abused Pell Grants, on teachers for the lack of clear correctional objectives in their courses, and on an unwillingness of teachers and prison staff to work toward common goals (Coffey, 1994, p. 76; Gehring, 1997).

Advocates for participatory education can make a sound argument for struggling to reinstitute these semiautonomous forms of schooling. But those who would focus their energies in this direction must take into account not just its accomplishments but the forces that affected its demise and the correctionalism that quickly appeared in its discourse. It is important to recognize moments like the Santa Cruz Women's Prison Project, the strong support university programs enjoy among prisoners, and the alliance between outsiders and prisoner-educators outlined by Stone. However, it is implausible to assume that a resurgence of prison higher education will reproduce the level of development that was wiped out by funding cuts in the 1990s. Nor can we assume that if programs were to reemerge in these more reactionary, repressive times, when prison labor and chain gangs are reappearing and institutions are being privatized, the correctional ethos would be less influential than it was in the past. New higher education curricula would likely be shaped to serve the instrumental and correctional mandates that are affecting literacy and basic skills training programs, also being starved for funds. Finally, it is essential to recall Faith's crucial point that even in programs as extensive as the SCWPP, outsiders burn out and drift away when practical considerations and logistical barriers turn their attention in other directions.

A common denominator in all of these cases is that prison higher education did not belong to prisoners. Unlike the Irish Republican's educational systems that were sustainable at some level even in the midst of the most repressive conditions, prison higher education can be taken away because it is fully dependent on agreements between universities and departments of corrections. When it is politically or fiscally expedient to do so or when changes take place in the lives of outside supporters, these agreements are canceled. The only forms of participatory adult education that have been able to adapt to shifts in the social spaces in which prisoners exist are the educational programs that are independent of these outside arrangements and rely solely on prisoners' struggles to create conditions that allow for some level of educational practice.

CONCLUDING REMARKS

There are accounts of other prisoner-organized educational activities. I have mentioned Hammond on Salvadoran's programs and Rivera's important discussion of a nontraditional approach that individuals created "so that upon release they can take up their lives in a way that will benefit themselves and their communities" (Rivera, 1995, p. 160). One program not yet mentioned brings to focus a central issue raised in this chapter: the possibility for participatory education within the structure of conventional prison schools and the necessity of working outside those schools with prisoners' own educational practice. Boudin worked on her master's degree in education when she first entered prison. In her studies she was introduced to Freire's "problem solving approach to literacy education" (Boudin, 1993, p. 209). Boudin became a teacher's aide in a prison school, which, thanks to the goodwill of the school's staff, opened up a "space to do meaningful work":

> Would it be possible in a prison classroom to create conditions for self-awareness, a space where people felt safe to identify and address their own problems and then struggle toward solutions, to imagine the world as it could be otherwise? (p. 209)

Between 1986 and 1990 at Bedford Hills Correctional Facility within an adult basic education classroom, Boudin worked to create such a program. It was "peer education" on AIDS in which women "related to real life emotional and social issues: they began addressing problems that they faced both individually and communally" (Boudin, 1993, p. 218). The program grew into AIDS Counselling and Education (ACE), which integrated literacy skills activities "into a critical-thinking curriculum ... [that captured] the dynamic unfolding process of curriculum development in which both teacher and student play an active role" (Boudin, 1995, p. 141). The class wrote a play to build literacy skills and "develop the strengths of working in cooperation with others" (Boudin, 1993, p. 219).

Support for the "peer education program" was withdrawn by the prison's administration in 1990. During its operation Boudin (1993) "found that the primary tendency of the system was to define me as a prisoner" (p. 226). She was prevented from having any real responsibility because administration felt it was a threat to security for prisoners to have even quasiauthority in a classroom. She attributed the program's closure to the contradictions among the goals of security, punishment, and rehabilitation, an argument made repeatedly by correctional educators and proponents of prison higher education (Williford, 1994). In this case, the contradiction was resolved in favor of cancellation because a key administrator, a supportive educational supervisor, took a job elsewhere. Moreover, New York State cut funds to educational programs, and "the general political climate was more antagonistic towards prisoners, inmate initiative, and program innovation" (Boudin, 1993, pp. 228–229).

Boudin did not dismiss the possibilities for further reform. However, when the reasons she gave for the demise of the AIDS project are read against the backdrop of current trends in prison schooling, there is cause for a more dire conclusion. The question to be asked here is what might have happened to Boudin's project had it been formulated like Stone's classes in jailhouse lawyering or the Irish Republican's political education programs? Formulated as it was within the context of the prison school, the project experienced a history not unlike that of the SCWPP, progressive classes in prison higher education programs, and Legere's "center of revolutionary Socialist and industrial union propaganda." The question is this: If the AIDs project and others like it operate as prisoners' own educational practice instead of reformed schooling, is there reason to suggest they have a greater likelihood of continuing, recognizing that their forms will vary depending on the social space prisoners are able to create and hold? Can we formulate a reasonable response to this question based on the information presented here?

It may be an exaggeration to say that prisoners' own educational practices are intimately connected to processes of politicization. Yet it is difficult to imagine that such programs could exist without some degree of political sophistication. Minimally, the existence of those examined here depended on carving out a social space through varying levels of organized resistance to penal authority. Under severe forms of repression, ingenious methods were devised to keep these programs alive. When the continuous conflict between keepers and kept created more space for political organization, prisoners' educational practices were quick to expand.

As for the relationships among prisoners' educational practices, outside adult educators, and prison schools, in the accounts that describe these relationships schools have often suppressed prisoner-organized education. Stone spoke to the necessity of keeping his course independent of the school's control. Cummins placed prisoners' systems in opposition to schools operated by conventional educators and described the role educators played as censors. On a more subtle level, the defense of prison higher education in the name of its effect on recidivism undermined higher education's more progressive gains in favor of the correctional ethos. It is difficult to see how prisoner-organized education could have something other than an antagonistic relation with forms of schooling that function to domesticate prisoners, serve as a form of prisoner management, and perform an insidious, behavioristic role in the operation of parole and classification boards.

But outside educators have also been supportive. Some teachers in higher education programs have contributed to prisoners' practices by providing prisoner-educators with a formal liberal arts education, introduction to Freirian pedagogy, advice on content and teaching methods, access to libraries and guest speakers, and by promoting prisoner writing and offering means for its publication. Boudin was introduced to Freire in the context of a prison higher education program; Stone and his students complemented their legal education by participating in Boston University's program; the *Journal of Prisoner on Prison* relies on the resources of the university-based members of its editorial board to keep it alive.

The analysis of prisoners' own educational practices presented here—juxtaposed against a critique of correctional schooling that demonstrates the improbability of their housing participatory practices—suggests that an affirmative reply to the question about the survival of Boudin's AIDs program as a prisoner-organized effort is a plausible response, and that its demise within the context of a prison school reform was predictable. Further research based on participants' and outsiders' analyses of these practices is needed before we can claim more. But this introduction into those practices suggests they may be relatively autonomous of penal authority and thereby more elastic in the face of repressive forces. Most certainly they have been capable of sustaining curricula for prisoners' politicization.

A question that remains is what the outside educator's role might be in relation to these practices. Clearly that must be worked out through praxis; however, in closing, I want to note that to confine the analysis of adult education in prison to programs delivered by sanctioned schools is to do the work of suppressing a much broader conceptualization of adult education that includes prisoners' practices. Altering the borderlines that define adult education in any setting is an essential if not sufficient part of a process that locates adult education in a struggle for genuine democratic social relations. Quoting Foucault, to fail to recognize and recount marginalized practices is to "locate . . . low down on the hierarchy, beneath the required level of cognition of scienticity" blocks of "historical knowledge which were present but disguised within the body of functionalist and systematising theory" (cited in Giroux, 1997, p. 103). To include prisoners' educational practices in a discussion on participatory education will not in itself transform practice and create the collaborative relations that may help to sustain those that are democratic, but surely it is a step in that direction.

ACKNOWLEDGMENTS

A catalyst for this chapter is Ed Sbarbaro's essay on educational activities organized among imprisoned members of the *intifada* (Sbarbaro, 1995a). I want to thank Robert Gaucher, Bob Brydon, and Marcia Stentz for their critical comments.

REFERENCES

A Lifer. (1989). Are we paddling uphill??? Against the current CSC realities???. *Tightwire*, *23*(3), 12–13.

A voice from prison (1919, October). *Mother Earth*, *7*, 252–253.

Abu-Jamal, M. (1991). A blast into dark immortality. *Journal of Prisoners on Prisons*, *3*(1&2), 65–69.

Abu-Jamal, M. (1995). *Live from death row*. Reading, MA: Addison-Wesley.

American Correctional Association Program Committee. (1989). *Literacy: A concept for all seasons*. Washington DC: American Correctional Association.

Arbour, L. (1996). *Commission of inquiry into certain events at the Prison for Women in Kingston*. Ottawa, Canada: Public Works and Government Services Canada.

Attallah Salah-El, T. (1992). Attaining education in prison equals prisoner power. *Journal of Prisoners on Prison*, *4*(1), 45–52.

Baker, J. E. (1985). *Prisoner participation in prison power*. Metuchen, NJ: The Scarecrow Press.

Barton, B. E., & Coley, R. J. (1996). *Captive students: Education and training in America's prisons*. Princeton, NJ: Policy Information Center, Educational Testing Service.

Blinn, C. (1995). Teaching cognitive skills to effect behavioral change through a writing program. *Journal of Correctional Education*, *46*(4), 146–154.

Boudin, K. (1993). Participatory literacy education behind bars: AIDS opens the door. *Harvard Educational Review*, *63*(2), 207–232.

Boudin, K. (1995). Critical thinking in a basic literacy program: A problem-solving model in corrections education, *Journal of Correctional Education*, *46*(4), 141–144.

Buck, P. D. (1994). "Arbeit Macht Frei": Racism and bound, concentrated labor in U. S. prisons. *Urban Anthropology*, *23*(2&3), 331–372.

Bureau of Justice Statistics (1995). National prison population growth. *Alaska Justice Forum*, *12*(3), 1–3.

Campbell, D. (1998, August 2). Police stop blacks eight times more than whites. *Manchester Guardian*, p. 8.

Cervero, R. M., & Wilson, A. L. (1994). *Planning responsibility for adult education*. San Francisco: Jossey-Bass.

Christie, N. (1994). *Crime control as industry: Towards gulags western style*. London: Routledge.

Coffey, O. D. (1994). A view from corrections. In M. Williford (Ed.), *Higher education in prisons: A contradiction in terms?* (pp. 73–85). Phoenix, AZ: Oryx Press.

Collins, M., & Niemi, J. A. (1989). Advanced adult basic education in prisons: The recruitment, selection and training of inmate tutors. In S. Duguid (Ed.), *Yearbook of correctional education 1989* (pp. 193–208). Burnaby, Canada: Institute for the Humanities, Simon Fraser University.

Collins, M. (1991). *Adult education as vocation*. New York: Routledge & Kegan Paul.

Correctional Services Canada. (1994). *The correctional planning process*. (Available from Correctional Services of Canada, 340 Laurier Ave West, Ottawa, Ontario).

Cummins, E. (1994). *The rise and fall of California's radical prison movement*. Stanford, CA: Stanford University Press.

Dana, J., & McMonagle, S. (1997). Deconstructing "criminalisation": The politics of collective education in the H-blocks. *Journal of Prisoners on Prisons*, *8*(1&2), 67–74.

Davidson, H. S. (1991). *Moral education and social relations: The case of prisoner self-government reform, New York (1895–1923)*. Unpublished doctoral dissertation, University of Toronto.

Davidson, H. S. (1995). An alternative view: Revisiting the Mutual Welfare League (1913–1923). *Journal of Correctional Education*, *46*(3), 169–178.

Davidson, H. S. (1997). Political processes in prison education: A history. *Journal of Correctional Education*, *48*(3), 136–141.

Davidson, H. S. (1998). Adult education in transition: The influence of social context on teaching prisoner. In S. Scott, B. Spencer, & A. Thomas (Eds.), *Learning for life: Canadian readings in adult education* (pp. 223–235), Toronto, Canada: Thompson.

Devor, H. (1989). Teaching women's studies to convicted sex offenders. In S. Duguid (Ed.), *Yearbook of correctional education 1989* (pp. 129–154). Burnaby, Canada: Institute for the Humanities, Simon Fraser University.

Duguid, S. (1992). Becoming interested in other things: The impact of education in prison. *Journal of Correctional Education, 43*(1), 38–45.

Duguid, S. (1993). Planning for student success: A review of the character and objectives of prison education. In R. Semmens (Ed.), *Yearbook of correctional education 1993* (pp. 177–188). Laurel, MD: Correctional Education Association.

Duguid, S. (1997a). Cognitive dissents bite the dust—The demise of university education in Canada's prisons. *Journal of Correctional Education, 48*(2), 56–68.

Duguid, S. (1997b). Confronting worst case scenarios: Education and high risk offenders. *Journal of Correctional Education, 48*(4), 153–159.

Duguid, S., & Hoekema, H. (Eds.). (1986). *University education in prisons: A documentary record of the experience in British Columbia 1974–1986.* Burnaby, Canada: Simon Fraser University.

Editor's desk. (1997). *Out of Bounds Magazine, 14*(3), 4.

Fabiano, E. A. (1991). How education can be correctional and how corrections can be educational. *Journal of Correctional Education, 42*(2), 100–106.

Faith, K. (1995). The Santa Cruz Women's Prison Project, 1972–1976. In H. S. Davidson (Ed.), *Schooling in a "total institution": Critical perspectives on prison education* (pp. 173–192). Westport, CT: Bergin & Garvey.

Foran, T., & Reed, M. (1996). The correctional system. In L. W. Kennedy & V. F. Sacco (Eds.), *Crime counts: A criminal event analysis* (pp. 293–311). Toronto, Canada: Nelson Canada.

Forester, J. (1993). *Critical theory, public policy and planning practice.* Albany, NY: State University of New York Press.

Frank, G. (1919, June). Self-governing industry: A plea for realism in politics. *Century Magazine, 98*(2), 225–234.

Franklin, H. B. (1982). *Prison literature in America: The victim as criminal and artist.* Westport, CT: Lawrence Hill.

Freire, P. (1996). *Pedagogy of hope.* New York: Continuum.

Garland, D. (1990). *Punishment and modern society: A study in social theory.* Chicago: University of Chicago Press.

Gaucher, R. (1988). The prisoner as ethnographer: The Journal of Prisoners on Prisons. *Journal of Prisoners on Prisons, 1*(1), 49–61.

Gaucher, R. (1989). The Canadian penal press: A documentation and analysis. *Journal of Prisoners on Prisons, 2*(1), 3–24.

Gaucher, R. (1990/1991). Organizing inside: Prison Justice Day (August 10th) A non-violent response to penal repression. *Journal of Prisoners on Prisons, 3*(1&2), 93–110.

Gaucher, R. (1993). Too many chiefs. *Journal of Prisoners on Prisons, 4*(2), 135–139.

Gehring, T. (1997). Post secondary education for inmates: An historical inquiry. *Journal of Correctional Education, 48*(2), 46–55.

Giroux, H. A. (1997). *Pedagogy and the politics of hope: Theory, culture, and schooling.* Boulder, CO: Westview Press.

Gosselin, L. (1982). *Prisons in Canada.* Montreal, Canada: Black Rose.

Gutman, H. (1976). *Work, culture and society in industrializing America: Essays in American working-class and social history.* New York: Knopf.

Hammond, J. L. (1996). Organization and education among Salvadoran political prisoners. *Crime, Law & Social Change, 25*(1), 17–41.

Harer, M. D. (1995). Recidivism among federal prisoners released in 1987. *Journal of Correctional Education, 46*(3), 98–128.

Heberle, R., & Rose, W. (1994). Teaching within the contradictions of prison education. In M. Williford (Ed.), *Higher education in prisons: A contradiction in terms?* (pp. 97–106). Phoenix, AZ: Oryx Press.

hooks, b. (1994). *Teaching to transgress: Education as the practice of freedom.* New York: Routledge.

Infinity Lifers Group, Collins Bay Institution (1988/1989). Can you hear us? *Journal of Prisoners on Prisons, 1*(2), 45–57.

Innes, J. (1983). The King's Bench prison in the late eighteenth century: Law, authority and order in a London debtors' prison. In J. Brewer & J. Styles (Eds.), *An ungovernable people; The English and law in the seventeenth and eighteenth centuries* (pp. 250–298). London: Hutchinson.

Jones, R. (1992). A coincidence of interests: Prison higher education in Massachusetts. *Journal of Prisoners on Prisons, 4*(1), 3–20.

Jones, R. J., & d'Errico, P. (1994). The paradox of higher education in prisons. In M. Williford (Ed.), *Higher education in prisons: A contradiction in terms?* (pp. 1–16). Phoenix, AZ: Oryx Press.

Kasinsky, R. G. (1977). A critique on sharing power in the total institution. *Prison Journal, 57,* 56–61.

Kerka, S. (1995). *Prison literacy programs.* ERIC Digest no. 159. (Report No. EDO-CE-95-159). Office of Education Research and Improvement, Washington, DC.

Lawrence, D. W. (1994). The scope and diversity of prison higher education. In M. Williford (Ed.), *Higher education in prisons: A contradiction in terms?* (pp. 32–51). Phoenix, AZ: Oryx Press.

Legere, B. J. (1914). The red flag in the Auburn prison. *The International Socialist Review, 15*(6), 337–341.

Linebaugh, P. (1995). Freeing birds, erasing images, burning lamps: How I learned to teach in prison. In H. S. Davidson (Ed.), *Schooling in a "total institution": Critical perspectives on prison education* (pp. 65–90). Westport, CT: Bergin & Garvey.

Lynes, D. (1992). On prison education and hope. *Journal of Prisoners on Prisons, 4*(1), 53–55.

Mason, C. (1994). A prisoner's view. In M. Williford (Ed.), *Higher education in prisons: A contradiction in terms?* (pp. 135–138). Phoenix, AZ: Oryx Press.

McCollum, S. G. (1993). Literacy programs in the federal prison system. The State of Corrections. *Proceedings American Correctional Association Annual Conference,* 1992, 25–29.

Morin, L. (1981). Inmate right to education. In L. Morin (Ed.), *On prison education* (pp. 23–33). Ottawa, Canada: Minister of Supply and Services Canada.

Murton, T. (1976). *The dilemma of prison reform.* New York: Holt, Reinhart & Winston.

Muth, W. R., & Gehring, T. (1986). The correctional education/prison reform link: 1913–1940 and conclusion. *Journal of Correctional Education, 37*(1), 14–17.

National conference on offender literacy (1987, July). *Let's Talk,* pp. 7–8.

Pfohl, S. J. (1985). *Images of deviance and social control.* New York: McGraw Hill.

Ratner, R. S., & Cartwright, B. (1990). Politicized prisoners: From class warriors to faded rhetoric. *Journal of Human Justice, 2*(1), 75–92.

Reiman, J. (1990). *The rich get richer and the poor get prison* (3rd ed.). New York: Macmillan.

Rivera, J. A. (1995). A nontraditional approach to social and criminal justice. In H. S. Davidson (Ed.), *Schooling in a "total institution": Critical perspectives on prison education* (pp. 159–171). Westport, CT: Bergin & Garvey.

Roberts, L. H. (1985). John Howard, England's great prison reformer: His glimpse into hell. *Journal of Correctional Education, 36*(4), 136–139.

Samenow, S. E. (1991). Correcting errors of thinking in the socialization of offenders. *Journal of Correctional Education, 42*(2), 56–59.

Sbarbaro, E. (1995a). A note on prison activism and social justice. In H. S. Davidson (Ed.), *Schooling in a "total institution": Critical perspectives on prison education* (pp. 141–145). Westport, CT: Bergin & Garvey.

Sbarbaro, E. (1995b). Teaching criminology to "criminals." In H. S. Davidson (Ed.), *Schooling in a "total institution": Critical perspectives on prison education* (pp. 91–101). Westport, CT: Bergin & Garvey.

Scharf, P., & Hickey, J. (1977). Thomas Mott Osborne and the limits of democratic prison reform. *Prison Journal, 57*(2), 3–15.

Schlossman, S., & Spillane, J. (1992). *Bright hopes, dim realities: Vocational innovation in American correctional education.* Santa Monica, CA: Rand.

Schneider, A., & Ingram, H. (1993). Social construction of target populations: Implications for politics and policy. *American Political Science Review, 87*(2), 334–347.

Shor, I., & Freire, P. (1987). *A pedagogy for liberation: Dialogues on transforming education.* Granby, MA: Bergin & Garvey.

Steurer, S. (1991). Inmates helping inmates: Maryland's peer tutoring reading academies. In S. Duguid (Ed.), *Yearbook of correctional education 1991* (pp. 133–139). Burnaby, Canada: Institute for the Humanities, Simon Fraser University.

Stone, J. (1995). Jailhouse lawyers educating fellow prisoners. In H. S. Davidson (Ed.), *Schooling in a "total institution": Critical perspectives on prison education* (pp. 193–201). Westport, CT: Bergin & Garvey.

Stone-Bey, L. (1997, June 9). Personal communication to Howard Davidson.

Thomas, J. (1995). The ironies of prison education. In H. S. Davidson (Ed.), *Schooling in a "total institution": Critical perspectives on prison education* (pp. 25–41). Westport, CT: Bergin & Garvey.

Torres, C. A. (1993). From the pedagogy of the oppressed to a luta continua: The political pedagogy of Paulo Freire. In P. McLaren & P. Leonard (Eds.), *Paulo Freire: A critical encounter* (pp. 119–145). London: Routledge.

Tracy, A., & Steurer, S. J. (1995). Correctional education programming: The development of a model evaluation instrument. *Journal of Correctional Education, 46*(4), 156–166.

U.S. Department of Justice (1996). *Correctional population in the United States 1980–1993* [On-line]. Available: http://www.calyx.net/^...er/govpubs/corr93.html.

Werner, D. R. (1990). *Correctional education: Theory and practice.* Danville, IL: Interstate.

Williamson, G. L. (1992). Education and incarceration: An examination of the relationship between educational achievement and criminal behavior. *Journal of Correctional Education, 43*(1), 14–22.

Williford, M. (Ed.). (1994). *Higher Education in Prison.* Phoenix, AZ: Oryx Press.

Wright, R. L. (1997). Towards integrative correctional education programs: Some obstacles, some suggestions. *Journal of Correctional Education, 48*(1), 10–22.

REFLECTIONS ON PRACTICE

13

"Yes, but ...": Problematizing Participatory ESL Pedagogy

Elsa Auerbach
University of Massachusetts, Boston

"In America, Democracy; in the classroom, no."

—ESL student[1]

Putting participatory ESL into practice isn't easy. ESL learners have their own ideas about what counts as language learning, and having a democratic classroom, as this student says, may not be one of them. They may want traditional, teacher-directed, grammar-focused instruction and rote learning. And teachers, too, may have their own issues relating to participatory education; like students, they often hold deeply ingrained beliefs and experiences that are at odds with participatory practices. And when they do embrace this approach, they inevitably encounter complex dilemmas (like dealing with student resistances!) as they try to put the lofty ideals of participatory pedagogy into practice. In this chapter, I explore some of the resistances, challenges, and problems that teachers struggle with in participatory ESL, as well as my own journey as a teacher educator in trying to address them.

I came to ESL from a history as an activist: I tried to join the NAACP when I was 12, marched against apartheid when I was 18, joined an antiimperialist research group when I was 22, and worked in an auto factory for 5 years as a would-be labor organizer after getting my Ph.D. No matter what I was doing, I was sure that I was doing the right thing: I approached all my

---

[1]Thanks to Linda Werbner for sharing this quote.

political work with passion and single-mindedness. Even when I criticized previous incarnations of my own politics, I was sure that my critique (whatever it happened to be) was correct. When I first started teaching ESL, I set out to adapt Freirean perspectives in my classroom. This, to me, was the perfect way to marry my political and my academic background: I saw teaching ESL as a pretext for doing political work with immigrants and was convinced that whatever we did inside the classroom would be worthwhile to the extent that it led to collective action outside the classroom. I was convinced that Freire-inspired pedagogy was the "correct" approach to adult ESL, and that my job was to spread the word. So, when I got the chance to do workshops and conference presentations, as well as to teach a course on "Adult ESL in Theory and Practice" at the University of Massachusetts at Boston, I saw it as an opportunity to promote a participatory approach to ESL and foster critique of other approaches.

Now the real story of this chapter begins. As I began to teach this course and to do workshops, the model I was promoting was often met with great enthusiasm (reflecting my own enthusiasm): If participatory education is responsive to learners, grounded in critical and humanist theories, culturally sensitive, engaging, relevant, and ultimately transformative, how could there be anything but enthusiasm? But there always was. As one of my graduate students said, "Participatory ESL really looks good on paper, but then again, so have other approaches that we've studied." Over and over, I heard the same two words, "Yes, but . . ." and then would come the concerns, the worries, the hesitations, and the outright challenges:

> But my students want grammar.
> What right do we have to bring political issues into the classroom?
> My students don't want to think about their problems. They think their life here is OK.
> My students don't know enough English to do this stuff.
> I'm scared that I won't be able to handle the issues that arise.
> I don't want to be a social worker.
> There's not enough time.
> It's just too complicated.

My own reactions at first were to counter these challenges with unwavering enthusiasm on the one hand and defensiveness on the other (just like in those family discussions at Thanksgiving when someone would say, "Why on earth are you working in a factory with all your education?" and my answer, implicitly, would be, "You just don't understand. Once you do, you'll agree with me"). In other words, I know the best way, and my job is to convince you that I'm right. I saw the "problem" as being located in the person who was resisting. For every "yes, but . . ." I would counter with my own "yes, but . . ." to show students why this approach really was "correct."

But several things happened. First, the questions just kept coming. No matter where I taught, or whom I was working with, the same issues popped up over and over. I was confronted with a virtual litany of resistances. It became clear to me that these resistances, in fact the whole process of resistance, were not peripheral, incidental aberrations, but central, critical aspects of any dialogue about participatory education. I couldn't ignore or downplay them.

Second, I felt increasingly uncomfortable responding in a defensive way and trying to explain away the concerns. I didn't like the *us–them, either–or, right–wrong* dynamics that got set up. I felt that this dynamic positioned me as an expert and reinforced my power as the teacher. In essence, it was antithetical to a problem-posing stance because it set me up as the one with the answers who took on the task of transmitting them to the novices. But, at the same time, I did have a wealth of ideas and experience and to deny my own knowledge wasn't a solution either.

The more I struggled with how to address these questions, the more I came to understand that my defensiveness was rooted in a misunderstanding of how participatory praxis develops: it's not a matter of grasping the approach and then implementing it (or reading a book like this one (!) and then "doing it"). Rather, praxis evolves through an ongoing process of embracing certain aspects of the approach on one level, attempting to apply this preliminary understanding in practice, bumping into problems that trigger further reflection, then applying this new understanding, bumping into new problems (or the same ones), and so on. This is an inevitable developmental process for everyone; it was as necessary for me in figuring out how to address teachers' resistances as it is for them in figuring out their own ways of addressing teaching issues.

So what follows reflects my own cycle of praxis, of reflection-action-reflection as a teacher educator trying to address a range of resistances to participatory education. I started with some theory, conviction, and commitment—an ideological stance and a sense of purpose. As I tried out my understandings with students, I encountered problems and had to revise what I did, and the process doesn't end. In fact, writing this chapter is part of it, helping me clarify some of what I've been doing and how it has evolved over the years. I am going to focus on my graduate course in Adult ESL at the University of Massachusetts at Boston, where I worked with novices (people with little or no teaching experience), experienced teachers who were new to participatory education, and teachers who already had some experience or familiarity with this approach.

Before I go on, I need to say that I face the same dilemma in writing the chapter that I do in teaching: What should I do with the problems once they have been named? Should I step in as the expert and provide "solutions" or strategies for each problem based on my accumulated experience and reflection? Or should I abdicate this role and leave the problems for you, the reader, to struggle with? Of course I have my own ideas about how each of the issues named here might be addressed. But if I respond by proposing my strategies, I fall into the mode of problem *solving*, of asserting my "expertise." Yet, if I withhold my ideas, I am denying others the benefit of what I've learned over the years. So I have chosen to negotiate this tension by doing two things in this chapter. On the one hand, I present some of my students' reflections and their strategies for addressing dilemmas interwoven with my own analysis of ways to address these problems (*teaching strategies*); on the other hand, I present the strategies I have developed to avoid a defensive and problem-solving stance in my teaching (*teacher education strategies*).

There are two teacher education strategies I want to mention because they provided the basis for this chapter. The first is making space for resistances in my teaching, inviting them into the dialogue, and recognizing them as an integral component of what goes on. I build in ongoing time to elicit and address resistances in my graduate courses. I do this by asking participants to write honestly in journals about reactions to readings and critique coursework in light of their own experience as learners and teachers. I also always ask for permission to copy excerpts from participants' journals so I can share them as handouts for the whole group to consider. Thus, a second strategy (after eliciting individual responses) is to name and make public these responses by reproducing journal excerpts (anonymously) and discussing them together. Dialogue around this collective text serves to legitimate resistance and models a problem-posing process. At the end of the chapter, I discuss other strategies for addressing problems once they have been named.

I started writing this chapter by rereading handouts drawn from journal responses that span about 10 years. I was struck by the insight and wisdom of these journal entries and decided to center the chapter around them: The voices of these prospective ESL teachers are much more powerful than mine could ever be in expressing the dilemmas confronting participatory educators. Then I began to group resistances by theme (with color-coded post-its!!): problems relating to student–teacher roles, problems relating to political analysis, problems relating to "hot" issues, and so on. However, as I was doing this it occurred to me that these themes fall into categories according to the origin of the resistance: They arose for different reasons. Some originate in misconceptions about participatory pedagogy, some were reactions to the ways I was teaching, others are probably inherent in the participatory approach itself (inevitable aspects of implementing this approach), and still others are problems that exist with any approach to teaching adult ESL. So I'm going to organize this chapter around these categories. Of course, despite my attempts to separate them, these categories and themes spill over into each other and are interrelated.

FREIRE TALES: MYTHS AND MISCONCEPTIONS

The first group of resistances or challenges to participatory ESL I want to address are those rooted in what I consider to be misconceptions or myths about Freire's work. I call these "Freire tales" because they are based more on the ways Freire's work has been interpreted and adapted over the years than on what he himself suggested. In fact, I think one of Freire's gifts was the fact that he left so much open to interpretation: He did not tell people what to do or how to do it. As one of my graduate students said, "Freire's greatness is not what he has done, but what he leaves behind for us to do." Freire-inspired educators have had to struggle to make sense of participatory practice in our own contexts. The myths in many ways reflect the history of this struggle: They arise from ways in which practitioners (like me) have attempted to put our own understandings of Freire's work into practice. The mistakes that we made and the lessons we learned by practicing in exactly some of the ways that my students critiqued have caused us (or me—I guess I should only speak for myself) to revise our thinking. This has been a productive process: It has helped us to figure out what we want to make of participatory pedagogy. I start the chapter by examining some of the misconceptions that have engendered resistance to participatory ESL and go on to explore challenges I think are central to this approach.

The Teacher Is Supposed to Be Some Kind of Political Activist

The first of these myths relates to *politics*. It goes like this: *Freirean pedagogy is more political than other approaches, and it often entails introducing a left political agenda whether or not students are interested. In fact, in some cases, it's just an excuse to indoctrinate students in left politics.* One student expressed discomfort with this stance as follows:

> The teacher is supposed to be some kind of political activist. I think this should be looked at more closely. The implication is that a teacher who doesn't raise students' political consciousness is a villain. . . . For a method that claims to eschew imposition of teacher worldview, this is awfully pushy. . . . Will a student get an "F" if he/she doesn't rebel against the establishment? I'm joking, but only just.

Others embraced an overtly liberatory political stance, but questioned whether it is realistic in North American contexts:

> How correct is it to call any educational process or program in an industrial-ized country "Freirean" (or those inspired by him, "Freirean practitioners")? The more I read about Freire, the more I regard him as an essentially political figure. True liberation from oppression was the only motivation and to try to adapt him to, say, ESL in Canada seems so implausible.

Of course, the short answer to these resistances, as Freire argued, is that addressing social issues explicitly is no more political than teaching lan-guage functions or survival vocabulary: Every pedagogical approach is po-litical in that it prepares students for particular life roles. But I think these challenges get at the more profound question of what it means to be a "po-litical" educator. They are reactions to reductionist views that see trans-formative pedagogy as promoting a particular perspective in the class-room, and the teacher as someone who leads students toward this politic. This, in fact, is exactly how Freirean pedagogy has been practiced in many contexts. On a macro level, in some cases left political content has been substituted for the traditional content of education, and Freire's name has been invoked to promote particular political movements or perspectives. On a micro level, teachers often try to lead students to their own analysis or perspective on an issue. I certainly have been guilty of this at times. For example, when I first started teaching I remember choosing a picture of a Kentucky Fried Chicken place in Japan to raise the issue of U.S. imperialism with a group of Latina women; needless to say, the discussion bombed (my issue, not theirs)! Likewise, as the following quote indicates, I have been known to convey the message in my teacher education courses that my in-terpretation is the right one, and that students should agree with me: One of my students wrote:

> My sense is that after doing the readings I was supposed to laugh and con-demn this book. Or rather that you wanted that type of response. I have tried to think as critically as possible (to think about the book from different per-spectives). Perhaps some of it seems trivial or silly, but I don't have a great objection to that in small doses and particularly if it is offset by more signifi-cant or meaningful topics. . . . At any rate, there it is. I have this feeling that I am writing something that you will reject as uninformed, politically incorrect, etc. I also wonder if I am paranoid and if I am unfairly judging you.

Thus, to the extent that I and others have perpetuated the view that par-ticipatory ESL involves imposing left politics on the class, these resistances certainly make sense. But how can I say that these are reactions to "misin-terpretations" because there can be no doubt that participatory pedagogy is profoundly political, and that indeed its ultimate goal is social transformation? I say this because the essence of this approach, as I understand it, is not to transmit a worldview or a particular analysis of the social order, but to enable participants to develop their own capacity for critical analysis. Promoting a predetermined perspective is antithetical to this process. Thus, the dilemma for partipatory educators is how to acknowledge and embrace the profoundly political nature of participatory pedagogy without imposing a particular political analysis. This is a dilemma I struggle with in all my teaching (and that I will come back to later in the chapter).

Does Everything Need to Be a Controversy?

A second "Freire tale" relates to *pessimism*. It goes like this: *Participatory pedagogy focuses too much on problems; it's too negative and depressing. Students don't want to think about their problems. They want to be hopeful.* The following excerpts illustrate this view:

> I want to teach language because words and meanings are delightful and powerful and beautiful—and fun. Everyone's life is so hard. Students know they work two jobs and/or don't get paid enough. Of course I want things to be different for them, for everyone, but I want to teach ESL not as explicit activism, but as a way to help people hear themselves, as a way in to . . . VOICE and IDENTITY. The participatory approach is so gritty—it doesn't seem at all fun to me. . . . Why is any tired, over-worked, stressed-out adult going to do anything that stresses them out more? I want to alleviate, not burden. . . . It's not their fault America is racist, why am I making them change it?

> To what extent do we begin turning a language class into a "therapy session" by focusing so much on students' problems/issues? I have this image of endless class sessions of feeling weighted down by the burdens of everyone's social problems. Let's face it, this can become very tedious and overwhelming for both teacher and students and I'm not afraid of admitting it.

> Maybe the students would also like to discuss things that are not necessarily rooted in a social controversy (if such a thing exists?). Let me see, ways to start a small business, creative writing, the scientific basis for why a hurricane or earthquake occurs, etc. Does everything need to be a controversy?

One reason that teachers may see participatory ESL as negative is that they confuse the *what* and the *how*. As the following quote suggests, it is entirely possible to address weighty issues in a humorous way:

> B., a student from Brazil, raised his hand up to the sky and said, "I'm proud to be a wetback from Brazil!" and the other students asked what the definition of "wetback" was. So B. told them that it meant you were an illegal immigrant and he went around the room laughing and calling everybody a wetback! We

laughed so hard we were crying, all of us. Then P. from Hong Kong said that she was not a wetback and that she had a green card. B. looked at her and said "so what, you are still a wetback; nobody wants us here and that is why they call us 'wetback.'" P., the meek, piped up and said "this is why I like to come here, I laugh so much here, I cry every night at midnight because I miss my sister, I miss Hong Kong, but I laugh here."

But I think resistance to the "pessimism" of participatory education may come from cultural factors as well. North Americans are often culturally predisposed toward optimism, and, as the following student said, like to avoid conflict or focusing on problems:

From my viewpoint, from the eyes of the non-American, the present conditions of ESL education seem to be deeply rooted in the two main characteristics of Americans, superiority complex and optimism. . . . Americans are optimistic. Since they do not like people complaining and criticizing, they do not teach ESL students how to justify their positions by thinking critically. It is also convenient for someone exploiting LEP [limited English proficiency] people. ESL textbooks are no exception, and they are full of optimism. The textbook tells the students "don't worry, be happy," simply presenting only good, problem-free topics which are not realistic at all. . . . I feel that ESL teachers themselves must first become critical thinkers in order to teach their students how to think critically.

As teachers come to see participatory ESL as a means of dealing with the issues that come from the students themselves (rather than as dwelling on burdens), the myth of pessimism falls away:

I have learned that it is very important to recognize the need to put other activities aside in order to talk about what is on [learners'] minds. These events are of great interest to the class because they are real issues which impact their lives.

Thus, one of the things that I've come to through the years is framing participatory education not so much as problem focused, but as making space for students to look at what is, ask why it is that way, and what can be done about it. Framing it in these terms helps teacher-learners see it more as a pedagogy of optimism and possibility.

Should Lessons for Literacy Be Therapeutic?

Related to the myth of pessimism is the myth that participatory education entails delving into students' personal lives and asking them to disclose personal problems. This misconception leads to a concern that participatory ESL can be intrusive in inappropriate ways. As one student wrote:

> The participatory approach promotes disclosing personal information. . . . I
> assume this would embarrass some students, especially immigrants . . . who
> have gone through unusual experiences.

Another wondered:

> If I try to get a student to discuss or become aware of her cultural or family
> context, am I crossing over her boundaries of intimacy? . . . Should lessons for
> literacy be therapeutic, leading a student to consciously make changes in her
> life and social context?

When students raise concerns like this, we often discuss the difference
between personal and social issues—that participatory pedagogy invites exploration of issues that are common social problems, not individual problems. We problematize the notion that teachers should probe students' personal lives. Nevertheless, teachers often worry personal issues will surface
that they won't know how to "handle":

> Fortunately, her situation [with her husband] resolved itself—but what if it
> had not? Would I have been able to help her? Would it have been in my place
> to initiate dialogue that might encourage her to change her reality? What
> would the consequences have been? To be honest, I was relieved that his
> change of heart got me "off the hook." But what if a similar situation presents
> itself in the future, which is always a possibility when students and teachers
> open their lives to one another?

In cases like this, teachers often believe that they have to somehow fix
students' problems or act as social workers. This question draws them
even more deeply into questions about the teacher's role. In this case, we
talk about the difference between *problem solving*, where the teacher steers
students toward remedies, social service agencies, and so on, and *problem
posing*, where the teacher poses issues back to the class for reflection, analysis, and strategy building. We talk about the implications of a "helping"
stance. But this, in turn, gets at deeper concerns:

> I can see that we must be careful not to try to be social workers and/or psy-
> chologists. But what is our place as teachers? How involved should we get
> with our students? When will we have crossed the line?

These questions raise a key issue about the teacher's role, which I'll come
back to later.

You're the Teacher, You Decide

The flip side of the politics myth is the *process* myth—the myth that the *how* is more important than the *what* in participatory education. There are a couple of versions of this myth. One goes like this: *A participatory classroom is one in which students participate a lot. Whatever the students want to do is fine. They just tell the teacher and this is the lesson. Teachers don't need to plan; they just get students talking.* This leads to comments like the following:

> How much participation? Doesn't the teacher still need to start a direction— otherwise why have a teacher? What if students aren't used to participation and don't know what to do? What if they want to be spoonfed?

> I remember one time during my student teaching when I had asked the students to vote on something (I can't remember what) and one of the students said, "You're the teacher—you decide." Here I was trying to "empower" the students, and some didn't want this power.

> The only thing I don't agree with is how do the students know what kind of curriculum they need or want? Suppose they have just arrived in this country and they want to learn English and get a job.

> Doesn't it sometimes feel like you're teaching without preparation or organization? Like a lesson on the fly?

The problem with the view that focuses entirely on process is that it can end up liquidating both the political aspect of Freirean pedagogy and the teacher's role. The goal of participatory education, as I see it, is not to promote individual self-realization or "empowerment" (as if it were possible to do this), but rather to promote critical reflection with a view toward acting for change. The teachers' role in this process is to identify shared problematic aspects of learners' day-to-day lives, re-present them to learners as content for dialogue and literacy work, and guide reflection on individual experience of these problems to more critical social analysis. Participants jointly construct an understanding of the social conditions affecting them and develop strategies for addressing them. This process entails not just sharing stories about learners' lives or asking them what they want to do, but introducing new content and skills that will enable students to understand and act on issues if they choose to do so. Participation and learner involvement in curriculum processes are not an end in themselves, but a rehearsal for changing power relations outside the class. What this means is that content and process are inextricably intertwined in participatory pedagogy: They exist in a yin–yan relationship. Perspectives that focus on either content or process to the exclusion of the other set up a false dichotomy that triggers many of the resistances that practitioners voice.

Where Is My Voice in All This ESL Trendy Ideology?

A related issue concerns the question of *learner centeredness*. Here the myth that engenders resistance goes like this: *Because Freire suggests transforming power relations in the classroom, participatory classrooms are truly learner centered, which means the teacher relinquishes all authority. Teachers and students are colearners, interacting as equals.* When I've contributed to the view that participatory pedagogy is "truly learner centered" (by using the terms *learner centered* and *participatory* interchangeably at times), my graduate students have reacted strongly, wondering, for example why teachers' knowledge should be diminished:

> This is an abstraction that I can't grasp. Are the learner and the educator supposed to be equally knowing about the subject matter being taught? Does this apply to a calculus class?

They may worry that participatory education means giving up (or losing) control:

> What kind of "co-learner" is the final authority for resolving student problems? I've been uncomfortable with this term for a while. It seems to represent an effort to maintain that "We're all equals here," which may very well be true, but I don't think much is gained by the fuzzy suggestion that students are teaching the teacher as much as s/he is teaching them. As a student, that's not what I come to class for, and, while I recognize that people all learn from each other in a multitude of situations every day, and that teaching is a wonderful way to learn, I think if a teacher claims to be a co-learner, she/he needs to clarify exactly what that means. Otherwise, I'm afraid it may sound patronizing.

Teachers from non-North American (non-Western) cultures may see this as liquidating the teacher's role:

> While I read these articles . . . I do not find the position reserved for the teacher. While a lot of attention is paid for the interest of the students, the image of the teacher is a blurred one . . . I think it is unfair to ignore the role of the teacher. Americans tend to go to extremes to lay much stress on the students' interest and unfavorably push the teacher far down in the corner, standing like a servant watching the whole master's household dancing, feasting in the living room—something which is quite the opposite of the Confucianist hierarchy, and I don't like it that way, to tell the truth.

Some felt this approach demands too much of teachers:

The constant reminder of having to put myself out makes me uncomfortable. If I don't visit the students' homes, explore their neighborhoods, do ethnographic and literacy studies, familiarize myself with their cultural habits, learn their languages, and teach English using their real-life realities timed momentously to a concrete situation in addition to having political clarity, cross-cultural skills, etc., I am a failure as an ESL language teacher. I am beginning to feel strangled professionally. Where is my voice in all this ESL trendy ideology?

My own view is that juxtaposing learner- and teacher-centered ESL creates a false dichotomy. The real question is what each participant contributes and how. Clearly teachers have their own goals, their own understandings of effective second language pedagogy, and, most important, they have power. To deny this is both irresponsible and disingenuous: Students know it and teachers act on it whether or not they acknowledge it. At the same time, part of having power is making space for students to exert their power and to participate in decision making. The dance of teachers and students as they negotiate their respective goals, expectations, and understandings is central to participatory ESL. Once we begin to problematize the dichotomy in my graduate class, teachers can get beyond it, and their responses become more nuanced, embracing the complexity of their roles:

> The more I think about how this might be done, the more I'm realizing that it's not a "laissez-faire" attitude of teaching (expecting student issues to fall from the sky) but rather it's quite a complex and conscious process of action and reflection on the teachers' part. I'm thinking, geez, it's harder to let go of controlling a curriculum than to control it, because it will probably go in so many different directions.

Some explored the roots of their fear of letting go of control:

> It seems to me that many of our questions regarding student participation in curriculum development spring from a fear that informs so much of what we do as teachers. We are afraid of losing our (already rather tenuous) status as professionals. If students can be involved in the process of curriculum development, then what good is all our experience and hard work? If students' input is as important as our own, how do we maintain our credibility as professionals who have an expertise? I think this is a misguided fear, but nonetheless it's very powerful. We are conditioned to view the teacher/student relationship in a particular way, and it's hard to change. Even when we do recognize the limitations of the traditional conception of the relationship, we're reluctant to share our thoughts with colleagues—and supervisors—out of fear that we might be perceived as lazy or flaky.

Once teachers come to realize that being a colearner and accepting responsibility as a teacher are not oppositional, the way is open for them to

explore various aspects of their role for themselves. A lot of this comes
about through listening to students, trying things out, negotiating, and allowing for the gradual evolution of relationships in the classroom. It's much
more complicated than giving students choice versus asserting authority.
Often, as these excerpts indicate, it involves knowing when and how to
share of oneself:

> There are many occasions when I feel strongly identified with my students and
> never know if I should cross the line and share my deep feelings and experi-
> ences with them. Will it make me more human or will they no longer be able to
> see me as a teacher (too far gone from the traditional role of teacher). Over
> time, I have let my barriers down.

> When I first started teaching ESL, I ran like a scared rabbit from questions like;
> why don't you have a boyfriend? Why don't you get married? Why don't you
> have children? I guess I'd always laughed off these questions when traveling
> abroad and now in the ESL classroom I felt put on the spot and slightly
> ashamed of my lifestyle before traditional family people. But then I realized
> that my avoidance of these questions was speaking for me and that, in fact, my
> changing the subject was answering the questions for the students: the teacher
> expected personal information from the students yet provided none herself,
> the teacher was not honest and therefore not trustworthy. When I decided to
> change and share equally with my students, I felt their openness blossom be-
> fore me. We became less in opposition to each other (although without a doubt
> I still hold an unfair amount of power) and more like confidants who could
> speak without fear of judgment. They didn't fear me and I no longer feared the
> inevitable questions. Now we talk about lifestyle of women in the U.S. and ques-
> tions flow more freely. . . . I hear more from my students in their journals and in
> class when the information flows two ways.

Often they arrived at their own guidelines, which go far beyond a simplistic opposition between teacher- versus learner-centered pedagogy:

> If I see myself as another real person in the class, if I really perceive myself, and
> act, as a co-learner, while showing my respect for the others, there's no prob-
> lem with being clear. . . . Maybe there's some kind of intellectual honesty in-
> volved in this that brings me back to two of my current preoccupations: *think-*
> *ing of authority in terms of responsibility rather than power or control*, and the basic
> humanness of all this stuff that gets talked about as methods, principles.

I Get the Impression I'm Supposed
to Do Something Else

Another version of the process myth is what I call the myth of *method*. It
goes like this: *There is a lock-step sequence of steps in implementing a*
Freirean method. First you identify a generative theme (often by introducing a

structured activity to get at students' concerns); then you transform it into a
code; then you facilitate dialogue around the code in which students name the
problems, relate them to their own experiences, examine underlying socio-
political causes, strategize possible actions, and finally engage in collective ac-
tion to address the issue. If the outcome isn't action for social change, it doesn't
count; it's not truly Freirean. Of course this view becomes problematic
as soon as teachers enter the classroom because nothing ever follows a
neat process or develops the way one has planned, as the following quote
suggests:

> These structured activities didn't work in this class; it seems to me that issues
> don't get put on the table in such a direct way. Issues come up when someone
> gets an idea out of the blue and they want to share it with everyone.

Similarly, teachers often feel as though they have done something wrong
if they don't get to a particular stage in the process (for example, if the discussion ends before any action results):

> My question is: what now? Issue raising is not a problem, the best ones came
> out when I wasn't trying to elicit them. . . . So what do I do with them? I am not
> supposed to solve them, which is good because I can't (God knows every in-
> stinct in me screams to try), but I get the impression I'm supposed to do
> something else. I remember reading in *Making Meaning, Making Change* about
> issues "dying" at the discussion stage. Perhaps I read it wrong, but I'm not so
> sure that only discussing an issue is a flop. Already students like N. have be-
> gun using more English in class, and students like J. have *participated.* And yet
> there's another voice inside that says that getting them to use the language
> isn't enough.

The notion that "it doesn't count if it doesn't result in action" further in-
duces frustration, particularly when "action" is narrowly defined as collective political action:

> I must admit, however, that I still experience some discomfort when it comes
> to the implementation phase—the "what can we do about it?" phase of the
> process. This is the point where it somewhat feels like the greatest potential
> for frustration and anger lies. That is, what happens if people can't come up
> with "solutions" for their problems (I know what I just said is awfully "prob-
> lem-solving" rather than "problem-posing", but won't people be looking for
> concrete solutions? Isn't there potential for more frustration and anger if they
> feel like they've come to a "dead end")—or is it enough to give people a sense
> to begin to *envision* differences in their lives?

Here again, teachers' resistance is not so much to participatory pedagogy but to a misconception about it, namely that problem posing can be

reduced to a method that entails following a set of prescribed steps to reach a certain outcome. I certainly have contributed to this myth in my own work (e.g., with one-shot workshops that focused on developing codes and dialogue questions rather than on exploring a range of ways students' realities can become curriculum content). And, of course, publishers are all too happy when problem posing is reduced to a method because this makes it easier to commodify: Neat methods that follow a lock-step process are much more amenable to commodification than approaches that are messy and demand thinking. The irony, of course, is that to the extent that problem posing is reduced to a method, it ends up disempowering teachers in the process of claiming to empower learners.

But, I Love to Teach Grammar

Another misconception relates to the role of grammar in participatory ESL. It goes like this: *You don't teach grammar in participatory ESL; all you do is talk and hope that communication will enhance the acquisition of English.* To this, my students responded with comments such as:

> While this approach seems to provide a lot of practice in language as communication, is there any chance that it interferes with the development of "correct" language? . . . Are we in some way making unfair choices or decisions if we use this approach for adult education programs but teach students in community colleges or other colleges grammatical forms? Are we handicapping people in any way?

> The other & final thought I have is really a confession: I'm not only not opposed to teaching grammar, I love to teach grammar. It's fascinating—how language is constructed, the power of words. I wholeheartedly agree with whoever said that grammar is essential . . . and not to provide students with grammar is to do them a great disservice.

It's not clear to me where the view that participatory ESL precludes grammar comes from. It may be that participatory education is sometimes seen as aligned with whole language pedagogy, which, in turn, is seen by some as excluding grammar instruction. Or perhaps because those of us who write about participatory ESL spend so much time on the ways this approach differs from others in its goals and substance, we perpetuate the idea that grammar instruction is antithetical to participatory ESL. However, rather than being antithetical, I see it as integral. That it is not the organizing principle of curriculum development does not mean there is no place for it in the classroom. Learning to contextualize grammar instruction is an essential skill for teachers who espouse participatory pedagogy. For me, the best way of addressing this is with examples from practice; books like *Talking Shop* (Nash, Cason, Rhum, McGrail, & Gomez-Sanford, 1992), which give teachers' accounts from their own classrooms, show multiple ways of using grammar lessons to get at students' concerns and to integrate them with reflection and with action.

A related concern is based on the view that all one does in participatory ESL is talk about students' lives:

> I believe [the participatory approach's] principal virtue is also its weakness. If all the course content is to be drawn from the students' lives and problems, that means that there is never the opportunity to inject something completely novel, to introduce them to other lives, other experiences, things beyond their ken.

The views that neither grammar nor content beyond the students' reality can be introduced in a participatory classroom are part of the larger myth of method: They rest on the notion there is a prescribed method for "doing it," which doesn't include teaching grammar or new information. Anyone who listens to students knows that they see both of these aspects of language learning as critical to enabling them to take action in their lives.

INHERENT DILEMMAS

In the previous section, I argued that many of teachers' resistances to participatory ESL result from misconceptions and false dichotomies that have somehow become integrated into the discourse of participatory ESL: political versus apolitical teaching, the primacy of content versus process, learner- versus teacher-centered pedagogy, and so on. At the same time, however, exploring each of these myths and their roots inevitably raises important questions: What does it mean to be a politically conscious educator? How can we both respect students' goals and move toward critical analysis if it's not what students want? What is our role as teachers? Even though these questions may come from reactions to Freire tales, they are critical, central issues for participatory ESL. These are the questions to which I now turn, but as you see, they are closely related to those I have just discussed.

Whose "Hope for Change" Is It?

Perhaps the most basic question teachers face is: *What right do we have to make critical analysis of the social context central in our teaching?* Teachers worry about the ethics of promoting a critical stance when students may not want to challenge the way things are. They wonder what their stance should be when students' goals have nothing to do with social change:

While I think this is the ideal to aspire to, is it what the students want? Is it what they are there for? Obviously, a group of students will have very different personalities and needs among them, some open to social analysis, and other, perhaps who are quite conservative or too afraid to consider criticizing life in America. Even if we have determined that there is no line between teaching English and working for social action, how do we make sure we are not imposing our liberal/leftist middle-class politics/ideals on our students?

I'm reminded of a Cape Verdean student who was perfectly happy to be a card-carrying (Visa, Mastercard, American Express) member of this society as it is. His new car was the symbol of his financial success. . . . He enjoys the material fruits of his 60 hours of labor a week—a new house, a car, a stylish Cape Verdean wife.

Aren't many of our learners so happy to be in a land of comparative freedom that they are uncomfortable questioning the system?

Some teachers worry they are setting their students up for disappointment or promoting false promises:

Do teachers have the right to introduce conflicts or desires that can't be fulfilled due to familial/social constraints?

However, after students finish the class, going out to the real world, they will find that the power relations which do not exist in class between teachers and students in this participatory approach are everywhere in the society. While changes in classroom take a long time and many efforts, changes in society take generations.

There need to be such large changes outside the classroom. It seems almost cruel to have awakened a hope, a dream that things might be different knowing that the small flame needs careful nurturing to grow into reality and that outside the classroom it will be extinguished and leave perhaps a bitter sweet memory.

Others wonder about the ethics of raising issues in a vacuum, without considering the consequences or making connections with concrete possibilities for collective action or change:

If literacy is a liberating force, it also unleashes hostilities. Both student and teacher are forced to anticipate the full consequences . . . particularly if the student's role has been prescribed by his cultural and social environment. What a tall order for both teacher and student.

If such a critically minded educational approach does not, at the same time, provide an **infrastructure** for "critique" to the student, it has not enough moral force to claim itself critical. By an infrastructure for critique, I mean a very basic thing: Connection to, say, trade unions, legal services (progressive ones, of course) and the like, that make it possible for the student to connect with people who also concern themselves with progressive change in the U.S.

These are not issues that have easy answers. I see the process of acknowledging and struggling with them as part of the teachers' own conscientization. Through the dialogue, teachers offer new insights to each other, insights that are invaluable as they explore the question of their own positioning and how their ideas may work out in their practice. They consider questions like who they are in the social order, as well as both their limits and their responsibilities:

> As a white American ESL teacher I must always keep this in mind for I am in some ways part of and a result of the power structure that oppressed these people in the first place.

> I think it's important to recognize the limitations of our role in their lives. Although I definitely think it's important to express our opinions in an open and honest way, I don't think it's appropriate for us to see ourselves as saviors coming to free them from the oppressive forces in their communities.

> Who is to define what is "liberating" for an individual student? The student alone? The student *and* the teacher? Is it enough if the student feels his life has been enlarged? What if the teacher feels the student has greater potential?

Beyond the macro-level question of whether it's ethical to "impose" a participatory approach, teachers often wonder, on a more micro level, if their identification and selection of issues are a form of imposition:

> But what makes me uncomfortable is the implication that the educator can identify the "issues" that are important in students' lives, make decisions about what to codify & develop curriculum based on these decisions. Having a more noble ideological view, a supposedly broader view of society, does not prevent us from barging in on someone else's reality any less than a more traditional dictatorial approach does. It is always our version and while we may be informed by all kinds of experiences and social-political theory, we are no less capable of knee-jerk reactions to someone else's reality, no matter how well intentioned.

> Some reservations about the participatory approach that have been resting in the back of my mind now have come to be clearer. The "issues" are interpreted differently from teacher to teacher. What I feel are significant and relevant issues may not be so for the next. After meeting with John (after he observed my class) I realized he caught on to some things that I either didn't catch all the way or caught, but not in my net of importance. What does this mean? Are participatory models even more teacher chosen curricula than CBAE? How do we choose an issue? Can we always go by instinct? These are questions I am trying to sort out.

I am having a hard time not pushing what I see as issues in D's life. . . . So this is my challenge, to not push my own agenda on her, and let her with my help express what her reality is. And then develop learning plans with it.

How to strike that delicate balance between students' identifications of problems vs. teacher's anticipation of what students will identify as their problems? i.e., Whose "hope for change" is it?

Teachers offer various ways of addressing this concern. Some accept their role in "proposing" issues and evaluate through student reaction whether the issues are genuinely relevant:

I have analyzed my "curriculum" to see if it addresses racism, classism, sexism, but then I think, "but these issues didn't come from participants." But then, again, I think to the extent that they get engaged with a topic once I've raised it, then it's theirs, e.g., as they have with questions of discrimination in housing or in the workplace.

Others suggest making space for issues without directly introducing them:

In approaching this lesson, I would allow room for, and in fact encourage, a discussion of the social realities that students face, but I don't know if I would make discrimination the focus if the students themselves didn't bring it up. I'm not sure how much to push a political agenda when it is not spontaneous from among the students, though clearly they must be made aware that the classroom is a safe place for all these issues.

It's All Such a Risk

The flip side of imposing issues is not knowing what to do with them when they arise, or feeling overwhelmed by the complexity of issues that learners face. For example, if teachers are especially successful in creating an atmosphere that encourages participation, they may be stymied by the richness of possible directions:

Too many issues are coming out all at once. How do I deal with all of them? How do I deal with the spontaneous issues that come out in the middle of a lesson?

Or they may worry that there are not enough *common* issues, issues that pertain to the whole class, and that, instead, each of the issues that arises only interests a subgroup. Some worry that when we make space for the realities of students' lives, issues may emerge that are overwhelming:

Yet the community that we have in our ESL class is very fragile. It is very easy to lose someone and never know why. People just disappear from class and you are left wondering if there was some betrayal, or something said or not said, if there was a topic that was too painful. Because of this fragility, I often want to use materials that are far away from the students' experiences of everyday life. For example, *Side by Side* is a great book for avoiding the realities of life. However, there is so much more we can do.

Teachers often wonder what their responsibility is for the powerful reactions that issues may elicit:

Race relations in the States, for example, is such a national preoccupation that it seems quite an ordinary topic to talk about, no matter how people feel about it. But, it might be a very trying subject to certain immigrants. This is the dilemma I have about any possibly controversial topic in the classroom. How far should it be pursued? What does one do if some students are clearly uncomfortable with it? To what extent am I responsible for any emotional Pandora's box that might open?

They may feel unprepared for the issues that surface:

And what if the teacher herself knows nothing about block organizing or tenants' rights? As a native English speaker—especially middle class—we don't often run into these problems. Students may expect the teacher to have the answers.

And I'm uncomfortable encouraging people to bring up their problems in class because many of those problems are going to be way more than I can handle. I can hardly keep my own life "together."

Teachers may be uncomfortable embracing the political aspect of participatory ESL because they don't have experience problem posing the issues they face in their own lives. They may worry they won't know how to move issues toward political analysis because acting on their own behalf, in a political way, doesn't grow out of their own strengths. If they never have advocated for their own rights, they may be uncomfortable asking students do so. How can they encourage students to fight for health benefits if they haven't been able to win them for themselves?[2]

A big question is—can't it snowball on you? Can't you end up "empowering" people and motivating them to social change to a point that is way over your head? . . . I could see it happening to me! I don't feel as if I know enough about life to help people make some of these big changes in their lives. It's all such a risk.

---

[2] Thanks to Diane Paxton for this point.

And, of course, their fears are real. Teachers are confronted with enormous issues and constantly have to struggle with the balance between the risks and benefits of exploring the realities of learners' lives, as this story shows:

> In the very first ESL class which I taught, there was an older Haitian gentleman whom we all loved. I call him a gentleman because this adjective fits him so well, especially because he was such a natty dresser—he always came to class in a suit and tie. One time, he was absent from class for two weeks and when he came back we asked him about his absence, especially because he look so tired and thin. First he told us he had big problems because his car had been stolen, for the second time, from in front of his house. Everyone expressed their sympathies and one student, a woman, told him he needed to move, since the car had been stolen twice. . . . He answered that he wanted to because his neighborhood was "bad" but he couldn't afford it. . . . A couple of people then made suggestions about where he needed to go to find a better apartment. . . . But he kept shaking his head and finally said that he had even bigger problems. It turned out that his wife, also elderly, had suffered a stroke that had totally incapacitated her. They had no near relatives so everyday he would get up at 4 in the morning to prepare all her meals and leave by 7 am. The facts of his story really impacted us, not just because they were horrendous but because he was so weary and sad as he told us. The classroom got very quiet like no one knew what to say or suggest for him to do. We, the teachers, felt like the students were waiting for us to say something, offer something, more than just our sympathies. I asked him if he had ever heard of the Visiting Nurses Association or of housing for the elderly. He shook his head but added that there were even bigger problems that he couldn't talk about. At this point, the head teacher initiated a continuation of the class. . . . After class, he confided that the reason he was afraid to seek help was that his wife was here illegally. He had papers but couldn't extend them to her because they had never married legally.

When I hear stories like this, my first instincts are to fall into stunned silence, to move on, or to come up with a "solution" (e.g., How about getting an immigration lawyer to come to your class?). These stories raise issues (How can teachers respond in situations like this?) that overwhelm me as a teacher educator. But when I remember to pose the question back to my students, they often resist the urge to move immediately toward solutions. As one teacher said:

> Individual teachers have to work out their own ways based on knowing who they are, what their strengths and limitations are, trusting themselves and their experience, and relying on that trust to pull them through whatever painful situation may emerge.

They come up with responses like the following as they explore this issue:

> Who knows what memories I could be dredging up, so I need to feel the students have a way out of my intended way in.

Many teachers feel that once they are able to connect on a human level with their students, and embrace the risk of allowing space for their realities, the benefits are huge:

> Some might say I've stepped way out of the bounds of teacher–student relationships. I don't think so. Real learning occurs when the urgent themes of one's life are being addressed. [Students'] grammar skills could be improving more quickly, perhaps, but their (our) souls are being fed in our class. Real learning is happening.

Yet I Want to Say, This Is America, You Can't Abuse Your Women Anymore

Another dilemma arises when students say something that challenges the teachers' belief system or when students have conflicting positions about charged issues:

> The issues that come up are often loaded ones. Sometimes students have conflicting opinions on how the problem is defined and what the solution might look like to the extent that they might wind up in an argument. Or, what if the teacher has a strong opinion that is very contrary to what most students think correct or proper? Should she state it at the risk of losing their respect and maybe losing them as students? For example, I know many gay teachers who are struggling with the issue of whether or not to come out to their students, knowing that most cultures are extremely homophobic.

Students may express opinions that are racist or based on stereotypes:

> Sometimes seemingly mundane questions brought up deeper issues. I remember one class when the teacher had asked "How do you get to class?" One woman became very upset when talking about riding the train and alluded to being accosted by men and not knowing what to do. Other students at this point assumed she was referring to African-Americans and began talking about various "unpleasant" and "frightening" behaviors they had observed in many people of that race.

Teachers may disagree with students' perspectives or practices regarding male–female roles, or the issue of domestic abuse may arise. Teachers wonder how, on the one hand, to respect students' cultural values and, on the other, to challenge those that conflict with values of equality and social justice. One teacher framed this dilemma as follows:

> I'm torn. Here we are advocating that newcomers value their culture as we try to keep from indoctrinating our values in them. Yet I want to say, this is America, you can't abuse your women and children anymore. While the impact of the dominant culture's stereotypes and prejudices are greater and more damaging on our oppressed students, we must have some obligation to address all stereotypes.

Often my students think that there is a "right" way to address these issues, and that I, as the professor, know it. They often ask me to tell them what to do, as in the following example:

> One point in that article, "Things that may happen," reminded me of an incident in my classroom when an argument broke out. I had only been teaching the class for a few weeks, and my students had been discussing the welfare system (casually, before class began). One woman stated that she felt people on welfare were lazy and taking advantage of the people who pay taxes. Another student became very defensive, saying those on welfare need assistance and that people like the first student only add to their shame. The argument became heated, and despite my attempts to intervene ("There are two sides to this . . ." etc.), the second student became angry and stormed out of the room. He never returned to class. I wanted to bring him back, but I didn't know how. When dealing with emotionally charged issues, the teacher may have to defuse situations in which anger or other emotions erupt. I see that incident as a failure on my part, and hope to learn to handle such situations more successfully in the future. I'd be interested in knowing how you would have handled this situation, or how I could have dealt with it more successfully (and hopefully avoid such negative outcomes in the future).

Invariably, if I suggest solutions, they don't work. I learned early on that if I said, "Here's what you should do," whatever it is will not work. When teachers bring in stories like this (and like the one about the Haitian gentleman), they provide opportunities to model problem posing in class. What can the teacher do in a situation like this? What would happen if she takes a stand? Or what if she remains silent about her own view and just asks questions? Although most teachers agree that offering one's perspective authoritatively suppresses dialogue, their strategies are often different. Some argue it's critical not to take an "interventionist" stance:

> Admittedly, it's very frustrating to watch some students sacrifice themselves for the selfish and sexist men in their lives, but on some level that is their choice. I think it's important to recognize the limitations of our role in their lives. Although I definitely think it's important to express our opinions in an

open and honest way, I don't think it's appropriate for us to see ourselves as saviors coming to free them from the oppressive forces in their communities.

Others argue that not offering one's perspective is tacitly reinforcing the status quo:

> [Ann Cason] is probably on target when she says that she may be privileging her authority status by removing herself from the discussion and having a veneer of objectivity.

Another position is that teachers need to be careful not to set up false dichotomies or succumb to stereotyping. They need to look more deeply at the context of the issue:

> I also think that we need not to see these issues in black and white terms. All men in poor and immigrant communities are not domineering, abusive and/or violent. The relationship between violence & oppression & economic need is real.... What kinds of support were available to these women? their husbands? were family situations as fixed as they sounded? What helps immigrant/poor communities cope with these personal changes? ... How do we simultaneously have compassion for women in oppressed situations **and** for men?

The Teacher Should Be Like a President

Another dilemma relates to students' versus teachers' conceptions about classroom *processes*; just as teachers can impose content related to social issues, they can impose their ideas about language learning. But students come with strong internalized models of what language learning should look like. They often expect rote learning and drill. To some extent this is an issue for any teacher who embraces communicative language teaching; but when the approach advocates respecting learners' goals and involves them in pedagogical decisions, the contradiction may seem even sharper. What is a responsive, nontraditional teacher to do if the students want nonresponsive, traditional teaching? Or if the students say (as one teacher reported), "The teacher should be like a President. In America, Democracy; in the classroom, no."? This is a common theme in my graduate students' journals:

> How often, as teachers, do we impose our approaches on our students? Student-centered? No way! We [students] want grammar, translations and rote memorization! Just give us the basics.

> I've seen students reject critical thinking even in a classroom where a learner centered lesson is taking place. This may be due to an inability to understand or feel comfortable with "inquiry." In an ESL classroom, how can a teacher help

the students and how can the students help each other to learn and be open to the process of thinking critically?

In addition, if teachers want to be sensitive to the cultural practices and expectations that students bring with them, and build on what is familiar to them, introducing dialogical and participatory practices can pose a dilemma. Don't the cultural practices of some groups prevent them from being comfortable in a nontraditional classroom? This was an issue often raised poignantly by non-American teachers:

> As a language teacher, I feel confident about my teaching job only when the class is centered on language learning. If the class focuses on the discussion of problems caused by other factors, rather than language, which are not within my ability to solve, I will grow a sense of helplessness, which will make me uncomfortable as a teacher standing in the classroom even though I understand I am not required to provide a solution. Perhaps this feeling is rooted in my culture. In Chinese culture, teachers are expected to solve the problems students raise in class. On the part of the students, if they raise a question, they expect it will be solved satisfactorily in class. Otherwise, they feel the class is a failure.

Again, teachers often work out their own strategies when the problem is posed back to them. Here, a Vietnamese teacher looked at the roots of student resistance to discussing problems and suggested talking openly about differences in cultural contexts:

> Unlike the U.S.A., where people can voice their opinion against state and public officials without taking risks, Vietnam has less freedom in writing and speech. We have only one political party and those who criticize the party are in danger of getting into big trouble. ESL teachers in the U.S.A. who have students from countries like Vietnam should explain to them that they can just feel free to express their critical thoughts without being afraid to make trouble in this country.

This teacher suggested going slowly:

> Maybe starting out with smaller problems and working up to the larger ones would be a way of familiarizing the students with the participatory process in which the teacher doesn't have the answers, but helps to guide discussion and discovery amongst the students so that they become comfortable with the process and realize their own capacity to take charge of their learning.

Another teacher reflected on this dilemma in light of the question of the teacher's role:

> The question of how to deal with students' models and expectations of education and language learning has concerned me for as long as I've been a teacher. On the one hand, I want my students to be involved in the decision-

making process regarding what goes on in their classroom. On the other hand, they often don't want to participate in the decision-making process. Even more frustrating for me is when they do want to participate and they make the *wrong* choices. What do I do then? I want to give my students what they want, but maybe only when it coincides with what I think they should want. And, in a way, I don't think that's entirely inappropriate. Sometimes I really do know better than my students do, and it isn't because I'm superior; rather it's just that I have more experience, and I've probably given more thought than most of my students have to the issues involved in second language acquisition. Having said this, I should also say that I am conscientious about incorporating student input. Basically, my goal is to strike a balance between students' expectations and my own approach and philosophy. Of course, it isn't always easy to do.

Does It Work for All Students?

There are many other pedagogical issues that recur as teachers move toward a participatory model. One of the biggest issues relates to the question of beginning ESL students, who may not be able to express much in English. This problem is compounded when students speak different languages or the teacher does not know their language:

> How do you do this with beginners whose first language you know nothing about? Can you? Does it work for all students?

> The participatory approach seems to require students to talk almost right from the beginning. Is that a problem for some students? Also, sometimes when a topic is especially emotional it seems that although that generates a lot of talking, it makes it difficult to talk in the second language.

Of course, these sorts of questions arise in any communicative approach, but they are more problematic when the approach is centered on drawing out the issues and concerns of learners. How can you find themes if students can't express themselves in English? Discussing this problem often leads teachers toward the question of first-language use in the ESL classroom. They have to confront the pervasive belief (which many of them hold) that "English only" should be the rule in ESL instruction. Yet, when teachers make space for first-language use and try to connect it to instruction or to draw out themes for further exploration in English, new problems may arise:

> When I stop and ask them if they want to share what they are speaking about together whether in jokes, pair conversations or group discussions, I usually get a shake of the head, shrugs of feigned ignorance or blank stares. Although their conversation could be related to the topic at hand, they may not have the words to express their feelings in English. This has been a long-term frus-

tration. How do I get them to reveal what they are speaking about when they may not have the language to express it or may feel that I am an intrusive force in their free conversation?

Although students may be most animated and engaged when their first language is accepted in the classroom, they themselves often react against first-language use, seeing it as exclusionary in mixed-language groups or an impediment to learning. These dilemmas, in turn, lead back to the question of the teacher's role: Should teachers make rules about language use and enforce them? In my classes, by posing this issue back to graduate students, we model a process they might use with students. We explore the pros and cons of various strategies without prescribing any. Participants come away with a range of possibilities which they can draw on, depending on the context of their practice. They often propose nonverbal ways of finding themes, reliance on more proficient students to facilitate, problem posing this issue with their students (exploring with them when it is and isn't useful to use the first language), and so on.

The Rest of the Group Become the Spectators

Other pedagogical challenges are not unique to participatory pedagogy, like the problems of uneven participation, difficult classroom dynamics, and multilevel classes:

> Also it was hard to draw in those students who have difficulty expressing their own opinions.
>
> In a group discussion, the fluent person is the one who talks the loudest and the longest and the rest of the group become the spectators of the show.
>
> Is this really the optimum way to do things in a multi-level class with learners from diverse economic, social backgrounds? This is the case in my situation. It's possible, but it takes a lot more thinking, I think, on the part of both the learner and the instructor.

One of the strengths of a participatory approach, I think, is the notion that teachers are not the only ones responsible for "fixing" problems like these. As my graduate students strategize about how to handle these issues, they often arrive at the idea of addressing them *with* students, rather than *for* them. A wonderful contradiction becomes apparent: On the one hand, participatory ESL requires, as one student said, a lot more thinking (it's demanding), but, on the other, it lets teachers off the hook because they don't have to solve all the problems of the classroom by themselves.

There are a host of other logistical questions that teachers pose; many of these relate to contextual constraints. What if you are teaching in an institution that mandates certain practices or outcomes that contradict participatory pedagogy?

> Can a teacher effectively challenge a particular system? If a newly hired teacher discovers the prescribed ESL curriculum to be value-laden, authoritarian, hierarchical in its sociopolitical outlook regarding immigrants, [what can she do about it]?

> How is work to be evaluated when grades are required? Evaluation of "objective" tests and structured assignments may be easier for the teacher. What, though, does she or he need to keep in mind when evaluating units and activities that have been shaped by the learners themselves?

> My number one question is will I be able to fit the lessons that I need to back into the experiences and problems of the students without it becoming a huge mismatch of grammar, vocabulary, skills. . . ?

Teachers worry about time constraints:

> I agree with the effectiveness of teaching literacy based on student needs. But such customized teaching needs more time and labor, and it would be particularly difficult for the teacher working with a large class..

> If it's a short course, by the time you really identify their needs, the course is almost over.

By now you've noticed that I'm not providing answers to these questions. In fact, as I was rereading what I've written so far, I started to get nervous; it seemed like a laundry list of problems without answers (and it doesn't even include half the problems that teachers encounter!). But, in thinking about this, what struck me was that these questions don't have generic answers that fit any context. The answers can't come from a chapter in a book. They need to come through a process of struggling with the questions. The quotes represent a window on this process and, as such, what my students have said in exploring these issues is more useful than anything I could have said. In the next section I discuss some of the strategies I have used to support teachers in this process, as well as what teachers themselves have said about the process.

TEACHER-EDUCATION STRATEGIES

So far I have mentioned three teacher education strategies I have used in my graduate courses to address student resistances: inviting students to write about their concerns in journals; re-presenting journal excerpts back to the class as a collective text; and modeling a problem-posing process by naming issues, looking at their roots, and eliciting strategies for responding to them. Several other strategies have allowed me to transfer the challenge of responding to problems back to the teachers themselves: (a) connecting learning and teaching; (b) doing a structured problem-posing activity; and (c) having students respond to their own journals at the end of the term.

There's a Lesson to Be Learned From What Worked in My Own Education

I often invite my students to see their own *learning* experiences as the object of reflection. This enables them to discover ways of addressing *teaching* issues they have raised. For example, here a Japanese student came to the realization she is her own best "laboratory" in thinking about how critical thinking develops:

> I was perspiring [as I read the articles for class]. . . . The second obstacle was my lack of skills in reading critically, thinking critically. And as I was contemplating Freire's description of Banking concept of education, it hit hard that I am mostly a product of this type of education, especially in Japan. . . . But then I must find out what sort of practice will free this cultural barrier. I must define what it is which makes people think more critically and analytically. This is going to be my second theme in participating in Elsa's class.

Many get insights about the question of how to promote new roles for teachers by looking at their own educational experiences:

> When I look back, the undergrad classes I got the most out of were those where the prof didn't "play prof" but guided us as we wrestled with the issues that came up as a result of our reading and other classwork. Homework in these classes felt like an extension of the classroom struggle—I paid attention to what I was doing and in the end I grew a lot. And (miracles!) I learned from my peers as much as my prof. Since we acted like adults . . . and because he/she treated us like adults, when the prof **did** speak, I **listened**. There's a lesson to be learned from what worked in my own education.

Graduate students may mine their own experience to understand learners' reactions, as this teacher did:

> A number of the excerpts from the journals seem to be addressing the issue of students expecting the teacher to play the traditional role of giver of knowledge. In response to this issue, I would like to say that that is what the students expect because that's all they've ever experienced in a classroom. . . . Speaking from my own experiences, it was not until this semester that I ever had a teacher who didn't overwhelmingly embrace the traditional teacher role. In both my classes this semester, the teachers to varying degrees em-

brace the Freirean approach in the classroom. At first I wasn't sure what to do because it was a brand new experience. . . . In the beginning, I wondered how long it would last before we'd be getting lectured, tested, forced to figure out what the teacher wanted us to say or write or spit back. But as time went on I relaxed as I realized that this new approach was going to last all semester. I've come to really love it—no longer is the classroom a separate entity from my life—it has become part of my life because I get to express what knowledge I've already gained from my life experiences and discuss issues which are real and important to me. . . . I also feel more relaxed and much more in control— no longer am I consumed in the game of figuring what the teacher wants to hear. I am learning for myself **today**.

Shifting the Expertise: Problem-Posing Trees

I always devote one session in my graduate course, about two-thirds of the way through the semester, to using a tool called the problem-posing tree. This is a tool I first learned about from my colleague, Cathy Walsh, which is used widely in popular education as a concrete device around which to explore a community problem. I introduce the tool as a way to address teaching issues (in our class) while modeling it as a tool that teachers can use to address students' issues (in their classes). Before the class, students divide into self-selected groups centered on issues we have identified together. At home, members of each group read assigned articles related to that issue. In class, participants are instructed to draw a tree, which becomes a visual symbol around which to discuss the issue. The trunk is the problem (here participants name the problem in its various aspects); the leaves and branches represent the manifestations of the problem (how it presents itself in teaching); the roots are the origins, causes, or underlying reasons for the problem; a watering can represents strategies for addressing the problem. After each group has discussed its issue, the students present the tree and their discussion to the class as a whole. This process often serves as a way of examining more deeply issues that have surfaced along the way (including many of the issues mentioned in this chapter) and bringing in new perspectives from readings. The group members become the "experts," and I contribute my own experience or ideas during discussion along with the rest of the class. I have included one example of a tree (Fig. 13.1) as well as notes that one group wrote up about the progression of their discussion (Fig. 13.2).

You've Mixed in the Yeast and We're in the Process of Rising

The last strategy I want to mention is inviting my students, at the end of the term, to reread and respond to their own journals. In their final journal entry, they not only address issues that have arisen, but, more important,

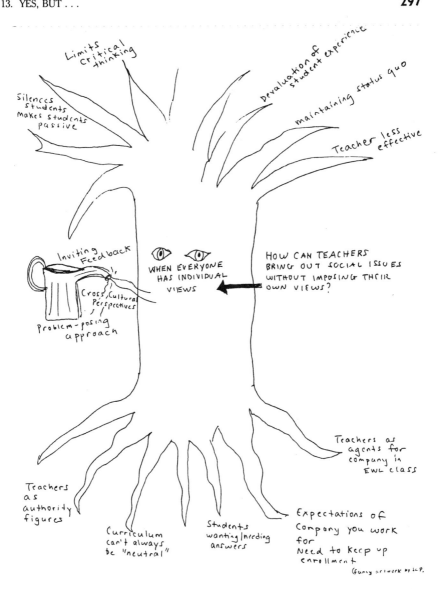

FIG. 13.1. Example of a tree.

they reflect on their learning processes. This helps them to solidify their own stance, to realize that their thinking (and sometimes their practice) has changed, and to see that becoming a participatory educator is a process. Often they identify for themselves where they are in that journey, where they want to go, and how they might do this. Of course, their reflections are much wiser than any feedback I could give. One student wrote:

Initially I felt overwhelmed by the basic goals of the participatory approach. While I could see the relevance of Freire's philosophy of education and could appreciate the ultimates that drive the process that he espouses, the words *empowerment* and *action* seemed radical and frightening. Learning how to pose the problems that would lead to a dialogue about their reality so that

Issue: What is the role of the teacher in a participatory classroom?

Questions:

— How much control is too much? How much is too little?
— How do we establish a genuine and positive sense of authority?
— What are the boundaries of the teacher's role?
— How do we negotiate the differences between our sense of the teacher's role and the students' sense of the teacher's role?
— To what extent are we teachers? To what extent facilitators?
— How much responsibility do we assume for student success and failure?
— How do we evaluate student success and failure?
— How political is our work?

Manifestations of problems and uncertainty about the teacher's role:

— Student silence, passivity
— Lack of confidence in the teacher
— What are the boundaries of the teacher's role?
— Students feeling invaded, uncertain
— Students feeling intimidated
— Classroom chaos, revolt
— Teacher anxiety
— Teacher feeling lack of control
  Teacher falling back on traditional methods
— Teacher burnout
— Teacher becoming problem solver
— Teacher feeling overwhelmed, frustrated
— Teacher feeling like a social worker

Roots of the problems:

— Cultural differences between teacher and students
— Different educational backgrounds among students and between teacher and students
— Economic pressures on students
— Organizational pressures on teachers
— Political climate in the United States
— Individual personality differences and preferences
— Previous teaching experiences
— Stereotypes about others/other cultures
— All sorts of emotional baggage

Some suggested solutions:

— Teacher/student communication and negotiation of classroom roles
— Co-teacher support
— Openness to learning with students and experiences
— Ongoing self-reflection and re-evaluation
— Tapping into one's own strengths as an individual and a teacher
— Ongoing curriculum development
— Trying what your comfortable with

FIG. 13.2. Notes about progression of discussion.

students would begin to perceive critically the way they exist and then feel challenged and obliged to respond seemed to me a frightening and unrealistic responsibility for a teacher. Gradually, however, it becomes apparent in my journals that there are many ways to initiate the process without feeling at risk of failure. Through the readings I have come to a clearer understanding of the possible meaning of action. Empowerment can begin with students gaining self-confidence to speak up without fear of making mistakes—or at the other end of the scale, it can mean a high level of involvement in community action. "Allowing for the knowledge of the students" takes the burden off the teacher. At this stage of my development as an ESL teacher, the challenge is to learn to be an effective problem-poser—to learn to ask the right questions.

Another experienced teacher reflected on where he had been and where he was going. After initially interpreting participatory education to mean he had to just let students take the lead, he became self-critical of his prior teacher-centered practice. But at the end of the term he wrote:

I need to have more faith in my authority as a teacher, to initiate activities even though they may at times override the direction that the students wish to go. This, of course, is an internal conflict that I have to work out as I change as a teacher.

Students identify challenges and processes that will help them move from here to there, including knowing their limitations, setting realistic goals, and learning to observe practice:

It's not that we have **not** become this sort of social fieldhand—the ones to blame when the crop fails—it's not that we aren't paid poorly, but we contribute to this somehow by overextending ourselves and setting up false expectations or unrealistic goals, don't we? Is it just new teachers who have unrealistic goals? Is this overextension and overempathy "a woman thing?" I don't know. I think the best solution (for me) is to observe my practice and to know my resources well enough not to feel overwhelmed with tasks that are placed in front of me.

Students develop the sense that it's not about doing things "correctly," but rather about trying and evaluating what they do:

Overall what I think is happening to me with this material is something like a roller coaster. First I'm thinking I can't do this, it's too hard, it's not what I expected, it's not teaching English; then I read further, or it just sits with me or we talk about it and then I get excited about it. Then I might read something else new and frightening and go down in a trough again, then something will happen to bring me back up. Today I sat in one of R.'s classes and it was such fun and I thought, I can do this. I loved the statement in the intro to the multi-level class book that teachers can't expect to always teach the perfect or near-perfect class, the idea ... that it's ok to try things out, they won't all work, don't be afraid of feedback from students, use that to change what you're doing, to evolve.

Likewise, as my colleague, Diane Paxton, pointed out, they come to the realization that being a participatory educator isn't an either/or thing (either you are one or you aren't); it's a constant process of becoming:

You can't force yourself to be a participatory educator just because it seems like a great idea and fits with your world view. Putting it into practice has to be built from where you are as a person, a teacher, a problem poser and from who you are ... use your individual strengths to get you to your own interpretation of participatory ed, but don't try to force the fit in a way that doesn't honor your own skills and strengths.

Many teachers talk about envisioning a gradual process of taking small steps:

"Students need to be successful taking a small risk in order to gain confidence for larger ones.". . . This is a good line to apply to ESL-teachers-as-students, especially in developing and implementing a curriculum that includes a language of action. Just as the ESL student can become empowered gradually through small personal victories which can lead to self-confidence and self-esteem, so, too, can ESL teachers take "small steps to initiate changes."

They recognize that they can't make all the changes at once:

I think also I need to go through an evolutionary process as a novice teacher. From everything I understand, progressive pedagogies require highly skilled and very experienced teachers because it takes time to become used to classroom dynamics (and the management of those dynamics). I **know** I am going through an evolutionary process. I am just stepping out of square one. I tried to begin at square ... what ... 250? 500? Square one, I believe, is traditional education—teacher as knower/students as learner with textbook. I tried to begin with what I understood to be student-centered education.

Students often come to realize that it's fine that their questions aren't answered, that they don't know how to "do it all," but that they have developed a stance and a process to guide them:

What I think I have gotten from this course is a sense that if I were faced with a class I would have some idea where to begin, what to do, some overall philosophy about teaching a language and working with adults. I don't think all the questions that were raised ... were answered completely, but I think they were touched on in a way to make us think about the question and how to get at answers. I don't think there are complete answers to many of these questions. I think the important thing is to be aware of the process of asking them and looking for the answers while one is teaching. If you think you know all the answers then I don't think you'll be open to learning from your students and modifying what you do as a result of your experience. I thought I would like to teach somewhere where they gave me a syllabus and materials to use. . . . I still hate to throw that idea out, because it's a lot more comfortable than thinking there isn't an authority who knows everything and I have to make up my own syllabus, etc. So now when I face a class I have to worry about everything, not just the presentation of predetermined material. While I love the idea of trying things out and seeing what works, the classroom as an ongoing experiment in learning, changing, evolving with input from the students, I've already caught myself thinking if I just planned a better lesson Nurisa would get it. There must be a way of presenting this material that will click for her so that it all makes sense. . . . It's not unlike the feeling that has kept me out of counseling—if I just say the right thing all this person's problems will be solved, it's all up to me and it's my fault if it doesn't work. I know it's a stupid attitude, but I know it's deep in me and it gets in the way of doing things, whereas if the materials are provided, I don't feel as if it's up to me to come up with the perfect lesson. I want very much to be able to adopt the attitude that I'm going to try this out and see how it works. Keep it if it does, toss it if it doesn't and try something different. I know it will be a conflict for me as I try to do this. So to some extent this course has made the whole idea of teaching English to adults more frightening, since . . . I can't count on authoritative texts but must, in collaboration with the student, find and develop the materials to be used. But, on the other hand, it has also made it more exciting, because it is less rigid, more open to new ideas, and more of an interaction between students and teacher.

Most important, the students talk about developing a sense of possibility and accepting that their evolution is a process:

> I think this participatory approach might be possible—I'm less muddled up than at the beginning. I think I feel like a loaf of bread. At present you've mixed in the yeast and we're in the process of rising.

The students also often reflect on what has pushed their praxis forward, seeing that journal writing is a tool they can take with them as they continue to learn and teach:

> I became aware at some point during this semester—and it was during one of the journal writings—that all this stuff has become personal. What happened in the last few weeks is that all that information has become internalized—the reality of being an ESL teacher has become real to me. It's become part of my identity, and I think overall that's what I've been struggling with all semester—what feels "native" enough to me that I can transport into the classroom? Some

of this is in part because of the journal. Writing is how I think things through, figure out how I feel, etc.

Keeping a journal also helped me to solidify my ideas and beliefs and caused me to change my mind about some of them. Journal-writing, as opposed to simple note-taking, forced me to read and think about the articles critically. As a result of this experience, I've once again begun dialogue journals with my class. This time, however, I have a clear sense of purpose; I'll use the journals to find themes and important issues as well as a way to pose questions back to my students individually, as you did.

Does Everyone Have to Do It?

All of this sounds wonderful. It sounds like everything we do in our class "works," that teachers end up growing into an understanding of participatory ESL and loving the process. But actually, that's not always true. In fact, what I have come to realize is that what people do with what I offer is up to them. The reality is that not everyone is comfortable with this approach, it doesn't fit all contexts, and people will take from it what they choose. Some of my students politely but firmly resist what I offer them, even when they understand it:

> I guess that what I am thinking is that the world of education has room for a variety of styles (both theoretical and personal). Participatory ESL sounds great, but does everyone have to do it or is it great for those people whose natural instincts lean in that direction?

Others tell me in no uncertain terms they know their own realities better than I do and can't imagine how participatory education could possibly fit their contexts:

> I can see in my mind an ABE class in Vietnam, an average-size class of 40 women, exhausted after a day of hard work on the field, fidgeting in their seats because they are not used to sitting in class as well as handling delicate objects like the pencils in their hands. Few of these Vietnamese peasants have ever gone to school, some don't quite know why they can stay there learning instead of serving dinner to their families. The teacher then asks them to form small groups to share their concerns, problems, or anything they think is important to them so that later they can tell her what they want to study or to work on. I can see their eyebrows raised in puzzle. Wash their linen in public? They are brought up to keep their problems to themselves. Besides there is nothing interesting or important in their lives to share. All of them have the same life style, the same daily routine. And what about the teacher? Isn't she supposed to be teaching them something? Doesn't she have a syllabus assigned by the principal? The peasants don't know what to learn, that's why they come. Now the teacher is standing in front of them asking them what

they want to learn. This is confusing! What will they tell their family, especially their husbands after class?! That they tell each other what happens to them during the day, what trouble they have, what problem they cope with? That they can tell their teacher what they want to learn and she is very likely to put the book aside and "go with the flow"? Even then they can hear their husbands' shouts: "You've spent all your class time gossiping? How disgusting! That's not a decent place for a wife and mother to go. I don't think you can learn anything from that class, so just stay home and take care of me and your children. They need you at dinner time, anyway."

Although I can think of lots of ways to respond to this and argue that participatory pedagogy really could be powerful in this context, I no longer see this as my role; rather, I ask questions and do a lot of wondering. The range of perspectives among students often brings out whatever I might have said.

For many students, the process is one of taking what they like, piecemeal, rather than buying the whole participatory ESL package, lock, stock, and barrel. On the one hand, this suggests a keen level of critical analysis; on the other, it often means students downplay the political nature of participatory ESL regardless of what I may say. This is where I have to let go of control. As one student wrote:

> Though I admire the PA [participatory approach] for teachers, I don't see how I could really implement it (all out) in my classes. . . . This is not to say that nothing from the PA is applicable. 1) classroom dynamics as described in *Making Meaning, Making Change* are something to be strived for in a big way . . . 2) a custom-tailored curriculum—each group has a personality. I really support the idea that the curriculum emerges, 3) emphasizing the connection between course content and outside world and the corollary—linking materials to their lives/experience—these practices are all highly doable in my teaching.

Everything Doesn't Revolve Around
What We Do/Do Not Do

So what are the lessons from all this? I started this chapter by explaining my own background as a political activist who was always impassioned about convincing others of my position, whatever it happened to be at the time. One of things that my years as a participatory educator have taught me is that not only are challenges, disagreements, and resistances to "my" position inevitable, but they are productive. They help me and my students understand our work more deeply. I've had to learn that it's not helpful for me to try to respond to challenges, hesitations, concerns, and resistances with *my* answers. First of all, I don't have to have answers, but, more important, if I did, I would be undermining my students' possibilities by presenting them. The learning that takes place in the process of struggling with the issues is as important as any outcome.

In addition to letting go of the notion that students' resistances mean I'm not doing a good job, I've let go of the idea that I should convince my students about the "correctness" of participatory pedagogy. Not only is that not my job, but it won't work. I can offer my students models and processes, but, as I said, they'll come to their own conclusions. Like ESL students, they'll learn through experience and make choices based on practice. So I've shifted from seeing my job as that of convincing people to that of offering food for thought, sharing insights and experiences, and guiding dialogue.

Along with this, I've had to let go of the idea that my students should go through some sort of transformative process and completely change their practice as a result of my teaching. Maybe they will and maybe they won't. I may never know. I have had to learn for myself the lessons about "action" that I convey to my students: Action or progress or "success" doesn't always take the form of concrete, visible changes or dramatic steps. What one of my students said about her own practice applies equally to me as a teacher educator:

> I think the toughest part of teaching is that we don't always get to see the results. We may not even be with someone long enough to notice a change ... but, in turn, this cannot stop us from doing what we do to the fullest extent.

These lessons have been gifts that my students have given me in my own political development. They have a common underlying theme—a theme about debunking our own importance and letting go of the need to have things go a certain way, or lead to a particular outcome. What one of my students said here could just as easily be said about the issues raised in this chapter:

> Sometimes it is helpful to acknowledge that not only is it OK to not exhaust an issue, but that maybe there's not "natural" closure to any of the difficult questions and topics treated in our classes. ... This quotation also led me back to times when I knowingly didn't push things that I thought could have gone on—I had to let myself see that there were not earth-shattering consequences! Maybe this is part of a teacher's responsibility—to just let things be sometimes?? It's one way of recognizing that everything doesn't revolve around what we do/do not do.

At times, while I was writing this chapter, I heard my English teacher's voice saying, "You're relying too much on quotes." But the wisdom in words like these—the words of my students—is why I did. Not only do they articulate the issues, but they embody a "way in" to addressing them. They demonstrate how teachers develop their own strategies and stances. By making these quotes public in this chapter, my hope is they will take on a new life of their own, becoming triggers for discussion and, taken together, modeling a process that others might find useful. So I want to end this chapter by thanking all the teachers who are writing this never-ending chapter with me and who have taken the risk of struggling with these issues.

ACKNOWLEDGMENTS

My students, who are my teachers, get my heartfelt thanks for their wisdom, commitment, and the inspiration they give me. I especially want to thank Diane Paxton, my colleague, former student, and fellow would-be participatory educator for her careful critical reading of this chapter and contributions to it.

REFERENCE

Nash, A., Cason, A., Rhum, M., McGrail, L., & Gomez-Sanford, R. (1992). *Talking shop: A curriculum sourcebook for participatory adult ESL*. McHenry, IL: Center for Applied Linguistics and Delta Systems.

14

The Many Faces of Participatory Adult Education

Barbara Burnaby
Faculty of Education
Memorial University of Newfoundland

In my career as a teacher and an academic, I have often found myself confused about the labels used to describe methods and approaches to classroom practices or more general aspects of education. More often than not, hearing a new label also makes me worry that I have missed out on some new knowledge I could have been using to make my work better. Where did this educational idea come from? Is it well founded? How do I find out about it? When I try to learn more, I sometimes discover it is based on an academic theory that has applications in the classroom. For example, in the teaching of second languages, there is the psychological theory of comprehensible input (Krashen, 1982), which suggests that second-language acquisition happens best when learners are exposed to examples of the language at just above the level of difficulty the students already control. Some other labels relate more to procedures and content of classroom teaching, such as the audiolingual method of second-language teaching (Fries, 1945), or even the organization of programs, such as immersion in a second language. I generally find there are descriptions and explanations for such labels so that I can learn their parameters and applications, get a sense of where they begin and end, and judge (often after trying them out) whether they might help in my situation. However, there are other labels I have encountered that seem to emanate out of a (set of) core principle(s) but that do not seem to have boundaries and are not as easy to define. They seem to be applied to a lot of situations, but the principle that ties them together is so elusive that I cannot always tell what these situations have in common. It appears I have to learn about these kinds of concepts experientially. For me, participatory practices has been one such label.

Working with the authors of the chapters in this book and reading their thought-provoking stories about their struggles and successes have provided me with a much-needed incentive to tease apart the tangle of my intuitions and biases about the essential nature of participation. The fact that all the chapters are based on actual practices in participation has made me especially conscious of the potential range of activities and stakeholders that can be drawn into more participatory work. Because every situation described in these chapters is real, I have become aware of the broad spectrum of factors that can and do come up and need to be taken into account. It is these many faces of participation that have challenged me in writing this chapter. I outline some of them here, knowing that there are many more and that each one has a much richer character than I can sketch in these few pages. Starting with problems of defining participatory education, I consider some dimensions that came off the pages to me as I read these chapters.

WHERE SHOULD WE LOOK FOR PARTICIPATORY EDUCATION?

Many discussions of concepts begin with attempts at a definition of the topic. Participatory education as an idea presents more challenges than most. As a one-time denizen and chair of an academic department of adult education studies, I am highly aware of the fact that aspects of adult education can be seen in virtually every facet of life. The idea of participatory education has more or less the same problems for conceptualization. Any activity that involves learning and (directly or indirectly) more than one person can be thought of in terms of participatory education if we examine how the learner is engaged in the learning. If we think of learning as some kind of activity aimed at changes in a person's concepts or skills, it seems the participatory part has to do with the relationship the learner has to change. In a search for participatory education, then, we are looking for activities, change, and relationships.

There is no reason to see the work described in this book as particularly representative of participatory education in North America because Pat and I, according to our own intuitions, gathered chapters simply by contacting colleagues who we felt were engaged in participatory education, and the authors agreed. However, for lack of a better, or at least more immediate, source of information, the chapters in this book can be used to see what ideas have been attached to participatory education. In all of the stories in this book, the people who are "participating" through their learning are seen as marginalized from decision making or control in some way, even doctoral students in one case (de Avila, Caron, Flanagan, Frer,

Heaney, Hyland, Kerstein, Kowalski, Rinaldi) or managers in a provincial government organization in another case (Pharness). Therefore, perhaps the changes we are looking for must involve learners moving from less inclusion to more inclusion. Because disparities in degrees of control exist in every situation, there must be many forms of participatory education that we do not recognize as such. It is worth considering the extent to which lessons learned from work with those most marginalized can be used in less obvious circumstances. I am reminded of all the decisions I made without reflection about what went on in my classrooms when I was teaching ESL to students whose languages I didn't speak. It long it took me a long time to even begin to take advantage of their input into how and what they wanted to learn. Because they could not express their perspectives, my control was not challenged. But I have learned just as crucial lessons working in a nongovernmental organization and trying to work with colleagues on a board of directors.

In some situations, the obvious focus of the activity is to increase the responsibility, or participation of the learners as with prisoners (Davidson) or literacy learners taking on new roles in the literacy agencies (Norton), but in others, the participation came in the process of learning as almost a byproduct by the rural community members at townhall meetings (Zacharakis-Jutz). Thus, we can look for participatory education happening even in activities that we would not immediately recognize as educational or where the inclusion of participants would not seem obvious. When we seek to identify participatory education, we can step back from the clearly marked goals in our everyday lives and see what unexpected outcomes there are in terms of enhanced or diminished participation.

In the chapters of this book, there are activities in which people in decision-making roles work with others who have not been in a position to make such decisions as in leadership work in literacy agencies (Campbell, Horsman) or workplace basic skills training (Belfiore & Folinsbee, Nash). However, other examples are given in which leadership develops from among the "learners" or the learners organize themselves (Davisdon, Zacharakis-Jutz). Therefore, we are looking at various relationships between the learners and the creation of the change process. We can be looking for participatory education without obvious "teachers" as well as in places that look like traditional "education" with people in the standard teacher and learner roles.

With this range of activity, relationships, and changes, it does not seem worthwhile to try to define participatory education, to draw a line around it, or to look for its presence and effects in terms of numbers. However, it is possible to look for its dimensions and character in the examples we have so we can recognize it elsewhere and bring its strengths into our projects. Experiential learning from our current practice, from reflection on past work, and from vicarious learning such as the examples in this book can help to firm up the concept for us.

KINDS AND DEGREES OF PARTICIPATION

As noted, among the chapters in this book there are examples of differences in relationships between the people who were learning and the sources of that learning. From my own work, it has taken me a long time to appreciate not what I "teach" in the formal classroom, but what my students are learning from many other sources. I think my teaching has been improved by my attempts to discover and encourage other avenues for learning about our topic in students' lives. In this book, we see the evident, conventional, "educational" intention of adult basic education in literacy programs (Norton, Barndt), workplace basic skills programs (Belfiore & Folinsbee, Nash), prison schools (Davidson), teacher training (Auerbach), and graduate programs (de Avila et al.). These sorts of educational aspects are less prominent in community development programs for marginalized women (Sauvé, Scott & Schmitt-Boshnick) or more mainstream groups (Zacharakis-Jutz). The authors for this volume have shown, however, that what they considered to be participatory about each of their situations was the stance taken toward the learners as actors in the learning process. Thus, in the more conventional education situations, it was not the basic skills training or whatever that was participatory so much as it was the roles that the learners were offered or took up as decision makers in what was to be learned, in what ways learning was to take place, and often how the whole organization was to be structured. In the circumstances that looked less like education in the ordinary sense, the point was not so much that there was participation, for example, in community action work (Barndt, Zacharakis-Jutz), but that it should be seen as education, as a source of learning for the actors. From this collection of stories, we see the need to appreciate the participatory potential of conventional education as well as the educational potential of participatory action.

Participation, as described in the chapters, not only took many forms but also differed in degree. One way of looking at it might be the degree to which the learners took part in the decision to initiate the activity. When I think of times when people came to me to lead a new educational activity, such as an extracurricular activity, or when I was caught up in a leaderless group to do action research to lobby for government policy change, I recall intensive learning because of the ownership in the project on everyone's part and having more fun doing it. In the prison example (Davidson), some projects were started by the prisoners themselves, and they kept control over the project throughout. In the example of the facilitation of rural community meetings (Zacharakis-Jutz), leadership may be asked for or chosen by the community. In many of the other examples, the initiative for learning and change came from outside the group of targeted learners. There is evidence in some of the stories that the learners resisted or at least struggled with the proposed changes (e.g., Auerbach, Campbell, Horsman). In each situation, there are reasons why some people do or do not take up the challenge to learn to increase their control, and other reasons why people with a certain degree of power do or do not assist people with less power to learn to take on more. There are lessons to be learned in our societies about ways to increase the likelihood of individuals' and groups' acting on their own for their own advancement. Clearly, some of these ways include creating the social environment where freedom to act and learn exists. In other situations, people with power can take the initiative to change the power balance. Social wisdom is perhaps in knowing when to let the initiative come from the group and when to insert catalysts from outside.

Finally, along with the issues of who is to take initiative and what kind of initiative to take is the matter of who is to evaluate the results and how. In my own experience, one of the best lessons I learned about evaluation came inadvertently when I kept a teaching diary. I started it just to keep myself organized about the content I was covering. However, as I took notes on what happened in class, not just the lesson plans, I had a revelation about the extent of the real learning that was going on. This, in turn, helped me give students feedback about essential aspects of the learning other than grammar and pronunciation. Examples in this book show that the original intentions of projects are often far from the actual results, and that this kind of change in direction throughout a process is often a good thing, at least in the eyes on some (Sauvé, Pharness). Evaluation of all the outcomes, especially those that are unanticipated, is an essential part of the examination of a process if we are to learn from it. Current resistance to draconian forms of evaluation, usually dictated by funding or other controlling bodies, in terms of the original objectives only and solely on the basis of "objective" measures such as test results, is a good start in the move toward true evaluation, but much more is needed.

The perspective of the initiators is important, but, in participatory terms, the assessment of other stakeholders is most telling. Virtually all of the chapters here were written by initiators and facilitators. Those of us who do that kind of work are more visible in society, as the experts, and the other stakeholders are less often heard or even asked. However, in these chapters we often hear the voices of other participants through their quotes. The ways public discussion of activities such as participatory education are carried out are strongly directed by conventions of communication (e.g., books like this one). For evaluation of participatory practices to take account of the assessment of all the stakeholders, it requires a sustained change in the way all perspectives are gathered and made part of the public debate.

In sum, what should and could be the kinds of participatory education is an open question with a great deal of scope for expansion. The chapters in this book show the potential in many circumstances, but the potential in many more fields could be explored and reported on. Within situations, participation can be enhanced in content, form of teaching and learning, and beyond what is obvious in terms of education. Degrees of participation vary not only in who takes the initiative, but also in how the participation of all stakeholders changes throughout the life of the activity. Finally, throughout the process and at the end, the various players have views about the success of the venture. Means of tapping the perspectives of all involved are slowly growing, but much more work is needed before the views of all are solicited much less brought to light and into the public debate that, in turn, shapes future decision making.

FACILITATOR/PARTICIPANT/ORGANIZATION RELATIONSHIPS

All the actors in a participatory (or any other) education situation bring to the encounter the characteristics and identities they have in their lives. It seems to me that the main point of participatory education is to alter some of the socially taken-for-granted ways they interact with each other. Also, the facilitator, by definition, is in a position to direct, at least to some extent, the activities of the learners. The facilitator is often in this position because he or she has knowledge the learners presumably do not have and skills in helping learners in the learning process. The kind of social institution in which the activity takes place also has its baggage in terms of the sorts of expectations individuals have about what it does and what authority it has. However, these assumptions are held up to scrutiny in a situation in which the goal is more participation.

The facilitator could be dispensed with in leaderless groups, although I find it hard to imagine a situation in which members do not take on roles that give them certain powers to influence other learners' actions. Self-directed learning (Tough, 1981), where an individual alone undertakes learning for change, could be considered to have both learner and facilitator in one person. In situations in which a group takes learning into its own hands, it is often one of the group that takes initiative or, later, leadership in directing and selecting learning activities, as in some of the prison situations described (Davidson). Other groups have more or less control over the hiring or other choice of facilitator for their activities, as in citizen action groups (Zacharkis-Jutz); the facilitator here might be presumed to have the skills to direct the learning or decision making but not necessarily any specialized knowledge about the actual topic. In the community women's groups described (Sauvé, Scott & Schmitt-Boshnick), the facilitator may take action to form the group as if it were a conventional educational activity and work to hand over the agenda to the group; such leaders may be seen at first to be acceptable because they have both the teaching skills and content knowledge needed to direct the educational activity. In the literacy agency (Campbell, Horsman, Norton), workplace (Belfiore & Folinsbee, Nash, Pharness), teacher training (Auerbach), and graduate education (de Avila et al.) examples, the organization leaders may focus on increasing members' participation in the actual teaching or in the direction and management of the organization.

Presumably, this kind of variation can and does exist because of differences among the individual leaders, the learners, and the organizations in which these events happen. As we have considered, leaders can take initiative themselves either to start projects or to change the relationships between themselves and the learners in some way. Thus, some courses and programs within institutions, such as universities, can be more participatory than others. Whole institutions can decide to change toward more participation, as in literacy agencies (Campbell, Horsman), whereas others become changed because of the ongoing effects of a process, as in some workplace projects (Belfiore & Folinsbee, Pharness). Surely, some kinds of institutions, by the nature of their purposes in society, are more likely to be amenable than others to participatory practices—compare prisons (Davidson) to community nongovernmental organizations (Belfiore & Folinsbee), for example. Learners, too, are different in terms of their relationship with the project. They have many possible relationships to the organization or project as well as interests in the kinds of learning, responsibilities, and change involved.

Among all these factors, a kind of chemistry must develop for all participants to set aside the expectations they have of one another, themselves, and the institution or circumstances of the project. The institution or circumstances must either be such that the participants feel free to risk taking on new roles or be so bad that the learners feel they have no choice but to change. Facilitators must be able to encourage trust and propose changes that seem acceptable and possible to the learners (and often other gatekeepers as well). They must show they have the skills and knowledge to do what the group needs, such skills and knowledge often being different from what they were originally hired for. Learners must be prepared to risk and make efforts to do things which they may not be accustomed to. In every case, for a project to be participatory, organizations and all participants must undertake new social roles; they must see themselves as at least possibly possessing characteristics and relationships with others they didn't have or express before. Those who led before must let go of some of that control; those who followed must take responsibility and ownership; those who knew must accept the knowledge of others; those who could act must stand aside for others to show their skills. Charisma and personality strengths of leaders are much talked about in public discussion of institutional and widespread change, but attention must also be paid to the role all the players have in making change possible and viable.

Thus, the relationship among the various constituents of participatory education is complex in any situation, and each is important to the effectiveness of change toward greater participation. The social matrix of organizations or broader society influences what individual participants may feel is possible or needed. Facilitators have differing potential for taking new initiatives or making change happen within old formats. Learners, too, can take initiative and shape the course and success of new undertakings through their insights and efforts. Trust or desperation concerning social institutions can be catalysts, and the personal abilities of individuals can influence the outcome, but it is a combination of factors within the circumstance and stakeholders that determines the overall outcome.

Personally, I have found that relationships among facilitators, participants, and organizations have been hardest to change when there is the most difference among them. In Japan, I worked in Japanese organizations with Japanese students, and my struggle was to separate the problem of differentiating my and their cultural understandings of teaching and learning from my ability as a teacher to effectively involve the students more in the learning process. Compromise and change on both sides was possible, but it had to be thoughtfully dealt with. In being an external evaluator of educational programs, I have been surprised at how willing organizations can be to making changes in the leeway they give to teachers and students. However, it took me, as an external authority, to bring certain possibilities to their attention. Since then, I have had occasion to use the strategy of getting outsiders' input on my own work and, in the process, making sure that administrations know of outsiders' perspectives on other ways of doing things, even to the extent of asking for an evaluation. In the long run, I have found it most difficult to act in a participatory way in my work when I was facilitator and the learners-participants were very different from me in class, gender, age, race, ethnicity, and so on, especially when I was cast in the role of "expert." If I am to facilitate in a participatory way under such circumstances, I feel the onus is on me to do the learning. I can only say that sometimes I think I have succeeded to some extent.

MOTIVATION FOR LEARNING

Following from this discussion about relationships among participants, it is essential that we attend to issues directly related to the learners. Leaders or facilitators often have the choice whether to initiate a project, although learners may take this step themselves. Once the project has been proposed, learners may or may not have much choice about whether to take part. Learners in literacy agencies and other community projects usually attend if they are attracted to the activity and if their personal situations permit, but targeted people in the workplace, for example, may feel they risk their jobs by taking part, not taking part, or both. For me, again, it is my experience as an evaluator of educational programs that has given me the impetus to examine my own practice. As an outsider in a situation, learners have often been surprisingly candid with me about their reasons for being in the educational situation, perhaps because they thought I could convey their ideas to the teachers or administration more safely than they could. As a facilitator, then, I have become more aware of how tied I am to the role I am perceived to have in the situation. I have experimented with ways learners could feel more safe in expressing their situations with me, but I am aware our relationship will always be a guarded one in some respects.

Discussion of reasons why people do or do not take certain actions, such as to be involved in an educational project, often include examination of push and pull factors. Push factors are factors in the present situation that make people look for a way to change. The kinds of push factors one might look for include poverty, undereducation, civil strife, frustration with government policies and the justice system, disaffection with the organization of work in organizations, and so on. Pull factors are factors in a proposed project that might draw people to take part. They are often the mirror image of the push factors, such as ways to make a better income, to become more educated, to escape or resolve civil strife, to influence governments or the justice system, to get work organized more satisfactorily in organizations, and the like.

However, we must be careful about whose judgment we rely on in assessing the reality and extent of the push and pull factors related to any participatory project. Few projects will succeed in attracting active participants if the target group does not see itself as being pushed or pulled in the same ways as the would-be initiators. There is no substitute for consultation with potential participants before and throughout a project to be sure the participants' interests are being addressed. Indeed, this is the core of participatory work, and all of the stories in this book show how activities work when there is an ongoing openness to the views of all involved.

In each of the chapters here, somewhere there is mention of ways barriers to participation are considered and worked on. Again, the literature on motivation often divides barriers into external and internal. External barriers are those perceived as being outside of the participants themselves. Examples in this book include prison regulations (Davidson), concerns about upsetting union–management relations (Belfiore & Folinsbee), physical and personal problems about attending meetings (Sauvé, Scott & Schmitt-Boshnick, Zacharakis-Jutz), the inertia of how things are usually done in an organization (de Avila et al.,Campbell, Norton), and many others. Internal barriers come from within a potential participant and have to do with personal dispositions toward the proposed change. The major internal barrier identified in the literature about adult basic education seems to be the level of confidence possible learners might have regarding their abilities to make this change. Such issues of confidence come up in many of the chapters (e.g., Barndt, Campbell, Horsman, and Sauvé). Other internal barriers might be strong attitudes and values that conflict with the (apparent) direction of the project, for example, those of teachers in training to their ESL students and the purposes of their teaching work (Auerbach), those of management about the organization of work (Belfiore & Folinsbee, Nash, Pharness), those of community members toward certain groups in the community (Zacharakis-Jutz), and others. Although the division of barriers into external and internal may be an artificial exercise and unhelpful in some cases, the concept still is a useful tool to assist in exploring the realities of a situation before, during, and after the activities of a participatory project.

In sum, the success of participatory work can be studied in terms of the kinds of motivations of the participants, or at least the potential participants. They may resist if they think they are being coerced. They may feel that they do not want or need what is promised. They may not be convinced the project will provide a solution. They may be prevented from taking part by any number of practical or organizational factors. And they may lack the confidence in their abilities or disagree with some principles that are central to the project. To my mind, some of the most interesting parts of the chapters in the book show how participatory activities have revealed such barriers and created solutions to deal with factors in situations that have blocked people from taking part and have broadened their possibilities in doing so.

LEARNING GOALS

It would be highly challenging to take full stock of the kinds of learning that were undertaken and achieved in the projects reported on in this book. In many cases, the most evident learning goals—such as increased basic skills in literacy agencies, community agencies, popular education, or the workplace—were supplemented and even surpassed by other kinds of learning—such as how education systems, formal meetings, the media, the documentation of traditional knowledge, and other things—work, and the development of personal skills for dealing with such things. In some of the projects described, the role of participation by learners was mainly in supporting the attainment of the obvious goal (e.g., Auerbach, Barndt, Norton, and Zacharakis-Jutz), whereas in others, participation helped learners get well beyond the first goal to other goals (e.g., Campbell, Horsman, and Pharness). In no case, as far as I can see, was the first goal not overridden at least to some degree. In other words, what was learned was more than basic skills, facts about law, knowledge about the media, and so on.

Various types of learning goals have different kinds of challenges associated with them. Some, such as basic skills, are often daunting because the goal seems a long way away in terms of the amount that has to be learned and the amount of time required. One way that participation by learners seemed to be useful was when groups could work together to mutually set shorter term objectives that seemed more easily attainable (e.g., de Avila et al., Belfiore & Folinsbee, Horsman, Pharness, and Scott & Schmitt-Boshnick). Other kinds of learning goals seemed to be difficult in terms of the amount of knowledge or sophisticated skills needed. Participation, in my view, was valuable in some cases described in this book because the participants (learners and facilitators) made the most of sharing the skills and knowledge they each possessed (e.g., Auerbach, Barndt, Davidson, Sauvé, and Zacharakis-Jutz). In some instances, the process of doing the group work was not much of an issue; it was the content that was the focus of participation (e.g., Auerbach, Pharness). In other instances, the participatory process was challenging and even counterintuitive to some participants (e.g., de Avila et al., Barndt, Campbell, Horsman, Norton). In all cases, I believe the greatest contribution of participation to the work was the authenticity that came into the activities when all learners actively brought their experience, knowledge, and skills to the tasks rather than passively taking part in something designed and originated by others (see particularly Auerbach, Avila et al., Barndt, Campbell, Sauvé, and Scott & Schmitt-Boshnick). Especially in situations in which I, as a teacher, have had a lot of freedom in the ways I teach and the kinds of progress evaluation I make, I have been most rewarded by the extent of the learning that takes place when students take real ownership of their projects.

The concept that political issues enter into every personal matter has often been raised in recent years. I am inclined to see this as a continuum between matters more concentrated on the interests of the individual at one end and those more concentrated on the social or political at the other; however, the purely personal or purely political are not possible in reality. In the examples of participatory practices here, some appear to involve activities that tend more to the political end (e.g., de Avila et al., Barndt, Horsman, Nash, and Zacharakis-Jutz) whereas others strike me as concentrating more towards the personal development of individuals (e.g., Auerbach, Belfiore & Folinsbee, Campbell, Norton, and Pharness). Nonetheless, strong elements of both individual and social change and development are evident in all the stories and are indivisible, especially as they relate to the participatory nature of the work.

Overall, these stories portray participatory practices as supporting a rich array of learning goals. Participation enhanced progress toward the obvious learning goals of formal education such as basic skills learning, teacher education, and graduate training, but it often went beyond commonly held expectations of education to learning through participation in peer teaching, leadership, administration, knowledge creation, and social action. Participatory practices made some long or difficult learning goals achievable. They permitted learners to get involved in processes that were highly challenging and enhanced all learning by making it authentic for learners. Finally, participatory components of the work promoted both personal and more broadly political and social learning.

CONCLUSION

Participatory practice in adult education can pervade a broad range of more and less traditional educational activity. Although its dimensions are not easy to identify in terms of the kinds of activities, participants, or processes involved, the examples in this book demonstrate an essential strategy that is a potent force in adult learning. This stance is that learning will be enhanced if control over and responsibility for learning is concentrated in the hands of the learners, or at least shared between learners and resource people. Through it, many individual and group learning goals are supported, indeed, sometimes made possible. It can broaden the scope of simple learning tasks step by step until the learners are shocked at the strides they have taken. It makes learning authentic at the personal level and at the level of social and political action. It exists in the tension between individuals' vision of changes for the better, and the strength, commitment, and resources of a group, without which the change could not be brought about. For myself, the best lessons I have learned are that this possibility of participation exists and that it will never be perfectly achieved. The discussion here raises as many questions as it answers about what kinds of situations participatory education is most effective in, and the limits of its usefulness, but the stories told here demonstrate it has much more potential than is being realized.

REFERENCES

Fries, C. C. (1945). *Teaching and learning English as a foreign language.* Ann Arbor, MI: University of Michigan Press.

Krashen, S. D. (1982). *Principles and practices of second language acquisition.* Oxford, England: Pergamon.

Tough, S. A. (1981). *Learning without a teacher: A study of tasks and assistance during adult self-teaching projects.* Toronto, Canada: OISE Press.